THE JAPANESE MYTHS

やまつら8
山童

THE
JAPANESE MYTHS
A GUIDE TO GODS,
HEROES AND SPIRITS

JOSHUA FRYDMAN

with 90 illustrations

Frontispiece: A one-eyed *oni* haunts the wild forests of premodern Japan.

For Nathan, for whom no temple is too remote or haunted

First published in the United Kingdom in 2022 by
Thames & Hudson Ltd, 181A High Holborn, London WC1V 7QX

First published in the United States of America in 2022 by
Thames & Hudson Inc., 500 Fifth Avenue, New York, New York 10110

Reprinted 2022

The Japanese Myths: A Guide to Gods, Heroes and Spirits
© 2022 Thames & Hudson Ltd, London

Text © 2022 Joshua Frydman

British Library Cataloguing-in-Publication Data
A catalogue record for this book is available from the British Library

Library of Congress Control Number 2021943177

ISBN 978-0-500-25231-4

Printed and bound in Slovenia by DZS-Grafik d.o.o.

Be the first to know about our new releases,
exclusive content and author events by visiting
thamesandhudson.com
thamesandhudsonusa.com
thamesandhudson.com.au

CONTENTS

TIMELINE

Jōmon Period: *c.* 45,000 BCE–*c.* 1000 BCE
Yayoi Period: *c.* 1000 BCE–*c.* 200 CE
Kofun Period: 200–538
Asuka Period: 538–710
Nara Period: 710–784
Heian Period: 784–1185
Kamakura Period: 1185–1333
Muromachi Period: 1333–1600
    Warring States Period: 1477–1568
Edo Period: 1600–1868
Modern Era: 1868–present
    Meiji Period: 1868–1912
    Taisho Period: 1912–1926
    Showa Period: 1926–1989
    Heisei Period: 1989–2019
    Reiwa Period: 2019–present

HOKKAIDO

HONSHU

Edo (Tokyo) ■

Kamakura ■

PACIFIC OCEAN

1

WHAT ARE THE JAPANESE MYTHS?

Japan has a long association with myth. One of the earliest English speakers to naturalize as a Japanese citizen, Lafcadio Hearn (1850–1904), made it his life's goal to learn the surviving folktales of rural Japan and transmit them to foreign audiences. His short-story collection *Kwaidan: Stories and Studies of Strange Things* (1904) became famous in the West, its tales of snow women and ogres in the hills adding to the exoticism of the Japanese woodblock prints and clothing that had recently become fashionable in western Europe and North America. Hearn's work began more than 150 years of Western obsession with Japanese myths. How many modern fans of Japanese cinema, anime, manga, literature or popular music thrill to the images of gods and monsters in the shrouded valleys and craggy peaks of the islands? Yet for all its modern appeal, Japanese mythology has a much longer history.

Japan today is a society navigating a complex historical situation. One of the most economically powerful and technologically advanced nations in the 21st century, Japan is firmly a part of the modern, global West. Yet it is also very much *not* a part of the West. The deep connections that now exist between Japan and the United States and Western Europe are only slightly older than Hearn himself, but the myths, folktales and stories that Hearn recorded go back much further. In addition, these stories are intertwined with Japanese religions such as Buddhism and Shinto, which are not well understood by many people in Europe or the Americas.

Mythology is never static, but it can often appear so in hindsight. Most of the famous mythologies of the world – such as Egyptian, Greco-Roman or Norse – belong to societies that either no longer exist or no longer practise the religions that were associated with those mythologies. We see these older mythologies as if they were frozen in time, when in reality they are sets of stories that may have been told at wildly different times with varying images of the same gods and heroes. In the case of Japan, however, the religions associated with the myths are still practised; their gods are still worshipped and their heroes are still relevant. Although the ways in which the modern Japanese understand their myths are very different today than they were even a century ago, let alone more than a millennium, the mythology itself is still very much a living force in Japanese society. In order to understand Japanese mythology, then, we have to understand the context of those myths: where they originated, why they were used in the past, and how they are still used today.

WHAT IS 'JAPAN'?

Japan today is neither politically nor culturally the same as it was 200, 500 or 1,000 years ago. At the same time, however, there is strong continuity: many contemporary Japanese are descendants of the Japanese people of 1,000 years ago; they live in (some of) the same areas and worship many of the same gods. In order to define what makes their beliefs Japanese, we have to then understand different ways to think of 'Japan'.

The country we know today as Japan is comprised of four main islands: from north to south, Hokkaido, Honshu, Shikoku and Kyushu. Honshu, which means 'mainland', is by far the largest, followed by Hokkaido and Kyushu, with Shikoku the smallest of the main islands. The Japanese archipelago also includes almost 7,000 smaller islands.

The archipelago lies to the east of the Asian continent and its name in Japanese, Nihon or Nippon 日本, meaning 'Origin of the Sun', reflects this geographical location. The English name 'Japan' is a 17th-century corruption of the Chinese pronunciation of those same characters; in modern Mandarin, *riben*, but probably something closer to *jeh-pen* in the Early Mandarin of the 1600s. Nihon is a royal name, fit for a royal kingdom. The name supposedly dates to the reign of Empress Regnant Suiko 推古天皇 (r. 593–628), the thirtieth monarch in the traditional order of succession. Suiko is said to have written a letter to Emperor Yang 陽 (r. 569–618) of the Sui Dynasty in China, proclaiming 'From the Son of

9

Heaven in the Land Where the Sun Rises (*Nihon*) to the Son of Heaven in the Land Where the Sun Sets'. This letter in its entirety appears in the *Sui shu* ('Book of the Sui'; 636), along with the aforementioned anecdote.[1] Once Emperor Yang heard the introduction, he was very upset that the ruler of a barbarian kingdom (and a woman no less!) claimed a title equal to the Emperor of China. He was so incensed, according to the *Sui shu*, that he ordered the letter burned, and sent no reply.

Regardless of whether the account in the *Sui shu* is true or not, the name Nihon was used both inside and outside Japan by at least the 8th century. It was the official name taken by the imperial court, and this is in part why it remains the name of the country today.[2] Yet neither the name Nihon nor the lands claimed to be associated with it had a stable definition until about 200 years ago. Take Hokkaido, for example, the northernmost of the main islands, famous today for its lavender fields, skiing and Sapporo beer. This island was not a part of Japan until the late 1700s; prior to that it was a mysterious barbarian region known by several different names. The indigenous people of Hokkaido, the Ainu, were seen as strange bear-worshipping savages for most of Japanese history – unfortunately until well after their island was taken and colonized.

Much of the northern part of Honshu was likewise a dangerous frontier for most of Japanese history. The entirety of the main island had been claimed by the imperial court since the 7th century, but everything north of the modern Tokyo suburbs was a hazy borderland, slowly subdued in a series of military campaigns that lasted until the late 1100s. The island chain that arcs south from Kyushu to Okinawa and then beyond all the way to Taiwan, and which today is split between Kagoshima and Okinawa Prefectures, was actually a separate country, the Ryūkyū Kingdom, from the 14th through 17th centuries. The Ryūkyū Kingdom was officially conquered in the early 1600s and has remained part of Japan ever since, except for a hiatus under American occupation between 1945 and 1972. Today all of the places mentioned above are considered 'Japanese'. Yet they were not historically a part of the islands, and the so-called 'Japanese' myths reflect that fact.

For much of its history, the definition of 'Japan' was the land ruled by the Japanese court. Even in periods when the government was con-

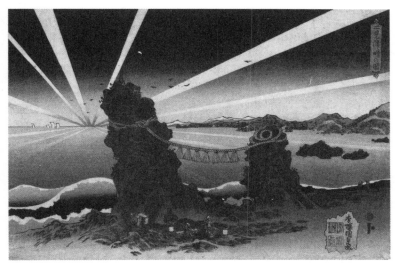

Dawn behind the sacred Married Couple Rocks of Futami, in modern Mie Prefecture. These rocks, linked by a sacred rope woven of rice straw, are worshipped at the nearby Futami Okitama shrine.

trolled by other forces, such as during the Shogunates (warlord-led governments during the medieval era), the Emperor and the court were central concepts. To many Japanese of earlier centuries, the country was the same as the land claimed by and for the Emperor, even when he was powerless in any real sense. In the modern era, the definition of 'Japan' has shifted to become the land controlled by the Japanese people, a term defined as those of ethnic and/or cultural Japanese descent who speak the Japanese language. What makes a 'people', or even a modern 'nation', is a complicated problem, even in the case of a country that seems relatively homogeneous, as Japan does to both many Japanese and many outsiders.

RELIGION AND FAITH IN JAPAN

A majority of modern Japanese claim to be non-religious, one of the highest figures for any country.[3] However, this is a modern phenomenon. As the many ancient temples and shrines across Japan clearly attest, the archipelago has a long religious tradition – several religious traditions, in fact. From its earliest recorded history, Japan has always maintained balance between multiple religions. This balance informs everything from the ancient myths of the 8th century to modern-day folklore, pop culture imagery and urban legends.

The two most prominent religions in Japan are Shinto and Buddhism. Shinto is the native belief system of Japan, but Buddhism arrived very early and the two religions have grown and developed around and in response to one another. Buddhism, originally from India, was transmitted to Japan from China in the mid-first millennium CE. It was not the only religion brought over from the continent; Confucianism, one of China's most important native beliefs, also arrived by this route. Confucianism was primarily a philosophy, only rarely practised as a religion, but it, too, left an important and enduring mark on Japanese faith and culture. Daoism, another important Chinese belief system, was also influential in Japan, but unlike Confucianism, it was not imported as a unified system of thought. In order to understand the Japanese myths, one also has to understand this web of intersecting religions.

Shinto

Shinto (properly Shintō 神道, 'The Way of the Gods') is Japan's only native belief system. In some ways it does not resemble a formal religion at all. Shinto has no sacred texts, and for much of its history its priesthood was organized under and through the imperial court. Most of its modern definitions are the result of scholars from the medieval era onward deciding what is or is not Shinto, and even today one can find arguments about what counts as part of the religion.[4]

Shinto is basically the worship of *kami*, or 'gods'. There is no easy definition of a *kami*. Some, particularly those in the ancient myths, are named and embodied, like Amaterasu, the Sun Goddess, or Susanowo, her younger brother who embodies violent natural forces. These *kami* are the most similar to the named gods of other pantheons, but they are far from the only ones. Natural locations such as mountains and rivers also have individual *kami*; so too do individual animals, plants and even man-made objects such as swords or mirrors. A given mountain such as Mt Fuji is not only the home of many *kami*, but also a singular *kami* itself,

A dragon (a *kami* of water and weather) parts the clouds around Mt Fuji.

and a place controlled by the *kami* of mountains in general, all simultaneously. This simultaneous existence of different *kami* is not a problem, because a *kami* is defined only by the fact that people believe in it and acknowledge its existence. Although *kami* fit into a loose hierarchy, no one can say for certain whether a *kami* that lives on a mountain is more or less powerful than the *kami* that embodies the mountain itself, and even if one could, it would not be an important point. This is because *kami* are not defined by *what* they are so much as *where* they are.

Shinto
- Japan's only native belief system.
- Meaning 'the way of the gods', it focuses on the worship of spirits known as *kami*; animals, objects and locations such as mountains can each have their own *kami*.
- Places of worship are known as shrines in English, and are staffed by priests and priestesses. They are marked by special gates called *torii* (bird landings).
- Focus is on 'purity' vs 'impurity' more than moral concepts such as 'good' and 'evil'.

Kami are local phenomena. The *kami* of a mountain is all-powerful on that mountain. In the case of one of the great *kami* of natural phenomena, they are all-powerful wherever they happen to be present, or want to be. Amaterasu is the Sun Goddess, but her powers do not necessarily involve the physical sun or its light; according to different legends, she has manifested as storm clouds, as a snake and as prophecy, among other things. In short, whatever a *kami* wants to happen can happen, but only within the area in which the *kami* is dominant. For the vast majority of gods, those of specific places, living things or objects, this dominance is limited to their immediate vicinity.

Kami are worshipped at what we call 'shrines' in English, to differentiate them from Buddhist or other religious sites. There are several words in Japanese for a Shinto shrine; *jinja*, 'god's mansion', is the most common.[5] Others include *taisha*, 'great mansion', or *jingū*, 'god's palace', for large or important ones. Shrines have both male priests, known as *kannushi*, and female priestesses, known as *miko*. For much of Japanese history, these

The famous 'floating' *torii* gate of Itsukushima Shrine, on the island of the same name (also known as Miyajima), in modern Hiroshima Prefecture.

titles were hereditary and the families who ran shrines were strongly associated with their shrine's god and its power(s). Most shrines feature one or more *torii* or 'bird-landings', thin wooden gates with two lintel bars on top, the upper larger than the lower. *Torii* mark the entrance to a sanctified space and are a common representative image of Shinto.

Trees, rocks and other, larger locations that embody *kami* can be cordoned off for worship by sacred ropes woven of pure hemp, rice straw or silk, with broad tassels at the knots. Cascades of folded paper and leafy branches of *sakaki* (*Cleyera japonica*), an evergreen flowering tree native to Japan, are also used as both ritual implements and to designate sacred spaces. These spaces are essential to Shinto; they offer, as well as define, space within which a given *kami* rules. Perhaps more importantly, these natural spaces also create areas where impurity is not allowed to enter.

Purity is one of Shinto's most important concepts. Purity can be defined as the natural state of the living world, when not dirtied by death, or things associated with death.[6] Blood, including from menstruation and

Petitioners wash their hands before entering a Shinto shrine, where a priest purifies a *sakaki* wreath hanging from a *torii* gate.

15

childbirth, as well as urine, faeces, vomit, rotted food, stagnant water, and any portion of a corpse, are all ritually polluted, and therefore cannot be brought into the presence of a *kami*. A washbasin featuring constantly running water often stands at the entrance to a shrine, enabling worshippers to ritually clean their hands and mouth – and by extension their body and spirit – before entering the sacred space. 'Purity' is not the same as 'good' any more than 'impurity' is equivalent to 'evil'; however, according to Shinto doctrine, *kami* love purity and abhor impurity. The clash between valuing purity over impurity, and good over evil, explains some of the events in the ancient Japanese myths.

Buddhism

Buddhism (Jp. *bukkyō* 仏教) developed in India for nearly seven centuries before it began to spread across Central and East Asia. It arrived in China sometime during the late Han Dynasty (206 BCE–220 CE) and by the Tang Dynasty (618–908 CE) had become one of China's major religions, a role it still plays today. The religion spread into what is now Tibet, Vietnam, Mongolia and Korea. It was a Korean kingdom, Paekche, which transmitted Buddhism to Japan at some time in the 6th century CE.

Buddhism changed as it encountered first China and then the rest of East Asia. The core of the religions, the doctrine surrounding Siddhartha Gautama, as well as other early works of philosophy and religious law – holy books called sutras (Jp. *kyō*) – were the basis of what we call today Theravada, or 'Words of the Elders' Buddhism. However, a number of other texts, some of which may not come from India at all, became

---

Buddhism

- Developed in India and spread across Central and East Asia; reached Japan from China during the 6th century CE.
- All beings, even gods, are trapped in an endless cycle of reincarnation; only buddhas, who have reached enlightenment, can be free of this.
- Places of worship are known as temples in English, and are staffed by monks (also called priests) and nuns.
- Focus on morality and philosophical issues such as the nature of reality.

The Historical Buddha, Śākyamuni (Jp. Shaka; see Chapter 5), preaches the concept of 'expedient means' on a painted copy of the *Lotus Sutra*.

more important to Chinese Buddhists, particularly one known as the *Lotus Sutra* (Jp. *Myōhō Hokkekyō*). The *Lotus Sutra* introduces the idea of 'expedient means' (Sanskrit *upāya*, Jp. *hōben*). These are ways in which one can realize enlightenment in one's own lifetime, skipping a long cycle of rebirths that lead eventually towards the truth and Buddhahood. The division of Buddhism that took up this idea as part of their focus is today known as Mahayana, or 'Greater Vehicle' Buddhism.

Buddhism does not technically feature its own gods. Instead the religion teaches that even gods are bound within the 'worlds of desire', as the universe is termed, and therefore subject to the cycle of rebirth. Gods from most religions can be subsumed into the Buddhist worldview, because they are limited beings, bound by their own existence – whereas buddhas, figures who have achieved enlightenment, are beyond even existence itself.

Buddhist religious complexes are known in English as temples, to tell them apart from Shinto shrines. They are known as *tera* or *jiin* in Japanese, and most have names ending in either the characters *-ji* 寺 'temple' or *-in* 院 'cloister'. Temples may feature male priests, also termed monks in English, and known by several names in Japanese, most often as variations on either *sō* or *bō* . Temples may also, or instead, be run by female

The five-storied pagoda of the Buddhist Kōfukuji Temple in Nara, the second-tallest of its kind remaining in Japan.

nuns, known in Japanese as *ama* or *ni*, both words using the character 尼. Buddhist clergy are far more organized than those of Shinto. Until the past few hundred years they took vows of chastity and were superficially similar to Christian monks and nuns. Attempts by the last Shogunate to control Buddhist institutions included requiring clergy to marry and temples to be passed down through family lineages, a practice that still continues today.

Unlike Shinto, Buddhism came to Japan with a long history, a multitude of written texts and a complex set of moral philosophies. Buddhism also differs from Shinto in actively engaging with deeper philosophical questions such as the nature of good and evil, or man's place in the universe. Each Buddhist school, including those that formed in Japan, further developed its own differences in philosophy and faith. As Buddhism was able to easily absorb the *kami* into its system, the two religions rapidly formed a coexistence, and soon afterwards a full symbiosis. Although there have been several historic attempts to separate them, including as recently as before the Second World War, Japanese forms of Buddhism and Shinto are so deeply interwoven that they affect each other's culture and art, as well as mythology. Today most Japanese tend to rely on Shinto rituals for birth or marriage, and Buddhist ones for funerals and other sombre events, although in many cases the rites themselves draw from the deep well of shared practices.

Confucianism

Confucianism (Jp. *jukyō* 儒教) is often called a 'school of thought' in English, but it has a long history of religious practice in China and across East Asia. Originally it was a set of philosophies attributed to the possibly fictional Kong Qiu 孔丘 (551–479 BCE), whose name was Latinized by European missionaries as 'Confucius'. Confucius was a scholar and advisor to courts during the period of multiple kingdoms prior to China's unification into a single empire. He travelled between different states on the North China plain, advising rulers how best to govern, and gathering disciples who followed his principles. His accumulated teachings were written down by his disciples in the decades following his life, primarily in the book known as the *Analects* (Ch. *Lunyu*; Jp. *Rongo*). These writings

---

Confucianism
- From writings attributed to Kong Qiu, or Confucius, a Chinese scholar and court advisor in the 6th century BCE. Many books, particularly the *Analects* (Ch. *Lunyu*, Jp. *Rongo*; *c.* 5th century BCE).
- Originally a philosophy, concerned with maintaining the balance between heaven and earth. Emphasizes morality, filial piety and respect for hierarchies.
- Eventually developed into a state-sponsored religion in China, with temples, priests and religious doctrines. This religious Confucianism was never fully established in Japan.

---

circulated over the next several centuries, and under the Han Dynasty were developed into the official philosophy for China's government. By the following Northern and Southern Dynasties Period (220–589 CE), Confucius himself became worshipped as a transcendental sage. His teachings developed a religious branch, distinct from those who followed them as pure philosophy.[7]

By the time of the Tang Dynasty – more than 1,500 years since Confucius' lifetime – his philosophical and moral teachings had developed into a state-sponsored formal religion. Confucian temples existed across China, with an active priesthood and religious doctrines. This religious Confucianism was what Japan first encountered, and which was imported to the archipelago during the Tang Dynasty. Confucianism never became widely established as a full religion in Japan, but it was also never treated as a solely philosophical pursuit. Several of its major tenets were incorporated into other Japanese belief systems.[8]

Confucianism's fundamental concern is the relationship between earth and heaven. Heaven is not necessarily a specific place, home to specific gods, but a conceptual realm, a perfect mirror of what the earth ought to be. As earth drifts further from heaven, both the natural world and human society get correspondingly further out of balance. The way to bring earth back into alignment with heaven is through acting righteously, which means both adhering to a code of universal morals, and protecting hierarchies. These hierarchies manifest on earth through specific relationships: parents to children, elder brothers to younger brothers, husbands to wives, lords to vassals

Confucius, here portrayed as late imperial Chinese royalty.

20

and the ruler to his subjects. Each hierarchy must be protected, because without them the fundamental harmony of society would crumble.[9] When earth and heaven fall out of balance, the result is not only moral lapses, but literal catastrophe, as natural disasters and rebellions.

In order to protect harmony, a good Confucian must practise filial piety, or respect towards their parents and ancestors. They must also respect other hierarchical relationships, take duty seriously and follow a strict moral code. In addition, a good Confucian must study; learning, particularly involving written texts, is an important part of cultivating one's morality. Because of Confucianism's emphasis on morality, respect and studiousness, and its lack of specific religious figures (other than Confucius and his disciples), it easily paired with Buddhism and other religions in Japan. Confucianism thus influences attitudes and ideas without necessarily appearing directly in either the ancient Japanese myths or more recent folktales.

Daoism and Chinese Folk Traditions

The last of the famous Chinese religions influencing Japanese mythology is Daoism (Jp. *dōkyō* 道教). Like Confucianism, it is often considered a school of thought rather than a religion; yet also like Confucianism, historical Daoism developed its own priesthood, temples and holy writings. However, in contrast with Confucianism, Daoism as we understand it today is not a series of developments from a single school of thought, but a synthetic grab-bag drawn from many different beliefs of premodern China.[10]

Daoism's main texts are a pair of works from approximately the same era as Confucius' *Analects*: the *Dao De Jing* and the *Zhuangzi*. The *Dao De Jing* ('The Classic of Virtue and the Way', Jp. *Dōtokukyō*, *c.* 7th century BCE), attributed to a figure known only as Laozi 老子 or 'The Old Master', is a collection of aphorisms and advice superficially similar to the *Analects*. The *Zhuangzi* (Jp. *Sōji*), attributed to Zhuang Zhou 荘周 (*c.* 3rd century BCE), is a more overtly philosophical work consisting of a number of musings on the nature of reality. The books may not have been originally related to one another, but by the 4th to 5th century CE they were considered to be a pair, and part of the same tradition.[11]

Daoism

- Originated in China around the same time as Confucianism, combining elements of many different premodern Chinese beliefs, including local folklore and traditions.
- Emphasizes living life according to 'the Way' – living in harmony with nature.
- Associated with magical traditions, fairy tales, Chinese astrology, divination practices and the gods of the house.
- Main works: the *Dao De Jing* (Jp. *Dōtokukyō, c.* 6th century BCE), and the *Zhuangzi* (Jp. *Sōji, c.* 4th century BCE).
- No known Daoist temples ever built in Japan, and no official priests, yet influence appears in other ways.

Each text discusses the concept of living according to 'the Way' (Ch. *dao*, Jp. *dō* or *michi*), which has many meanings, but generally refers to being in harmony with nature. Unlike Confucianism, which requires strict morals to bring earth in line with heaven, according to Daoist philosophy earth is always already perfect. It is only humans with their pesky thoughts that mess up the perfect – if messy – harmony of the natural world. Therefore, in order to live according the Way, one must give up the trappings of wealth, power and status in human terms, and simply exist. There are many different ways to make this happen, and neither the *Dao De Jing* nor the *Zhuangzi*, let alone the many later commentaries and derivative texts, presents a specific, clear path to do so. For some Daoists that confusion is itself a part of the Way.

Daoism began to incorporate local folklore and traditions at an early stage. Because of this association, as well as its connections to the natural world, Daoism has long been associated with magical traditions, fairy tales and any number of little-known gods. The most common of these are Immortals (Ch. *xianren*, Jp. *sennin*), people who become so at one with the Way that they transcend mortal life. Immortals live in the wilderness and can do essentially whatever they feel like. They are not gods of anything in particular, but they have strange and mysterious powers, such as riding on clouds or controlling the flow of time. Above the

Immortals are larger figures, such as the Queen Mother of the West 西王母 (Ch. Xiwangmu), an ancient and mysterious goddess whose powers are nearly limitless. The Queen Mother lives in the outermost west, as implied by her name, and sometimes is balanced by other mythic figures representing the other directions. However, like many Daoist deities, her role and powers change with each tale, myth or parable.

Daoist places of worship are referred to as 'temples' in English (Ch. *guan* or *gong*; there is no standard name in Japanese), and their male and female clergy as 'priests' or 'monks', and 'nuns', respectively. These are the same terms used for Buddhist institutions, and they can be confusing. In fact, Buddhist temples in China borrowed many architectural and artistic elements from older Daoist ones. However, the size and style of icons are different, as are the gods and figures worshipped in each religion, and certain types of buildings, such as pagodas at Buddhist temples, exist only at one or the other.

Daoism is also associated with Chinese astrology, divination practices and the gods of the house. Perhaps because of these associations, which were more the preserve of commoners than of the educated elite, it is the one important Chinese religion that was transmitted to Japan only in pieces. Although its important books, including both the *Dao De Jing* and the *Zhuangzi*, are known in Japan from as early as the 7th century CE, it appears that there was never any interest or attempt to

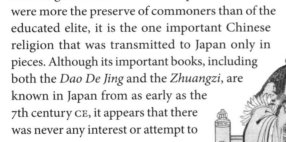

The Daoist Immortal the Queen Mother of the West (left) and an attendant, portrayed as Tang Dynasty Chinese nobles.

copy Daoist institutions. There are no known Daoist temples ever built in Japan, and no official priests practising the religion. In fact, many of its more magical elements were borrowed into other traditions, or fused with practices drawn from Shinto or Buddhism to make new ones. Scholars in both Japan and the English-speaking world like to talk about 'the disappearing Daoism'. By this, they mean the fact that a religion so important in China, Japan's greatest model for society, was completely absent as an institution in Japan. However, as we will see when we address various forms of magic, fairy tales and local folklore in Japan (Chapters 3 and 5), Daoist influences on the Japanese myths are wide and deep – just not set apart as clearly as those of other religions.

MYTH, HISTORY AND TRADITION

The Japanese myths developed in a culture with the complicated mixture of native and imported religions discussed above, and are soaked in their ideology and theology, even when the stories themselves are not religious in origin. *Kami*, for instance, are an inherently Shinto concept, but they are often treated according to Buddhist morals; likewise, Buddhist folktales from Japan often invoke purity, or have Buddhist deities behaving like *kami*. Filial piety, drawn from the ancient Confucian texts, is a recurring theme, as are Confucian texts themselves, which are universal symbols of learning across East Asia. Magic and its uses in Japanese myths are often Daoist, or at least derived from Chinese folklore. Without at least a basic understanding of the ideas in play, a reader who has not grown up surrounded by Japanese culture may find themselves at a loss as to what happens in a given myth, how it happens, and why.

Modern Japan has a strong continuity with the past, not only culturally, but also geographically, politically and artistically. Japanese myths are no exception. The 8th-century chronicles were reworked in the 13th, 18th and 20th centuries, gaining new aspects and interpretations each time. Urban legends in modern Tokyo draw on Edo Period ghost stories that reference medieval folktales, themselves all tying back into Heian lore. There is much that is new in each era, but also a strong effort to preserve and rework what is considered to be 'tradition'.

This book explores the Japanese myths along with the changing historical and cultural situations that surround them. The chapters that follow investigate Japanese mythology in chronological order. Chapters 2 and 3 discuss the myths laid out in the ancient chronicles from the 8th century. These form the basis of what can loosely be called 'Shinto mythology' and they are still widely known today. Chapter 2 discusses the creation of the world, the main gods of the ancient chronicles and the basic understanding of the cosmos in ancient Japan. Chapter 3 focuses on the first emperors, most of whom are legendary figures on the level of Greek or Norse heroes, looking at how and why these figures were important to the development of the imperial court and Classical Japanese culture.

Chapter 4 discusses the new mythologies of Classical and early medieval Japan (roughly 800–1300 CE), many of which saw new gods and heroes get added to, or even replace, some of the older myths. Chapter 5 looks at legendary figures who joined the Japanese pantheon from Buddhism, Confucianism and Daoism. Chapter 6 continues through the late medieval and into the early modern eras (1400–1850 CE). As printing and literacy spread, much of the folklore of commoners was written down for the first time: ghosts, monsters and lesser *kami* of all shapes and sizes join the body of mythology, and ancient myths get reinterpreted in new ways. Finally, Chapter 7 covers the intersection of popular culture and mythology in the modern era. The Japanese myths form a rich source for modern anime, manga, video games, live-action film and other modern art forms, and this chapter will look at how that happens.

Japanese mythology is not any one single, coherent body of stories, but many, some of which outright contradict one another. Most of these stories, and the gods, heroes, emperors and villains in them, have very long histories, but they have changed over time, and continue to change today. This book will show that process, exploring the deep links between past and present, and the ways that stories live and grow. Some elements of Japanese society, culture, history and folklore may be unique to Japan, but the larger ideas they reveal are not. It is my sincere hope that through this book, readers can glimpse not only the many worlds of Japanese myth, but the ways in which all stories – myths – live and grow in their own societies.

2

THE AGE OF THE GODS

Most of what we today call 'the Japanese myths' can be traced back to the 7th and 8th centuries CE. This is the oldest period of Japan for which we have written records. Their tales of gods and heroes are still retold today, and form the basis for other Japanese folklore (such as the heroic *kami* mentioned in Chapter 4). We are aware, however, that the stories portrayed in these ancient texts were understood very differently when they were created than they are today. What people considered important in the distant past is often very different from what modern scholars want to know. Although the details of these myths have changed and grown over the centuries, evolving along with Japanese society to mean different things, the core stories from the ancient texts have endured.

The two oldest surviving books written in Japan are historical chronicles that date to the early 8th century. These two works, the *Kojiki* and the *Nihonshoki*, begin with the creation of the world, and recount history through to the time of their writing. Their 8th-century Japanese audiences considered both texts to be 'history', and each presents its mythological portions as verifiable historical truth, not allegory or folktale. The later portions of each chronicle cover the early history of the imperial court and lay out detailed narratives that occasionally corroborate Chinese or Korean documents. However, they also include stories that are clearly fantastical.

The myths in the *Kojiki* and the *Nihonshoki* offer the best views we have into the beliefs of the early Japanese. Unfortunately, these texts are neither comprehensive nor always comprehensible. Historians have studied both works for centuries, and for modern scholars they remain objects of reverence, curiosity and even disappointment, often all at the same time. In short, the chronicles are messy – but they are all we have.

The *Kojiki* is the oldest extant work of literature in Japanese. It was compiled in 712 and its name means 'The Record of Ancient Matters'. It begins with the creation of the world and continues through the reign of Empress Regnant Suiko (r. 593–628), the 30th ruler of Japan. A relatively short document, it is divided into three books. The first or 'upper' book follows the Gods of Heaven – the Amatsukami 天津神 – as they come into existence and eventually send a pair of siblings, Izanagi 伊邪那岐 and Izanami 伊邪那美, to create the physical world. Izanagi and Izanami's children include the Sun Goddess Amaterasu 天照 and her estranged brother Susanowo 須佐之男. From this pair come a lineage of fertility gods, culminating in Ninigi 邇邇芸, the Heavenly Grandson, who descends to the newly created world, where his descendants become the imperial clan.

The second or 'middle' book of the *Kojiki* picks up with the reign of Jinmu 神武, the First Emperor, who is also Ninigi's great-grandson. The narrative continues throughout the first fifteen rulers, all of whom are heroes positioned between gods and humans. The third or 'lower' book continues for rulers sixteen through thirty. Many of the emperors in the lower book have shorter lifespans and more human concerns than their predecessors. If the middle book is that of demigods and legendary emperors, then the lower one is about human rulers. They are still descended from deities, but no longer supernatural beings themselves.

The *Kojiki* includes a preface that outlines the history of its compilation. The text was originally a series of oral histories, supposedly memorized in the 680s by a mysterious courtier named Hieda no Are 稗田阿礼, whose background and even gender remain unknown. A generation later it was copied down in writing by Ō no Yasumaro 太安万侶, a (male) civil servant.[1] The preface is written differently from the rest of the *Kojiki* and is suspected to be a 9th- or 10th-century forgery, but the *Kojiki*'s main text is cited in other works from the 8th century, which does suggest that it was already a well-known source and therefore as old as the preface claims. Nevertheless, modern scholars take most of the details in the preface with at least a grain of salt, if not an entire shaker, and the origins of the *Kojiki* remain mysterious.

The *Kojiki* has a strong central narrative, charting the origins of Amaterasu and her descendants, their descent to and pacification of the earth, and finally their rule as the imperial family of Japan. However, the work also spends a large amount of time recounting genealogies. Almost every deity who attends Amaterasu and her descendants, fights them, or simply exists in their world, gets a genealogy. Every one of these genealogies ends with a family known to exist in the imperial court of the 700s, and in all cases their predecessors are somehow bound to the Sun Goddess and her offspring. The *Kojiki* is not only a story of how the imperial family came to be, but of *why* they came to be, and how their rule over the court (and over Japan as a whole) is natural. After all, if one's ancestor swore fealty to the imperial family, then doesn't one's place remain at their side? Modern scholars believe that the *Kojiki*'s original purpose was not as a collection of myths, but as an official genealogy to prove that the aristocratic families of the court served the imperial family because their ancestors had done so ever since the age of the gods.

The *Nihonshoki* recounts similar myths in a very different way. The *Nihonshoki* was finished in 720; its name means 'The Chronicles of Japan', and it lives up to that title. A vast work of 30 books, the *Nihonshoki* is much longer and more detailed than the *Kojiki*. The first two books cover the 'Age of the Gods', while the other 28 cover the reigns of the first 46 emperors, ending with Empress Regnant Jitō (r. 686–696). In discussing the reigns of the emperors, the *Nihonshoki* follows the exact format of an ancient Chinese dynastic chronicle, with every ruler's annal divided into entries by year, month and day. This gives the work a historical feel even when it is discussing legendary events and makes the *Nihonshoki* sound superficially more 'accurate' than the *Kojiki*.

In the first two books of the *Nihonshoki*, however, those covering the 'Age of the Gods', the information is presented in a narrative that begins with the origins of the universe, like that in the *Kojiki*, from which it also differs in striking ways. One difference is that the *Nihonshoki*'s books on the gods regularly discuss alternative versions of the myths. These additions, written in smaller text, all begin with the phrase 'one book says', and often outright contradict the main narrative. The *Kojiki* is frequently one of these alternative accounts. A reader would therefore be able to cross-reference the main narrative of the *Nihonshoki* to other myths in the middle of reading it. No one knows for sure why the alternative myths

---

The *Kojiki* and the *Nihonshoki*

- The two oldest surviving written books in Japan (early 8th century CE).
- Main sources for what is known about ancient Japanese mythology.
- The *Kojiki* ('Record of Ancient Matters') has three books, ends with the 30th emperor (early 600s). It is a genealogical tale about how the imperial family came to dominate Japan, written in Old Japanese.
- The *Nihonshoki* ('The Chronicles of Japan') has 30 books, is much more detailed and continues through the reign of the 41st emperor (ending 696 CE). It is written in Classical Chinese and thought to have been an official history aimed at other countries, such as China.
- Both texts recount similar myths, but with differences. The *Kojiki* has a single narrative, but the *Nihonshoki* gives multiple versions of myths.
- Modern scholars see both texts as propaganda; the myths they recount legitimize the authority of the early Japanese court.

---

were included but listing them alongside the main narrative does give the *Nihonshoki* a more scholarly appearance than the *Kojiki*.

The *Nihonshoki* does not have a preface or an attribution. We do not know who compiled it, or where they found the records that they used. Unlike the *Kojiki*, the *Nihonshoki*'s history is recorded in a sequel, the *Shoku nihongi* ('Continued Chronicles of Japan'), written in 797. The *Shoku nihongi* is an even longer text than the *Nihonshoki* and covers events from 696 to 791 in excruciating detail. It is corroborated by other evidence, including archaeological discoveries and other 8th-century texts, such as the Shōsōin records (discussed below), and is considered to be more accurate. The *Shoku nihongi* records the compilation of the *Nihonshoki* and its presentation to the court in 720. It also discusses the earlier chronicle's contents, which match most of the surviving text quite well (although it mentions a final book of genealogical tables that has been lost).

The *Nihonshoki*'s age and authenticity are not in doubt, only the identity of its compilers. Its rationale is also not a mystery. The overtly historical style in which it was written, as well as the fact that it received a sequel, suggest that the *Nihonshoki* was intended to be the imperial court's official record of its own history. Genealogies are important in the *Nihonshoki*, but they are not the main theme of the text. Although its myths are also important, they are only the starting point for the historical volumes that follow. These historical annals go into more detail than the *Kojiki*, as well as far beyond the end of the other chronicle in time. In fact, the later parts of the *Nihonshoki*, those covering the events of the 6th and 7th centuries, are generally considered historically accurate even today.[2]

Modern scholars view both the *Kojiki* and the *Nihonshoki* as political works. Reading these chronicles as political documents may take some of the fun out of them, but it also lets us understand their limitations, which include their lack of interaction with the world outside the Japanese archipelago, and their focus on the Sun Goddess and her descendants above anything else. The ancient Japanese myths are not present in these chronicles to explain the existence of the world or the things in it, but to establish how all things come back to the emperors and their divine right to rule – they are basically propaganda texts. An astute reader will keep this in mind while reading the stories from the *Kojiki* and the *Nihonshoki*, as well as looking at how they develop in later centuries.

THE AMATSUKAMI AND THE ORIGINS OF THE UNIVERSE

The Japanese creation myths are messy and complicated, much like an actual birth. Originally, the world was formless, 'like tallow upon water, drifting like a jellyfish'.[3] At some point, the first god comes into existence. In the *Kojiki*, this first deity's name is Ame-no-Minakanushi 天御中主, ('Master Mighty Centre of Heaven'), who appears from nothingness.[4] In the main narrative of the *Nihonshoki*, the god's name is Kuni-no-Tokotachi 国常立 ('Land Eternal Stand of August Thing'), who grows out of the formless universe 'like a reed-shoot'.[5] This first deity is soon followed by between one and four more deities, depending on the version, all of whom come into being without gender or solid forms.

Like their number, the first deities' names, attributes and purposes vary in each version. These gods are not often worshipped today, and little is known about them. The only one who features significantly in later myths is named Takamimusuhi 高御産巣日 ('Lofty Growth'). Like the other first deities, Takamimusuhi represents the mysterious and powerful genesis of creative forces that underlie nature. Although they sit in the background for the remainder of the myths, these first gods are always there as the invisible source of the rest of the universe.

Following this first generation of gods are six more generations. Each of these generations consists of a pair of deities. Their specific names and functions vary according to the chronicle, but they are generally associated with sand, mud and creative forces. Each pair is a male-female couple, who then birth the following pair. In all known versions of the myth, the last pair is the same – Izanagi ('He Who Beckoned') and his sister Izanami ('She Who Beckoned'). The six previous generations of gods call Izanagi and Izanami to a council and command them to create the islands of Japan – and, by extension, the entire physical world. The other gods present the pair with the 'balled spear of heaven', from which two testicular jewels dangle. Izanagi and Izanami thrust the spear into the watery formlessness of the uncreated world, before pulling it up. Salt congeals on its tip and drips down, becoming the first island, Onogoroshima ('Self-Shaped Isle').

Izanagi and Izanami descend to Onogoroshima, where they erect a ritual pillar, and decide to wed formally. They circle the pillar and pledge themselves to one another in marriage, but Izanami speaks before her brother/husband. Soon afterwards, Izanami gives birth to their first child, and he is a failure. He lacks arms and legs, and is known as Hiruko 蛭子, the 'Leech-Child'. Izanagi and Izanami place Hiruko into a basket and release him onto the ocean, where he sails out of ancient myth (but will return in medieval folklore as Ebisu, the long-lost god of luck; see Chapter 4).

Izanagi and Izanami try again to conceive, and this time produce a mass of froth and bubbles as their second child. Upset over their continued failure to create something worthwhile, the gods ask the Amatsukami, the older gods back in heaven, for advice. The couple are told that their failure to birth 'good' children is due to Izanami, the woman, having spoken first during their marriage ceremony. The pair return to Onogoroshima, where they re-enact the ceremony. This time, Izanagi speaks first, and the children they create are healthy and useful: the islands of the Japanese archipelago.

Izanami (left) and Izanagi (right). holding the 'balled spear of heaven'
over the formless chaos that preceded creation.

The order of the creation of the islands is different in the *Kojiki* and in
both the main and side narratives of the *Nihonshoki*, but the key points
remain the same. Shikoku and Kyushu are among the firstborn, as is
Awaji, an island in the Inland Sea. Honshu itself is usually two 'islands'.
Several small outlying isles – such as Iki, Oki and Tsushima in the Korea
Straits, and Sado in the Sea of Japan – appear in the birth order as well.
After the islands are born, Izanami gives birth to various aspects of the
natural world, including seas, rivers, mountains, forests and plains.
These gods of nature are also born in male-female pairs like the earlier
Amatsukami. Unlike their parents or the gods of the islands, these paired
gods of the natural world are not famous. Although many of them are still
worshipped today at smaller shrines, their names are not widely known.
They are representations of natural landscapes, and rarely make further
appearances in myth or folklore.

According to the *Kojiki*, as the last of her many children Izanami gives
birth to Hi-no-Kagutsuchi 火之迦具土, the god of fire. Hi-no-Kagutsuchi
burns Izanami's genitals as he is born, and she vomits, urinates, defecates

and then dies. Her vomit, urine and faeces turn into more pairs of deities, respectively associated with mining and metal, rushing water and clay. Izanagi, enraged at the death of his sister/wife, promptly takes out his sword and kills Hi-no-Kagutsuchi, cutting the fire god so violently that his blood splatters on the rocks, where it turns into volcanoes.

Following this act of violence, Izanagi begins to search for Izanami. Eventually he learns that she has gone to Yomi 黄泉, a land of the dead. Izanagi makes his way to Yomi, where he finds Izanami hidden away inside a house. She begs him not to enter, as she is ashamed for him to see her in her dead state, but Izanagi barges in anyway, revealing Izanami as a rotted corpse. Horrified, Izanagi rejects her and flees.

Izanami, upset over her brother/husband's betrayal, pursues him along with an army of thunder deities and hags. Three times Izanagi removes accessories from his person – his hair tie, his comb and, finally, his sword – and throws them behind him; each one turns into a distraction to keep Izanami's armies from reaching him. Finally, Izanagi reaches the Slope of Yomi, the entrance to the land, and after passing it, he blocks it with a giant boulder. When Izanami reaches the far side, the two have a conversation – perhaps the earliest divorce in Japanese history. Izanami threatens to 'strangle to death 1,000 of your land's grass-green mortals each and every day'. In return, Izanagi promises to 'build 1,500 birthing huts each and every day'.[6]

Izanagi purifies himself in a river after his harrowing escape from Yomi. As he washes each part of his body, gods of time, tides and ritual purity spring into being. He cleans his eyes and nose last and creates the three most powerful deities of nature. From Izanagi's left eye comes Amaterasu, 'Heaven Shining', the sun goddess. From Izanagi's right eye comes Tsukuyomi 月読, 'Moon Counting', the moon god. Finally, from Izanagi's nose comes Susanowo, 'Reckless Rushing Raging Man', the god of violent natural forces. Izanagi is happy with these last three deities and appoints them as his heirs over all of the natural world that he and Izanami created. Amaterasu is granted rulership over the High Plain of Heaven (Takamagahara 高天原), Tsukuyomi, the night, and Susanowo, the ocean.

The story of Izanami's death and Izanagi's trip to Yomi is among the most well-known of the ancient Japanese myths today, but only in the *Kojiki* is it recorded as important. Izanami never dies in the main narrative of the *Nihonshoki*; instead she gives birth to all three celestial gods (Amaterasu, Tsukuyomi and Susanowo) before retiring alongside Izanagi. Outside of the extra narratives, several of which includes parts of the *Kojiki* story, the land of Yomi is never mentioned in the *Nihonshoki*. This may have to do with that work being more strongly influenced by Chinese themes. If we read Izanagi and Izanami as representations of *yin* and *yang*, the Chinese principles that together drive the universe, both must remain alive for things to function. Alternatively, the lack of the Yomi story in the *Nihonshoki*'s main narrative may just mean that it was less important at the time than the *Kojiki* makes it out to be. But in all versions, regardless of whether or not Izanami dies, the creator gods ultimately cede the world to their three children, and Japan continues to move closer to human rule.

Izanagi

Izanagi is a transitional figure. He is a member of the last generation of the gods of creation, but also the father of the rest of the world. He has few defined characteristics, and is not known as the god 'of' anything in particular. As a personality, Izanagi is strong and pure, the epitome of masculine godhood. However, he is also flawed, with desires and fears that the older gods do not have. These desires and fears will be imparted to all his descendants.

Izanagi is usually portrayed as a middle-aged man, often bearded and with a fierce demeanour. He may wield a spear. Starting in the 19th century, it became typical to picture him in clothing of the Kofun and early Asuka Periods, so that he appears more 'primitive' than other gods. When Izanagi is referenced in contemporary Japanese popular culture, it is most often in some sort of pairing with Izanami.

Many shrines across Japan worship Izanagi, but only some have him as their chief deity. These include Izanagi Shrine in Awaji, and Onogorojima Shrine in Minami Awaji, both on Awaji Island (modern Hyōgo Prefecture). This is supposedly the first island created by Izanagi and Izanami. Taga Grand Shrine in Taga, Shiga Prefecture, is another shrine dedicated to Izanagi, and supposedly the location where he returned from Yomi. Eda

---

Izanagi and Izanami

- Izanagi (He Who Beckoned) and Izanami (She Who Beckoned) are a brother and sister pair of creator gods who also were married.
- They created the islands of Japan, as well as other natural forces such as seas, rivers, mountains, forests and plants.
- In the *Kojiki*, Izanami dies giving birth to Hi-no-Kagutsuchi, the god of fire. Izanagi tries to follow his wife to Yomi, the land of the dead, but is horrified to see her there as a corpse and rejects her. After Izanagi flees the land of the dead, he purifies himself in water and other gods, including Amaterasu (the sun goddess), are born as he washes himself.
- In the main narrative of the *Nihonshoki*, however, these three celestial gods are birthed by Izanami, who has not died; she then retires peacefully with Izanagi.

Shrine in Miyazaki, Miyazaki Prefecture, is supposedly the location of the pool where Izanagi purified himself. In addition, Izanagi and Izanami are often worshipped alongside the main gods at shrines dedicated to Amaterasu, Susanowo and others.

Izanami

Izanami's story hints at her becoming a goddess of death, but she is rarely depicted that way. Instead, she is usually worshipped alongside Izanagi as a goddess of long life, marriage and motherhood. In contemporary and popular culture, Izanami is often paired with Izanagi. At other times she is a villain, particularly in fantasy works based on Japanese mythology.[7]

In art, Izanami is usually pictured as a middle-aged woman who accompanies Izanagi. She is worshipped at most shrines that also worship Izanagi (although not all). Shrines that give her more importance than her husband are Iya Shrine in Matsue, Shimane Prefecture, and the Hibayama Kume Shrine in nearby Yasugi. Iya Shrine supposedly is built at the Slope of Yomi, the very spot where Izanagi and Izanami divorced. In contrast, Hibayama Kume Shrine celebrates Izanami's female form and the act of birth.

The Names of Japan

Japan has several names in the *Kojiki* and the *Nihonshoki*. The archipelago as a whole is usually a stand-in for the entire mortal world. It is known as Ashihara-no-Nakatsukuni ('The Wide-Spreading Land of Reed Plains'), Yashima-no-Kuni ('The Land of Eight Islands') and sometimes as Akizushima ('The Dragonfly Islands'). The reasons for the first and third names are unknown, but the second has to do with the myth of the islands' creation.

The order in which the 'eight islands' appear differs in each text, but always consists of Awaji, Shikoku, Kyushu, Honshu, Oki, Iki and Tsushima. Shikoku is always divided into four regions. Its name, 'Four Provinces', refers to the four ancient provinces that became its four modern prefectures. Even in the myths, it seems to have been strongly associated with the number four. Although born as a single deity, the island of Shikoku has four faces, each of which acts as a separate god specific to one of the island's four provinces.

The other islands are traditionally embodied by single deities, except Honshu, which may be divided into two depending on the version. Some of these deities are later worshipped at shrines in their respective islands or areas. They rarely appear in myth again, and are not important outside of their local communities. One example is the goddess Ōgetsuhime 大宜都比売, one of the four 'faces' of Shikoku. She is associated with Awa Province (modern Tokushima Prefecture). A patron of modern Tokushima, the capital of the prefecture, Ōgetsuhime is worshipped at several shrines across the city, including its most important one, Ichinomiya Shrine.

AMATERASU, TSUKUYOMI AND SUSANOWO

After their creation the islands of Japan are still unclaimed and ungoverned, full of wild gods and unruly spirits, since rulership of the islands was not included in the original three-way division of the world. Amaterasu received heaven; Tsukuyomi, the night; and Susanowo, the sea, but Japan itself was ignored. Initially, Amaterasu and Tsukuyomi work alongside one another and share space in the sky. One day, Amaterasu asks Tsukuyomi to pay a visit to the islands below. He looks in on Ukemochi 保食, the goddess of food, and sees that she magically generates food from all of her bodily orifices. Tsukuyomi is horrified that he may have eaten or drunk something that came from an impure part of her body. He immediately slays Ukemochi, and in response, Amaterasu banishes him from her sight. The moon is then condemned to wander the nights even as the sun wanders the days, separating their domains permanently.

The disagreement between Amaterasu and Tsukuyomi seems the most like a traditional 'myth', but it appears only in the *Nihonshoki*. Both the *Kojiki* and the *Nihonshoki* instead devote more space to discussing Susanowo, who has his own conflict with Amaterasu. The youngest of the three great deities abandons his duty of ruling the sea. Instead, he storms about the land wailing and crying. According to the *Kojiki*, when Izanagi questions his son about his behaviour, Susanowo claims that he misses his mother, the dead (according to that text) Izanami. Hearing this, Izanagi flies into a rage and banishes Susanowo from his original realm of the sea.

Susanowo flees to the High Plain of Heaven, where he seeks out Amaterasu. At first Amaterasu does not trust her brother, but they agree to have children with each other as a test. They create three girls, whom Susanowo claims as his, and five boys, who become Amaterasu's heirs. None of the children are deformed, so Susanowo wins Amaterasu's trust, and she lets him into her domain.

Despite his promise to be good, Susanowo ends up wreaking havoc on the High Plain of Heaven. He tears up Amaterasu's carefully ploughed rice fields and defecates in her weaving hall. Finally, he skins a horse backwards (from tail to head) and throws it through the roof of Amaterasu's now much-abused weaving hall. This act scares Ame-no-Hatorime, the goddess of weaving, so much that she hits herself in the genitals with her shuttle and dies. Ashamed of her brother, Amaterasu retreats into hiding in the Heavenly Rock Cave, while the other gods of the High Plain of Heaven capture Susanowo and exile him.

With Amaterasu in hiding, 'endless night came to cover the world'.[8] The other Amatsukami gather and ponder what to do. Eventually they decide to lure Amaterasu out of hiding. They make a beautiful bronze mirror and a strand of gorgeous jewels and hang them in a tree outside the Heavenly Rock Cave. Ame-no-Uzume 天鈿女, the goddess of dance

Amaterasu emerges from the Heavenly Rock Cave, causing the sun to shine once again; the mirror hangs in the tree behind her.

and joy, strips down to her underclothes and performs a provocative dance which causes all the assembled deities to laugh loudly.

Surprised that anyone has reason to laugh while she is in hiding, Amaterasu peers out of the cave. Immediately the mirror catches her reflection, shining brilliantly. Enamoured with the mirror and the jewel strand, the sun goddess moves away from the entrance to the Heavenly Rock Cave. As soon as she does, the other gods close it behind her with a sacred rope, forcing her to stay in the world. Amaterasu's return brings back the light of the sun. The mirror and the jewel strand, now both imbued with her sacred power, became two of the Three Imperial Regalia. These items would be handed to the sun goddesses' descendants in the imperial clan, and still exist today; more will be said about them later (see Chapter 3).

Meanwhile, Susanowo goes to ground in the islands of Japan. He arrives in what is now Shimane Prefecture, on the Japan Sea coast of southern Honshu. Noticing a pair of chopsticks floating down a nearby river, he backtracks up its course to find an old man and an old woman crying as they embrace a younger woman. When pressed, the old couple explain that they are local gods of earth, Kunitsukami 国津神, the term for the descendants of the landscape gods born to Izanagi and Izanami. The old couple once had eight beautiful daughters, but the Yamata-no-Orochi 八岐大蛇, a massive serpent with eight heads and eight tails, has devoured one every year for the past seven years and is now coming for the eighth and final sacrifice.

The couple's last daughter is Kushinada-hime 櫛名田比売, the 'Comb-Stroking Princess.' She is due to be eaten by the Orochi at any moment. Susanowo is smitten with Kushinada-hime, and offers to save her if he can have her as his wife; once they hear who he is, her parents agree. Susanowo promptly changes Kushinada-hime into her namesake comb and sticks her in his hair for safekeeping. He then has her parents help him to build eight giant platforms and to place a huge sake vat on each one. The Orochi arrives and drinks deeply from each of the vats with its eight heads, soon falling asleep. While it slumbers, Susanowo takes his sword and proceeds to cut off all of the Orochi's heads and tails, killing it.

As he cuts into one of the Orochi's tails, Susanowo's sword snaps. Thinking this curious, he digs deeper inside the monster's tail, and uncovers a spectacular, gleaming new sword. This is Kusanagi 草薙, the 'Grass-Cutter', the last of the Three Imperial Regalia. Recognizing the sword's power, Susanowo presents it to Amaterasu by way of apology. He earns her forgiveness – provided he remains in the mortal realm. Satisfied, Susanowo and Kushinada-hime settle at Izumo, also in modern Shimane Prefecture. Susanowo then composes the world's first poem:

> Eightfold are the clouds that rise
> in Billowing Clouds, where eightfold fences
> to surround and shelter my wife
> are eightfold fences made by me
> Ah, those eightfold fences![9]

Susanowo abandons rulership of the seas to become the master of the islands of Japan. This act is a prelude to the official conquest of the earthly world by Amaterasu's children soon after, and begins to shift the narrative focus away from the great forces of creation to the smaller ones that will shape Japan and the imperial line. Susanowo's seeking support from Amaterasu, and her greater importance to the other gods, also set up the imperial clan's divine right to rule.

Of course, the story of Susanowo and Amaterasu does more than just establish the imperial clan as the future rulers of Japan. The myth also represents an early Japanese understanding of natural forces. Amaterasu is the sun, lifegiving and vital, but prone to vanishing in ways that may require rituals to bring her back. Susanowo, in contrast, is the storm and the flood, the violence of nature rampaging unchecked.

Amaterasu

Amaterasu, 'Heaven-Shining', is the goddess of the sun, and the ancestor of the imperial line. She is the ruler of the High Plain of Heaven. She is also the origin of the imperial family's divine right to rule through her position as chief over the Amatsukami. In art over the past few centuries, Amaterasu has often been depicted as a stern yet beautiful woman who wears radiant robes and emits light. Her portrayal in the ancient chronicles is more ambiguous, however, and she is rarely described in physical detail. In both the *Kojiki* and the *Nihonshoki*, Amaterasu wears male armour for her confrontation with Susanowo, and this has even led to a hypothesis that she was originally a male deity.[10]

Amaterasu's powers are likewise difficult to define. She is the sun, but aside from her presence producing light in the sky, she does not manifest traditional solar powers such as emanating heat or causing crops to grow. In book 28 of the *Nihonshoki*, Prince Ōama, the future Emperor Tenmu (r. 672–686), calls upon her to support his forces during the Jinshin War of 672. Amaterasu responds by sending a dark cloud to shroud the sky with storms, and revealing to Ōama his future victory. In the 13th through 16th centuries, Amaterasu becomes strongly associated with the Buddhist divinity Kannon 観音, the Bodhisattva of Compassion. In this form, she is known by the Chinese-style reading of her name, Tenshō Daijin.

Ise Shrine
- Main place of worship for Amaterasu, centre of her cult in modern Ise, Mie Prefecture.
- Is said to hold the Mirror of the Three Imperial Regalia.
- Consists of an Inner Shrine, dedicated to Amaterasu; an Outer Shrine, dedicated to the goddess of food; and several other subsidiary shrines.
- Between the 7th and 18th centuries CE, the High Priestess of Ise (the 'Ise Virgin') was selected from the unmarried women of the imperial family.

Amaterasu is worshipped at shrines across Japan, but the main source and centre of her cult is Ise Shrine, in modern Ise, Mie Prefecture. One of the three most important shrines in Japan, Ise supposedly holds the Mirror, one of the Three Imperial Regalia. The shrine is a massive complex containing several concentric holy precincts. The innermost of these is called the Inner Shrine (*naikū*) and is devoted to Amaterasu. From the 7th through 18th centuries, an unmarried female member of the Imperial family was chosen during every reign to serve as the High Priestess of Ise. Known as the *saiō* 斎王, sometimes translated as the Ise Virgin, this tradition eventually lapsed, but was very important for a long time. Today Ise remains a huge tourist attraction. In accordance with ancient custom, the entire Inner Shrine of Ise is rebuilt from scratch every 60 years, most recently in 2013.

Tsukuyomi

Tsukuyomi, the god of the moon, is the odd sibling out of the celestial trio. He is granted the domain of the night by his father Izanagi, and rarely appears in myth afterwards. In the *Nihonshoki*'s main narrative, Tsukuyomi is responsible for the death of Ukemochi, the goddess of food. Otherwise, it is Susanowo who gets the position of villainous counterpart to Amaterasu.

Tsukuyomi is rarely pictured in art prior to the modern period, and there are no consistent features to his portrayal. His name hints at an association with divination, but this too is not well-represented. His other powers remain largely unknown. He is worshipped at subsidiary shrines that usually appear alongside those honouring Amaterasu. The largest of these is the aptly named Tsukuyomi Shrine, which lies between the Inner and Outer Shrines of Ise in Mie Prefecture.

Susanowo

After Amaterasu, Susanowo is probably the most recognizable deity of the Japanese pantheon. He is a deity of innate contradictions: the spoiled child who abandons his realm and the villain who tricks Amaterasu, almost causing the loss of the world's sunlight; yet he is also the hero who slays the Yamata-no-Orochi. Scholars are not even sure what, exactly, he is the god *of*. Although initially connected to the sea, he has very little to do with it later; the role of god of the ocean is eventually filled by Watatsumi.

Susanowo's name implies speed and power, and his actions mimic destruction by wind, water and fire – the natural forces that terrorized early Japan. However, he is also full of ordinary human ingenuity, and defeats other, more deadly, natural forces – such as the Orochi, whose immense bulk, tree-covered back and glowing, bloody stomach are reminiscent of a volcano, the greatest danger of the Japanese archipelago. Contemporary scholars generally claim that Susanowo is the god of violent natural forces, in charge of both instigating

Susanowo, here styled in a pose from the Kabuki theater, defeats the Yamata-no-Orochi, and takes the sword Kusanagi from its tail.

and stopping them. This argument makes sense, but it is still a modern interpretation of a complex figure. In the end, Susanowo defies our understanding as readily as he did his sister Amaterasu's.[11]

Susanowo is often portrayed as a wild-eyed, bearded man. He usually has a straight sword in the style of the Asuka and Nara Periods. Less often, Susanowo is portrayed as a young warrior, more fierce than beautiful, armoured and ready to face his enemies. He has a strong association with swords, though not necessarily with swordsmanship.

Although Susanowo is associated with anger and ferocity, both righteous and unjustified, he is, perhaps surprisingly, also an occasional patron of poetry and supposedly created the first poem to celebrate his defeat of the Orochi and marriage to Kushinada-hime. This claim is mentioned not only in both chronicles, but also in numerous later documents, such as the famous 10th-century *Kokin wakashū* ('Anthology of Ancient and Modern Poems', 920).

Susanowo is connected to Izumo, in modern Shimane Prefecture, but his primary shrines are elsewhere. These include Yasaka Shrine in Kyoto, the patron shrine of the famous Gion district and known for its rowdy July festival. There is also Susanō Shrine in Fukuyama City, Hiroshima Prefecture, which purports to date to the 5th century or earlier. In Izumo itself, Susanowo has two smaller but still important shrines: Susa Shrine and Yaegaki Shrine, both associated with the larger Izumo Shrine complex. Yaegaki Shrine is supposedly the location of Susanowo's original palace after his marriage to Kushinada-hime.

THE KUNITSUKAMI AND THE WORLDS OF CREATION

Susanowo marries Kushinada-hime and settles in Izumo. From here on he is counted among the Kunitsukami, the 'gods of the land.' For the most part, the Kunitsukami are the children of the original islands and landscape gods birthed by Izanagi and Izanami. These deities, often specific to localities across the archipelago, become the ancestors of important local lineage groups. In contrast, the Amatsukami are the ancestors of the imperial court and of the clans who serve they imperial line; they are also the ancestors of the gods who live in heaven.

Susanowo's descendants from his marriage to Kushinada-hime are named in the *Kojiki*, which next focuses its narrative on his sixth-generation descendant, Ōnamuji. Ōnamuji is the youngest of myriad brothers; the text says 80,000, functionally equivalent to infinity. He is of good and kind heart, beloved by his mother over all her other children. Ōnamuji's brothers conspire multiple times to murder him, and each time his mother revives him, before eventually sending him off to escape his family.

After an episode in which he gives a rabbit its fur, Ōnamuji finds his way to Izumo, where he falls in love with Susanowo's daughter Suseribime, his great-great-great-great-aunt. Ōnamuji must pass several tests before Susanowo will let him marry Suseribime. He passes them all flawlessly, relying on his own wits, Suseribime's wisdom and the fealty of various animals such as mice and (of course) rabbits. Having proven himself worthy to Susanowo, Ōnamuji obtains the name by which he is known thereafter: Ōkuninushi 大国主, the 'Great Land Master.'

Ōkuninushi takes over the rulership of Izumo – and through it, the archipelago – from Susanowo. Susanowo then retreats to be closer to his mother, and becomes lord of an underground domain known as Ne-no-Katasu, 'the Hardened Root.' Ōkuninushi is now head of the Kunitsukami. As a god of earth and cultivation, he is more suited to this role than was his wild and destructive predecessor.

Ōkuninushi's first act as ruler of the earth is to pacify the land, finally and permanently completing the process of creation begun with Izanagi and Izanami. A newcomer from across the sea named Sukunabikona 少名毘古那, 'Little Name Lad', joins him in this endeavor. Initially a silent, mysterious deity, Sukunabikona's identity is revealed by Ōkuninushi's attendants, as are his mysterious creative powers. Together Ōkuninushi and Sukunabikona journey across Japan, making it ready for habitation and cultivation on a large scale.

Ōkuninushi

The closest thing in the ancient myths to a god of the earth, Ōkuninushi is the deity responsible for 'finishing' the creation of the mortal realm. He is also responsible for keeping the earth prepared until Amaterasu's descendants can take it over. Ōkuninushi plays many roles in the myths, from young and victimized hero – a sort of Japanese Osiris – to wandering lord, and then cautious master of his realm in the face of the demanding Amatsukami. Despite all this, his actual powers are less well-defined than many of the Japanese deities.

Ōkuninushi finishes creation, rendering the land stable and capable of growing crops. He also brings the Kunitsukami together under his authority. This calms the forces of nature. However, Ōkuninushi is not a god of agriculture. He is likewise not a god of mountains or plains, the natural landforms that make up the islands. Perhaps he is a holdover of a local god originally on the same level as Amaterasu, only for a different ancient kingdom, one that had to be put under imperial control – as Susanowo and Tsukuyomi may have been.

Ōkuninushi was rarely portrayed visually until the modern era. Today he often appears as a calmer version of Susanowo, as a serious man wearing Kofun or Asuka Period clothing, sometimes without a weapon. Statues and paintings of Ōkuninushi show him with a quiet pride in stance and gaze, in contrast to Susanowo's typically ferocious posture and expression.

Ōkuninushi, here portrayed as a wise old nobleman, with the rabbit that he saved.

45

Ōkuninushi's most important place of worship is the Izumo Grand Shrine in Izumo, Shimane Prefecture. The second of the three most important shrines in Japan, this is supposedly the location of Susanowo's first settlement, which later became Ōkuninushi's palace in the days before the arrival of Ninigi, Amaterasu's grandson and the founder of the imperial clan.

Today the Izumo Grand Shrine is a large complex of wooden structures in a style similar to the Ise Shrine, but more rustic. However, this was not always the case. The chronicles talk about Ōkuninushi's 'high house', and a Kamakura Period illustration appears to show a different shrine structure raised on large pillars. In one of the most spectacular archaeological discoveries ever made in Japan, a dig on the grounds of the Izumo Grand Shrine in 2000 revealed the remains of immense supports for the ancient building. These supports were formed by lashing many sets of three tree trunks together to make a single pillar. Each completed pillar was over 2 m (nearly 7 ft) in diameter. It appears that the 'high house' supported

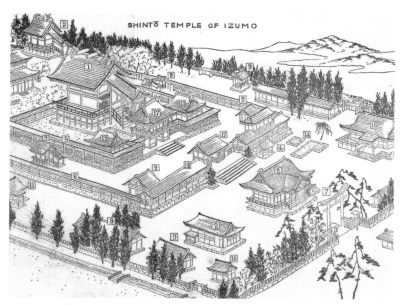

SHINTŌ TEMPLE OF IZUMO

Izumo Shrine in Shimane Prefecture, the main site of worship for Ōkuninushi, long after the great pillars had fallen. Scholars were unaware of its earlier size.

Izumo Grand Shrine
- Primary site for worship of Ōkuninushi; is also sacred to Susanowo.
- Marks location of Susanowo's first settlement, and Ōkuninushi's palace.
- Said to have been constructed in Ōkuninushi's honour by the legendary eleventh emperor, Suinin (trad. r. 29 BCE–70 CE), whose mute son Prince Homutsuwake then miraculously recovered the ability to speak.
- In 2000, archaeologists uncovered the remains of support pillars for an ancient version of the shrine; this original 'high house' would have been 20 m (65 ft) tall. The modern shrine is a large rustic wooden complex.

---

by these immense pillars was at least 20 m (65 ft) tall, putting it among the tallest premodern wooden structures ever created![12]

As with the stories of Izanami's death and Izanagi's visit to Yomi, the *Nihonshoki* more or less ignores Ōkuninushi in its main narrative; he is mentioned only in the smaller 'one book says' sections, and he does not appear to have been worshipped widely by the early Japanese court. However, there is evidence that Ōkuninushi was an important local god in southern Honshu, as he, and not Susanowo, is the dominant deity at Izumo Shrine. Ancient Izumo had a very different tradition of tomb-building and ironworking than the rest of the archipelago: the technology used at Izumo in the first few centuries CE is more similar to that of the ancient Korean kingdom of Silla.[13] Perhaps the Great Land Master Ōkuninushi was originally the patron of a kingdom subsumed into the Japanese court long ago and forced to pay homage to Amaterasu's descendants in myth as well as fact.

THE GEOGRAPHY OF THE JAPANESE MYTHS

The cosmology of the *Kojiki* and the *Nihonshoki* is confused. This is in part due to the lack of continuity between the texts, but there is also very little description in either work about *what*, exactly, is located *where*. The mortal realm – Ashihara-no-Nakatsukuni – is clearly identified with the archipelago of Japan. Unfortunately, the rest of the real world does not seem to exist around the islands. What we have instead are several 'countries' (*kuni*), the same word used for both 'province' and 'land' in ancient times. These 'countries' are joined to Ashihara-no-Nakatsukuni in certain places, but also coexist within fantastic spaces, such as the bottom of the sea.

The most important of these other realms is Takamagahara, 'The High Plain of Heaven.' This is the land of the Amatsukami, specifically of Amaterasu and her court. It is sometimes identified with the sky. However, it is not the same as Tsukuyomi's domain of night (which, interestingly, lacks a name). Takamagahara is described solely as being 'above' Ashihara-no-Nakatsukuni. Several different figures, including Izanagi and Izanami, and all of Amaterasu's envoys to the Kunitsukami, use a contraption known as the 'Floating Bridge of Heaven' (*ama-no-ukihashi*) to reach the mortal realm. The bridge's function is never described. In more recent times it has been pictured as everything from a regular bridge to a magical elevator.

When Izanami dies, she goes to the realm of Yomi. Yomi is physically reachable from Ashihara-no-Nakatsukuni, although the text never speci-

Izanagi (left) and Izanami (right) standing on the
Floating Bridge of Heaven.

fies where exactly the entrance – the Slope of Yomi – is located. The name uses the characters for 'Sulphur Springs', borrowing from a Chinese term for a volcanic hellscape. The pronunciation *yomi* is not Chinese and is probably a name native to Japan. Yomi is home to hags, old women beyond marriageable age, and thunder deities, who cause destruction. The land is rarely referenced at all outside of the ancient chronicles, whether in medieval stories or early modern folklore.

Yomi is usually considered to be the same place as Susanowo's eventual home, Ne-no-Katasu, or 'The Hardened Root.' Susanowo retires here after passing his rule over Ashihara-no-Nakatsukuni to Ōkuninushi. Strangely, nothing more is ever mentioned about it. The name is reminiscent of roots underground, and in an earlier scene, Susanowo explains his crying as a longing to be with his mother, Izanami, who is currently in Yomi. These two facts have led scholars to link the two places, although there are problems with this attribution. The most notable of these is that Yomi is not underground, but Ne-no-Katasu may be.

The final realm mentioned in the chronicles is the land of the sea god Watatsumi 綿津見. It is usually considered to be on the ocean floor, but it also has gardens, rice fields, palaces and other features of the terrestrial world. This realm appears to be that originally assigned to Susanowo before his tearful abdication. Like Tsukuyomi's domain, it lacks a specific name. It is populated by *kami* who double as creatures of the sea, perhaps drawing from Chinese associations of dragons with water and the ocean. Whereas Yomi and Ne-no-Katasu appear to be specific places, reachable from the mortal realm, the sea realm is, like Takamagahara, somewhere apart and inaccessible to humans. To reach it requires the tacit approval of its master, Watatsumi.

THE CONQUEST OF THE LAND

After Ōkuninushi completes the creation, Amaterasu decides to take over the islands and unite earth and heaven under the Amatsukami. She chooses the eldest of the five sons she produced with Susanowo, Ame-no-Oshihomimi 天忍穂耳, to persuade Ōkuninushi to give up rule of the earth. Ame-no-Oshihomimi does not want the difficult job of pacifying the restive gods of the earth, and refuses. In his place, Amaterasu decides to send the second of her sons, Ame-no-Hohi 天穂日.

Ame-no-Hohi dutifully descends to the mortal world. He meets with Ōkuninushi, and becomes enamoured with the Kunitsukami, refusing even to report back to Amaterasu for three years. Frustrated, Amaterasu sends a god known as Ame-no-Wakahiko 天若日子 to contact Ōkuninushi. Ame-no-Wakahiko, too, ends up siding with the Kunitsukami, and marries one of Ōkuninushi's daughters. After another eight years have passed, Amaterasu orders a pheasant to travel to Ōkuninushi's realm and find out why Ame-no-Wakahiko has also not reported back. Ame-no-Wakahiko shoots the pheasant, but the arrow turns around and hits him as well, killing him.

At this point, the Amatsukami convene an assembly to decide what to do. Eventually it is resolved to make a less diplomatic effort. Amaterasu contacts Takemikazuchi, a god of strength and storms whose father was the blade used by Izanagi to kill the fire god Hi-no-Kagutsuchi. Takemikazuchi's mission is to conquer Ōkuninushi's court by force.

Takemikazuchi travels down to earth with several companions, and parleys with Ōkuninushi on the coast of Izumo. Ōkuninushi confers with his own council of Kunitsukami. Chief among this council is his son Kotoshironushi 事代主, a god of knowledge. Kotoshironushi urges his father not to fight the Amatsukami and, after much deliberation, Ōkuninushi agrees. He accepts Amaterasu's demands and gives over rulership of the earth. In return for giving up rule of the archipelago, he insists on maintaining authority over the religious affairs of the *kami*, and a 'great palace' in Izumo for a home – the origins of Izumo Shrine.

The Amatsukami have officially won dominion over all creation for Amaterasu. Now the task of ruling the mortal world must begin. For this, Amaterasu turns to her grandson, the oldest son of Ame-no-Oshihomimi. This grandson has many names, but most of them contain the element Ninigi, and it is by this name that he is known today.

Ninigi, like his father, is a deity of rice cultivation. In addition to bearing Amaterasu's blood on his father's side, his mother is the daughter of Takamimusuhi, one of the deities preceding Izanagi and Izanami. Ninigi therefore combines within himself both Amaterasu's solar rule and

Konohana-no-Sakuyabime, Ninigi's wife and a progenitor of the future imperial clan.

the older creative forces that underlie the universe. Ninigi gathers some companions from among the gods who helped to pull Amaterasu out of the Heavenly Rock Cave, and goes down to earth. Before he leaves the High Plain of Heaven, he receives the Imperial Regalia from Amaterasu: the sword Kusanagi, the mirror with Amaterasu's image, and the jewel strand that lured her out from the Heavenly Rock Cave. Upon arrival in the mortal realm, Ninigi's group is joined by Takemikazuchi. The group settles in Himuka ('Sun-Facing'), modern Hyūga in Miyazaki Prefecture. Ninigi marries Konohana-no-Sakuyabime, a flower goddess and the daughter of the mountain gods birthed by Izanami. Their marriage firmly binds one of the major lineages of the Kunitsukami into Amaterasu's line, and joins the powers of nature to those of the sun.

Takemikazuchi

Takemikazuchi is a thunder deity, but very different from other thunder deities in the ancient chronicles, who appear as servants of Izanami and/ or destructive forces. Takemikazuchi is a god of bravery and righteous battle. He is also the messenger who finally makes Amaterasu's claims on Ashihara-no-Nakatsukuni known to the Kunitsukami. Takemikazuchi refuses to bend like the previous messengers did, and later serves as one of Ninigi's counsellors. He seems more like a god of war than of thunder. His war-leader status and original importance far from the imperial court raises questions as to whether he too was once the central deity of a smaller kingdom or region in ancient times. If so, this would mean that Takemikazuchi was also subsumed under Amaterasu as part of the new imperial order.

A procession of *miko* or shrine priestesses at the Kasuga Grand Shrine in Nara.

Starting in the late medieval era, Takemikazuchi appears as a patron of martial arts, particularly swordsmanship. From this point onward he is always portrayed as a swordsman, typically stern but calm. Takemikazuchi's original shrine was Kashima Shrine in Kashima, Ibaraki Prefecture, north of Tokyo. He was later re-enshrined at several other locations in southern Honshu, most prominently at the Kasuga Grand Shrine in Nara.

Ninigi

Ninigi has many names in the ancient chronicles, but most of them end in the three syllables by which he is known today. As the Heavenly Grandson, he is Amaterasu's heir on earth, sent to rule the mortal realm in the name of the Amatsukami.

Ninigi's longer names contain words for ears of rice, and scholars think he was originally a god of agriculture. However, agriculture is usually the domain of local *kami*. Ninigi is more often worshipped as a god of rulership. As a mythical figure, he is more human than deity in some ways, and his most famous role is as ancestor of the imperial clan.

Ninigi is not often portrayed in art, and images of him are rare even in the modern period. When he is pictured it is usually as a young man in ancient Japanese clothing. These images surprisingly have very few distinguishing characteristics.

Ninigi is worshipped at only a few shrines. The most important of these is Kirishima Shrine in Kirishima, and Nitta Shrine in Satsuma Sendai, both in Kagoshima Prefecture, as well as Imizu Shrine 射水神社 in Takaoka, Toyama Prefecture.

THE ORIGINS OF THE IMPERIAL LINE

Ninigi and Konohana-no-Sakuyabime have several children. Two of their sons are Hoderi 火照 ('Bright Flame') and Howori 火折 ('Flickering Flame'). Hoderi is born first; in fact, Konohana-no-Sakuyabime announces that she is pregnant with him the morning after her marriage to Ninigi! Ninigi is astounded at how fast this occurs. Worried that she is actually bearing the child of a previous lover, Ninigi forces Konohana-no-Sakuyabime into a birthing hut and then sets it on fire. The flames spare the goddess, who was telling the truth, and she is found amidst the ashes unharmed, cradling a baby boy. Hoderi's name reflects his birth in a fire.

Hoderi becomes a famous hunter, using the knowledge of the mountains inherited from his mother and maternal grandfather to find game. Howori, his younger brother, becomes an equally famous fisherman. One day the two get into an argument when Hoderi tries to prove that he can fish as well as his brother. Unfortunately he can't, and even loses Howori's special stone fishhook in the ocean. Hoderi tries to give Howori another fishhook, but Howori claims that, as all things have their own *kami*, it would be like throwing one child away for another. Hoderi then decides to dive into the sea to retrieve his brother's original fishhook.

Hoderi dives down into the ocean depths to search. Instead of the fishhook, the young god stumbles upon a marvellous palace at the bottom of the sea. This is the home of Watatsumi, the god of the ocean, who presumably inherits the realm after Susanowo abandons it. Hoderi stays with Watatsumi for several years. During his sojourn under the sea, he falls in love with Watatsumi's daughter Toyotama-hime 豊玉姫, a goddess of treasure. The two marry, and then decide to return to the surface.

Upon their return, Toyotama-hime gives Hoderi a magical jewel that controls the tides. He challenges Howori once again, and uses the jewel to catch more fish than his brother. Howori acknowledges defeat, and that Hoderi is better suited to rule. Hoderi then inherits Ninigi's mandate over the earthly realms of creation. Hoderi's marriage brings yet another force, the powers of the sea, into the nascent imperial line; Amaterasu's descendants not only have the mandate to rule over the islands of Japan and the surrounding seas, but have quite literally married into both the land and the water.

Toyotama-hime becomes pregnant and prepares to give birth to her and Hoderi's first child. She tells her husband that despite her pleasing form she is still a child of the sea, and so she must give birth alone in a secluded hut. She begs him not to look upon her when the time comes. Unbearably curious, Hoderi sneaks into the hut. He is shocked when, instead of his beloved wife, he sees an immense sea creature in the throes of labour! What exactly he saw differs between the texts, with the *Kojiki* claiming a shark, and the *Nihonshoki*, a dragon.

Toyotama-hime gives birth to a boy, whom she names Ugayafukiaezu 鵜萱葺萱不合, a reference to the cormorant feathers that thatched her magical birthing hut.

Toyotama-hime, daughter of Watatsumi, the god of the sea; her dishevelled hair and the dragon on her back hint at her true nature.

She gives the boy to Hoderi but tells her husband that she can never forgive him for his disrespect. She then leaves him for the oceans forever. In her place, Toyotama-hime sends her sister Tamayori-hime 玉依姫, a goddess of objects invested with sacred power, to take care of Ugayafukiaezu as he grows.

The boy bears within him the lineages of the Amatsukami, the Kunitsukami and the sea. Yet Ugayafukiaezu is unable to take up the mantle of emperor, the destiny of Amaterasu's descendants. No version explains exactly why, but it may be due to the promise that was broken between his parents. When he comes of age, Ugayafukiaezu marries his aunt Tamayori-hime, and finally the lineage of the sea is bound to the rest without incident. They have four sons, the youngest of whom is best known by his two-character imperial name: Jinmu 神武, 'The Gods' Weapon', the legendary First Emperor of Japan.

Watatsumi

Watatsumi, the god of the sea, makes surprisingly few appearances in the ancient chronicles. Of course, considering that Japan is made up of islands, *kami* of individual bodies of water have always had outsize local importance. Watatsumi goes beyond that, however, overseeing the greatest body of water of all.

Watatsumi is actually a triple deity. He first appears as three brothers born to Izanagi during his purification after visiting Yomi. The three brothers are: Sokotsu-Watatsumi 底津綿津見, 'Crossing God of the Sea Floor' (or Sokotsutsunowo 底筒之男, 'Man of the Bottom Crossing'); Nakatsu-Watatsumi 中津綿津見, 'Crossing God of the Sea Middle' (or Nakatsutsunowo 中筒之男, 'Man of the Middle Crossing'); and Uwatsu-Watatsumi 上津綿津見, 'Crossing God of the Sea Surface' (or Uwatsutsunowo 上筒之男, 'Man of the Upper Crossing'). These three appear as a single god in all other myths concerning Watatsumi.

Watatsumi is worshipped at many shrines across Japan. The most famous of these is the Sumiyoshi Grand Shrine in Osaka. Sumiyoshi Shrine was originally a huge shrine complex right on the beach, just south of the ancient port of Naniwa. Today the shrine is several kilometres inland due to land reclamation, but is still a major tourist spot, and the namesake of its entire city ward. Curiously, all three of Watatsumi's component gods are enshrined separately at Sumiyoshi. They are worshipped at identical smaller shrines placed next to one another, alongside one for Empress Jingū 神宮皇后, a figure about whom more will be said in the next chapter.

JINMU, THE FIRST EMPEROR

Jinmu is the figure who transitions between the world of the gods and the world of men. He takes his authority to rule from Amaterasu, the divine matriarch. He also contains all the other strands of creation within his bloodline. From his great-grandmother, Jinmu has the power of the Kunitsukami and their dominion over the land. From his mother

Jinmu, the First Emperor, defeating the Tsuchigumo with his longbow and a sacred wand. The 'Eight-Legged Crow' Yatagarasu perches on his bow, emitting the light of the sun.

and grandmother, he has that of the sea. Unlike his father, he is not the offspring of a broken promise. Jinmu therefore represents the unity of forces needed to bring a lasting peace to the archipelago.

He also represents the first character in the myths who is as much man as he is god. The First Emperor does not have a direct connection to the High Plain of Heaven except through his ancestral lineage. Everything he does is focused solely and completely on 'mortal' concerns, such as control over territory or the defeat of local enemies.

The name Jinmu is a Chinese-style name made up of two characters. This is a style of imperial name that became popular for rulers of the 8th century, and which remains the official format today. In the chronicles, however, he is referred to by his native royal name: Kamu-Yamato-Iwarebiko 神日本磐余彦, or 'Brave Prince of Iware in Yamato, Blessed By the Gods.' This impressively long name lists the village in which he will eventually build his palace, Iware, in modern Sakurai, Nara Prefecture.

The young prince is the fourth of four sons born to Ugayafukiaezu and Tamayori-hime. He grows up in Himuka, on the south-eastern coast of Kyushu. He has three older brothers: Itsuse, Inai and Mikeiri. Only Itsuse, the oldest, figures prominently in any narrative. Inai and Mikeiri barely appear in the *Kojiki*, whereas in the *Nihonshoki* they both vanish on errands. Inai travels to the bottom of the sea as a shark-god and Mikeiri goes in search of Tokoyo 常世, the land of eternal life. Itsuse, however, is very close to his younger brother, and remains by Jinmu's side.

Ugayafukiaezu and Tamayori-hime both die when their sons are in their forties. Soon afterwards Jinmu stumbles upon a man with a tail while hunting; this man is Shiotsuchi 塩土, a Kunitsukami, and he swears allegiance to the young prince. Shiotsuchi has had a dream that Amaterasu and Takemikazuchi spoke to him. They ordered him to tell the children of Ugayafukiaezu, and Jinmu in particular, to travel north. There, deep in central Honshu, they will find Yamato, a valley ringed by mountains and blessed by rivers. Amaterasu desires for Yamato to become the centre of the mortal realm. The way forward is filled with as-yet unappeased Kunitsukami. It will be up to Jinmu and Itsuse to quell them.

Shiotsuchi, whose name is associated with the tides, joins Jinmu as a master shipbuilder. To help the princes further, Amaterasu sends one

---

Jinmu, the First Emperor
- His authority comes from the sun goddess Amaterasu, who is his great-grandmother.
- He is as much man as he is god, and thus concerned with mortal issues.
- Leads troops in a conquest for Yamato (modern Nara Prefecture). Defeats various Kunitsukami ('gods of the earth') who are not subservient to Amaterasu and the Amatsukami ('gods of heaven').
- Marries Himetatara-Isuzuhime, who has the bloodline of a pure Amatsukami.
- Scholars dispute if Jinmu existed at all. Shrines dedicated to him, and a burial site, are all modern-day constructions.

---

other god: Yatagarasu 八咫烏, the 'Eight-Legged Crow'. Yatagarasu leads the way north, heralding the arrival of the Heavenly Descendants and their nascent court.

Jinmu and Itsuse travel up the coast, stopping at various places (the exact list is different between the chronicles). At each stop they find themselves opposed by the Tsuchigumo 土蜘蛛, the 'Earth-Spiders'. These are long-armed and long-legged Kunitsukami who resent the Amatsukami rule of the land. Some Tsuchigumo also end up joining Jinmu and Itsuse's army. Others fight back, but they are always conquered.

In time, the two princes and their forces reach Naniwa, the port that became the modern city of Osaka. Naniwa is the closest approach to Yamato by sea. As the princes try to land their boats, Nagasunebiko 長髄彦, one of the Tsuchigumo lords of Yamato, engages them in a vicious battle. During the battle, Itsuse is struck by a powerful 'whistling arrow'. Jinmu sounds a retreat. As his forces leave the field of battle, he realizes that they have been facing east, into the sun. Instead they should have been fighting with Amaterasu at their backs; not doing that has caused their defeat.

Itsuse dies of his wounds, cursing his fate with his last breath. Jinmu is left as the last heir of the sun. He gathers up his army and sails south around the Kii Peninsula to land at Kumano, now the city of Shingū in Wakayama Prefecture. According to the *Nihonshoki*, Jinmu receives a good omen from the Great God of Kumano, a mysterious local deity. In the *Kojiki*, the sign is a portent from Amaterasu herself. Regardless of who sent it, the omens are positive, so the Amatsukami army moves inland. They travel through the mountains of the Kii Peninsula, following the ancient pilgrimage route (and present UNESCO World Heritage Site) known as the Kumano Kodō.

The *Kojiki* account of Jinmu's conquest after this point is almost mercifully brief. The prince travels up through the mountains into the Nara Basin, where he engages Nagasunebiko's forces at Mt Kaguyama. This low mountain, at 152 m (500 ft) tall barely more than a hill, is nonetheless one of the Three Sacred Mountains of Yamato. Jinmu defeats Nagasunebiko soundly on its slopes.

The *Nihonshoki* account is much more detailed. It focuses on each of Nagasunebiko's subordinates, and how Jinmu and his forces defeat them. These stories feature some themes that will be repeated later, such as the existence of twin adversaries, one of whom turns out to be good and the other evil. Soon after entering Yamato, Jinmu encounters a pair of brothers named Eshiki and Otoshiki. Both brothers agree to swear allegiance to him at Eshiki's great hall. Otoshiki comes to Jinmu in secret, telling him that Eshiki has placed rock traps in the ceiling at the hall and plans to crush the prince to death during the ceremony. Jinmu sends his forces to investigate. In the ensuing battle, Eshiki accidentally triggers his own traps and crushes himself to death. Otoshiki swears allegiance in good faith and becomes one of Jinmu's generals.

In another trope that will be repeated further down the line, the *Nihonshoki* records that Jinmu wins a victory through deceit via crossdressing. He tries to scout out Mt Kaguyama, but finds it blocked by Nagasunebiko's forces. The prince then has Shiotsuchi and Otoshiki dress in the clothes of an old woman and old man. Thus disguised, the two proceed to the mountain claiming to be pilgrims wishing to pray to its god. The enemy troops laugh uproariously at how impoverished the pair appear, and then let them through. Once past the blockade, Shiotsuchi and Otoshiki steal holy clay from the mountain and return to Jinmu. Jinmu shapes the clay into a bowl, which he then uses to divine the conditions of his victory.

In both versions, the entry into Yamato culminates with the battle atop Mt Kaguyama. Nagasunebiko's forces are scattered across its flat, wide summit, while Jinmu's army has to attack straight up from the surrounding plain. The prince himself leads the attack and defeats the Tsuchigumo with almost no casualties. In both versions, he follows up his victory with several songs. Most of them are boastful claims about his skill with a sword, or the speed of Nagasunebiko's defeat. Known as *kumeuta*, they were thought to be ritual songs sung by a specific clan serving the imperial family. One example is the song below, sung by Jinmu immediately upon killing Nagasunebiko:

> Fierce and furious
> lads of the Fighters
> in a field of fox-tail millet thrives
> a stinking stalk of chive.
> Hunt for its roots,
> seek out its shoots,
> strike and put an end to it![14]

The First Emperor of Japan is enthroned on the first day of the new year following his pacification of Yamato. He builds a palace on the north-eastern slopes of Mt Unebi, another of the Three Sacred Mountains of Yamato. The modern Kashihara Shrine in Kashihara, Nara Prefecture, was built over what is supposedly the exact spot of Jinmu's palace.

Jinmu's first act as emperor is to search for an appropriate wife. Although he had married once before in Himuka, he now needs someone with pedigree worthy of Amaterasu's descendant. Rumours come to him of a beautiful woman, the granddaughter of a local lord, who was conceived through mysterious means. Some decades ago, the lord's daughter was defecating in a river that flowed from Mt Miwa, another sacred mountain to the east of the Nara Basin (although not one of the Three Sacred Mountains). The woman was seen by the god of the mountain, a deity called Monoshironushi 物白主. Monoshironushi was a descendant of Takamimusuhi, one of the original gods of the first creation, and therefore among the highest ranks of the Amatsukami.

Monoshironushi fell for the beautiful woman. He turned himself into a red arrow, which then flew down the stream and lodged in the woman's genitals. In shock she stood up, whereupon he turned into a beautiful man and professed his love for her. The child born from that union, a girl named Himetatara-Isuzuhime 姫蹈韛五十鈴姫, is extremely beautiful. She also bears the bloodline of a pure Amatsukami and therefore would be a perfect match for the new emperor. Jinmu sends messengers to verify Himetatara-Isuzuhime's beauty and lineage, and they return with proof. He then courts and marries her, beginning the lineage of emperors that supposedly continues in Japan to this day.

Jinmu rules for 76 years, until he is either 160 or 170 years old (depending on the chronicle). After his death, he is laid to rest in the first Imperial Mausoleum. This was supposedly a tomb mound at the foot of Mt Unebi, near his palace. Interestingly enough, there is no ancient tomb mound anywhere near the area where both chronicles record his burial – though one was constructed in the late 19th century, as part of the State Shinto project that ended with the Second World War.

The lack of a tomb for Jinmu was bewildering to premodern authors. Some questioned whether the First Emperor of Japan truly died; others, whether he was real at all (a position held by most modern scholars). Certainly Jinmu was never worshipped in the same way as his ancestors or other *kami*. Any shrines dedicated to him are also modern phenomena, just like his tomb mound.

The First Emperor is not a god like his ancestors and with his death their age comes to its final close. Whatever the future deeds of the imperial line, whatever adventures they have or powers they present, ultimately they belong to the human realm alone. It is to this realm that we next turn our attention.

3

THE IMPERIAL MYTHOS

This chapter continues looking at the ancient Japanese chronicles, the *Kojiki* and the *Nihonshoki*, as they leave behind the stories of the gods and begin those about humans. This next set of myths is about the emperors' ancestors and how they gained control over Japan. They also show an idealized image of the realm and offer guidelines for how the early Japanese understood kingship. Their ideas belong to the 8th century, when the *Kojiki* and *Nihonshoki* were written down, but they were revived century after century, even as Japan's society and culture evolved. In some eras the concepts were ignored, and in others, embraced. In the present era, they are treated as sources of history and past ideology that are mostly no longer applicable to modern Japan. The mythology of the early emperors is thus as much about the *ideal* of an emperor as anything else. That ideal remains important today.

WHAT IS AN EMPEROR?

Article I of the Constitution of Japan states that: 'The Emperor shall be the symbol of the State and of the unity of the People, deriving his position from the will of the people with whom resides sovereign power'.[1] This constitution, adopted in 1946 and written by the American occupying forces, has defined the government of contemporary Japan and the roles of its leaders since the disastrous end of the Second World War. The fact that the very first article begins by explaining the emperor and his role is a testament to how important a figure he remains today.

Article I of the Constitution contains two very important ideas: first, that the emperor is the symbol of Japan and of the Japanese people;

second, that his power comes from the people, not himself. The first idea, that the emperor is the symbol of Japan and its people, is an ancient one. The second, that his power comes from the people, is new, and different from anything that has come before – but not shockingly so. During the Second World War, the emperor was perceived as a living god, an ideal enforced by the government, the education system and many aspects of Japanese culture itself. However, this focus on the emperor as god-king had not been the norm for much of Japanese history. The emperors have been many things at many different times, and they were not often worshipped as deities. In many periods, they were not even truly in charge of the government! The American occupation used this historical understanding to shift the emperor back to being a figurehead, a symbol used to unite the realm.

There are several words in Japanese that are translated into English as 'emperor', and each of these has a specific meaning. The main one used

Enthronement ceremony of Emperor Hirohito (r. 1926–1989), illustrated like a classical scroll. In the back are two *takamikura*, covered daises for the emperor and empress.

today is *tennō*, which literally means 'heavenly sovereign'. The term was originally the name of a mythical early ruler of China. In later Chinese sources it refers to a ruler of heaven, or sometimes to the pole star. The pole star is the closest star to the Earth's axis and, from the northern hemisphere, all the constellations appear to rotate around the north pole star, known in the West as Polaris, in the constellation Ursa Minor. Ancient Chinese astrologers noted that the sky appeared to rotate around the northern pole star, and therefore believed that it was the throne of heaven.[2] This idea led to the belief that the ruler of heaven is like a pole star, if not literally the same thing – and thus that the ruler of earth, or at least its of its most important location (for them, China), must be as well.

Both the *Kojiki* and the *Nihonshoki* call all rulers starting with Jinmu 'emperor', but none of the terms translated as 'emperor' in English were used until the late 7th century CE. The first ruler to call himself an 'emperor' was Tenmu 天武 (631–686, r. 672–686), the fortieth ruler in the traditional count. Tenmu won the throne after a brief but intense conflict known as the Jinshin War in 672, deposing his nephew, who had been the crown prince. According to the *Nihonshoki*, Tenmu himself performed a divination using a series of wooden boards, and discovered that he was to be the next ruler. The sun goddess and divine matriarch Amaterasu herself verified the result by filling the sky over the province of Yamato with storm clouds.[3] Tenmu then proclaimed himself not an earthly ruler, but one drawing power from the gods and heaven – the *tennō*. All the previous rulers were known by the term *ōkimi*, or 'great lord'; 'sovereign' and 'king' are also acceptable translations. We will be using the word

---

The *Tennō*

- Main Japanese word for the emperor. Literally 'heavenly sovereign', it comes from the name of a mythical early ruler of China (Ch. *tianhuang*).
- Sometimes refers to the pole star, indicating the emperor's place at the centre of the Japanese realm.
- The *tennō* functions as the intermediary between humans and *kami*.
- Can control the Japanese calendar (see page 68).
- Has only ever been one dynasty, so the imperial family has no surname.

Emperor Hirohito (r. 1925–1989), portrayed after his enthronement surrounded by members of the military and the court.

'emperor' because the chronicles use it, but most reputable books of Japanese history do not use it for any ruler prior to Tenmu.

The name *tennō* implies the emperor's position at the centre of the Japanese realm. However, like the pole star, this is not an active position. The pole star does not *do* anything; it simply sits, and by virtue of what it is, everything else rotates around it. The *tennō* is theoretically the same: he exists at the centre of the government and all things orbit around him, but he himself does not need to *do* anything other than simply be. There are many historical examples of emperors taking action, and in the modern era, the emperor's practical responsibilities to the nation (such as greeting foreign leaders and being responsible for the management of historical sites related to the imperial family) have become more prominent and controversial, as in many modern European democracies whose royal families are ceremonial figureheads supported financially by the state. Yet on a fundamental level, the *tennō* is a static figure, an image that serves to orient everyone else.

Starting in the Heian Period, the term *mikado* became more widely used. *Mikado* is a native Japanese word that literally means 'the honourable gate'. It refers to the gates of the inner palace, inside which the emperor and his harem reside out of view. Although in the 7th and 8th centuries, the emperors were often leaders of large public events, by the 9th century they had begun to be cloistered more and more within the palace.

Traditionally, a male child of the imperial family would inherit the throne. Primogeniture, in which the *oldest* (male) child automatically inherits the throne, was *not* practised at the Japanese court. Any imperial prince could be chosen to be the heir, provided his mother was of high enough status herself. Emperors typically had a harem composed of many different women, but there was usually only one full empress, who was always of the highest levels of the aristocracy. Only her children, or those of the highest-ranking concubines, would be eligible to be the next emperor. This pattern was finally altered in the early 20th century, and today the emperor marries once, to whomever he wants (in theory; though in practice, public opinion limits the choice of potential spouses).

Women are not supposed to inherit the throne, but there have been seven cases of women becoming emperors. Five of these occurred during the Nara Period, when a dearth of male descendants of the ruling branch of the imperial family led to imperial princesses occupying the throne. The other two women who ruled were put on the throne in similar situations but much later, in the early 17th and mid-18th centuries, respectively. As the Japanese language does not have gendered words, these women were also called *tennō*. There is much debate as to how to refer to them in English, as 'empress' is usually used for the head of the imperial harem; this book will use the term 'empress regnant', although 'female emperor' is arguably more correct.

Female emperors
- There have been seven cases where women have become emperors.
- Five female emperors occurred during the Nara Period, including the only woman to pass the throne to another woman.
- Female emperors are also called *tennō*. In English the most common term for this is 'empress regnant'.

WHAT DOES THE EMPEROR DO?

Based on the important terms used, the emperor's two most well-known features were his role at the centre of the realm, and that he was often concealed deep within the palace. Both of these qualities are passive ones. The Japanese emperor was not usually an active leader like his Roman counterpart. He was meant to be an axis for the rest of the empire, not stand at the head of the armies. Yet he did have more to do than just exist. The emperor was not only the descendant of the gods, but their chief representative on earth. In this position, he was expected to perform ceremonies for the well-being of the realm. Many of these ceremonies, at least initially, were related to *kami* and what would become Shinto. However, ceremonies from other origins – Buddhism, Confucianism, and those of other continental traditions – were rapidly added to the mix.

In addition to performing these ceremonies, the emperor technically organized the entire calendar. As the metaphysical centre of the kingdom, he was responsible for controlling the proper order of events. In order to do this, the emperor picked an era name, which restarted the calendar from year 1. This practice remains in Japan to this day: in addition to the Western calendar year, the modern Japanese calendar also counts by eras. The current emperor, Naruhito, ascended the throne in May 2019. That year became the first year of his new era of Reiwa, or 'manifest peace'. 2020 then becomes Reiwa 2, etc. The year numbering changes on the day of ascension, meaning that January through April of 2019 are still recorded as the first four months of Heisei 31, the previous era (the reign of the now-retired Emperor Akihito).

Prior to 1868, the Japanese calendar was solely counted in era years. Although modern emperors are forbidden by law from changing the era name after their ascension, premodern emperors were not, and would ceremonially reset the calendar to reassure the nation whenever events went unfavourably, such as during an epidemic or a war. In one extreme case, a single solar year had up to three different era names: 749 began as Tenpyō 21; it was changed in summer to Tenpyō Kanpō 1; and was changed again a few months later to Tenpyō Shōhō 1! The decision to change the era name, as well as what two- or four-character name to give it, was made through the councils of state. Today a body of scholars and

The emperor and the Japanese calendar
- The emperor has the role of organizing the Japanese calendar.
- On ascension to the throne, he picks an era name, which restarts the calendar to year 1.
- Originally this could occur again whenever necessary, such as after great events (positive or negative), to give history a fresh start.
- Today this practice can only occur once per imperial reign.
- Modern era names are chosen by scholars and politicians, and only affirmed by the emperor (who no longer has any political power).

politicians pick the name, and in the case of Reiwa (Naruhito's current era) there was significant public debate after it was announced.

The role of the *tennō* was not necessarily that of a powerful ruler. The upper levels of the court, and in later times the shogunal government, handled most of the day-to-day affairs of state. The Japanese emperor was instead primarily a passive source of authority, cloistered away inside the palace so that he (or occasionally she) could interact with the *kami* and other forces that helped shape the realm. The emperor was envisaged as the axis around which the empire orbited, and as the most important connection between humans and the *kami*. These qualities come out clearly in the myths of the early emperors.

THE LEGENDARY EMPERORS

The first of the three scrolls of the *Kojiki* ends with Jinmu's birth. The second scroll of the ancient chronicle begins with the account of Jinmu's youth, his conquest of Yamato and his enthronement as the First Emperor (see Chapter 2). This scroll chronicles the events up to the reign of the fifteenth emperor, known as Ōjin 応神 (traditional regnal dates 270–310 CE). The third scroll of the *Kojiki* picks up with Ōjin's son Nintoku 仁徳 (trad. r. 313–399), and continues through the reign of the 30th ruler, Suiko 推古 (554–628, r. 593–628), the first empress regnant. Suiko and the five rulers before her are the earliest figures in the text whose existence can be proven. This means that the *Kojiki* covers up to the bare beginnings of what we would call 'history' in the present.

The *Nihonshoki* has a different organizational scheme, with many of its 30 books dedicated to a single emperor. However, it gives the same list and order of emperors as the *Kojiki*. The *Nihonshoki*'s third book is the annal dedicated to Jinmu, and books 4–10 cover the next fourteen rulers. This is roughly equivalent to the second scroll of the *Kojiki*. Books 11–22 of the *Nihonshoki* cover the same span as the third scroll of the *Kojiki*. The final eight books of the *Nihonshoki* detail the remainder of the 7th century, ending with the reign of the empress regnant Jitō 持統 (645–703, r. 686–696), the 41st monarch in the traditional order. The *Nihonshoki* is the only work in Japan that addresses the history of the 7th century. These annals are also its most detailed and are generally considered historically accurate. The rest of the chronicle, however, is considered as mythical as anything in the *Kojiki*.

None of the first fifteen emperors recorded in the *Kojiki* and the *Nihonshoki*, including Jinmu, are considered actually to have existed by modern scholars. They are generally referred to as the 'legendary emperors'. There is also no archaeological evidence from Japan, nor evidence in the much older records from China, that any figures even

A set of late 19th-century woodblock prints entitled 'A Mirror of Our Country's Revered Deities and Esteemed Emperors', presenting famous figures both mythical and historical.

vaguely similar to these first fifteen rulers ever existed. In some periods of Japanese history, however, particularly the time between the Meiji Restoration of 1868 and the end of the Second World War in 1945, the ancient chronicles were treated as literal history.[4] During this era, school textbooks taught the existence of the legendary emperors as historical fact, including mapping their extraordinarily long lives and reigns onto the Western calendar. Much of this education was propaganda designed to support State Shinto and the emperor system as imagined by the post-Meiji, pre-war government

The Eight 'Missing' Emperors

Jinmu dies after a 75-year reign and is succeeded by his second son with Himetatara-Isuzuhime, known as Suizei 綏靖 (trad. r. 581–549 BCE). Suizei is the first of a series of eight rulers about whom even the chronicles say next to nothing. These eight – Suizei, Annei 安寧, Itoku 懿徳, Kōshō 孝昭, Kōan 孝安, Kōrei 孝霊, Kōgen 孝元 and Kaika 開花 – are collectively known as the 'missing emperors' in modern scholarship. Both the *Kojiki* and the *Nihonshoki* record their names, the location of their palaces and tombs, the dates of their lives and their reigns, and the names of their wives and offspring, but nothing else. Each ruler is either the oldest or second son of the previous one. Taken together their reigns cover over 700 years – a very long time for nothing to happen.

Given the lack of information about the eight 'missing emperors', modern scholars have pondered why they were even inserted into the list of legendary emperors. One theory explains these 'missing emperors' as pushing Jinmu further into the distant past. By inserting eight rulers with long reigns, Jinmu's ascension goes from only a few hundred years

---

Why are some emperors legendary?
- Modern scholars doubt that the first fifteen emperors in the *Kojiki* and the *Nihonshoki* ever existed.
- There is no archaeological or historically verifiable evidence for them.
- The chronicles give these emperors outlandishly long lives and reigns of more than a century.

---

before the creation of the ancient chronicles to over a millennium earlier. This artificial lengthening would allow the Nara Period court to claim that they had a history as long as that of the imperial court of China, or even longer. Such a move also made it harder for other claimants, including those from competing clans with their own ancestor myths, to argue against the events portrayed in the early parts of both chronicles.

Building the Realm: Sujin and Suinin

The tenth emperor listed in the chronicles is known by the two-character name Sujin 崇神 (trad. r. 97–30 BCE). Sujin is the first ruler after Jinmu to have any details given for his reign besides the basics of his palace and burial locations, and the names of his wives and offspring. According to the chronicles, Sujin was the second son of the previous ruler, Kaika. In the fifth year of Sujin's reign, an epidemic broke out, ravaging the Home Provinces (the modern Kansai region). Despite prayers to Amaterasu and the other great gods, there was no relief. Sujin decided to dedicate a new shrine to Amaterasu outside the palace and sent one of his half-sisters to be the high priestess, but she fell ill. He chose another of his half-sisters, but not only did she too fall ill, but all her hair fell out as well.[5]

Soon after his second half-sister fell ill, Sujin's aunt was possessed, and began to speak in the voice of a powerful *kami*. The *kami* named itself as Ōmononushi 大物主, literally 'Great Master of Things', and claimed to be the god of Mt Miwa. Mt Miwa is one of the mountains that encircles the narrow basin of Yamato and overlooks the supposed locations of the palaces of Jinmu and his descendants. Ōmononushi demanded that Sujin worship him with the same veneration shown to Amaterasu. To do so, the *kami* demanded that the ruler locate a man known as Ōtataneko 大田田根子 and bring him to serve as his chief priest. In return, Ōmononushi would make the epidemic go away.

Sujin was shocked that such an important *kami* had gone unknown and unworshipped. He immediately issued orders to sanctify Mt Miwa and for a shrine to be erected at its base. In the meantime, the sovereign issued a search across all of Japan for the man named Ōtataneko. He was eventually found in Kawachi (the east part of modern Osaka Prefecture), brought to Mt Miwa and given the role of chief priest of Ōmononushi.

Emperor Sujin

- Tenth emperor listed in the chronicles, and the first ruler after Jinmu to have details given about his reign.
- During the fifth year of his reign there was an epidemic. His aunt was possessed by the *kami* Ōmononushi ('Great Master of Things'), who demanded that Sujin worship him.
- Ordered Mt Miwa to be sanctified to honour Ōmononushi so that he would end the epidemic; supposedly built Ōmiwa Shrine at its base.
- Died at the age of 118 according to the chronicles.
- Chose his younger son Ikume (who ruled as Emperor Suinin) as his heir.

As soon as Ōtataneko conducted the proper rites, the epidemic cleared up. The *Kojiki* explains that Ōtataneko was actually the son of a young woman who had been seduced by Ōmononushi. This made him the most appropriate person to serve the god, who was in fact his father.[6]

To this day, Ōmiwa Shrine ('Shrine of the Great God') stands at the foot of Mt Miwa. Unlike most Shinto shrines, Ōmiwa Shrine does not have a main hall. Instead, the entire mountain is its main hall, as well as being the *shintai*, or body of the god. There are hiking trails on the mountain, many of which follow ancient paths to the top. Men who wished to commune with the Miwa *kami* would climb them. Originally women were not allowed on the mountain itself out of fear that they would anger Ōmononushi, but in the past few decades this practice has changed.

Sujin is not only the first ruler after Jinmu to receive a detailed account in the chronicles, but also the first to continue Jinmu's process of consolidating rule over Japan. Once the Miwa crisis had been averted, he proceeded to send military forces to subdue the four quarters of the realm. Each of these quarters needed to be 'pacified', subjugated to Amaterasu's descendants. Although supposedly 600 years had passed since Jinmu's death, much of the archipelago remained wild and untamed from the perspective of the court. Today, scholars read these 'rebellious' forces as representations of smaller tribes and kingdoms, now long lost to history, that were subdued by the Yamato court probably no earlier than the 3rd or 4th century CE. Yet in the ancient chronicles, the lands that must be pacified are portrayed as evil and horrifying places that rebel against their rightful, *kami*-ordained rulers.

In the sixtieth year of his reign, Sujin wished to look upon treasures kept at Izumo Shrine. He ordered imperial messengers to travel to Izumo, some weeks' journey from the palace, and to bring the treasures back to the court. The lord of Izumo, a man named Izumo Furune 出雲振根, was the keeper of the treasures, but he was away on business in northern Kyushu, so his younger brother, Izumo Irine 出雲入根, turned over the treasures to the imperial messengers. When Furune returned he was furious. He invited Irine into a pool to bathe, and then secretly switched Irine's sword with a wooden one while he was in the pool. Furune then challenged his brother to a duel; Irine's fake sword broke and Furune killed him. When news of this came to the court, Sujin was so horrified that he immediately dispatched two generals and an army to bring Furune to justice, which they did.

According to both chronicles, Sujin died at the age of 118. To settle the question of succession before his death, he called his two sons by his primary wife to appear before him and recount their dreams. The older son, Prince Toyoki 豊城, dreamed that he climbed to the top of Mt Miwa. There, he thrust a spear into the earth eight times, and waved a sword into the sky eight times. The younger son, Prince Ikume 活目, also dreamed of climbing Mt Miwa. However, what Ikume found at the peak was an area bounded by sacred ropes, in which sparrows were eating millet. Ikume ran about the area, scattering the sparrows and saving the millet from being eaten. Upon hearing both of his sons' dreams, Sujin realized that Ikume was destined to help the people prosper, and chose his younger son as his heir.

Ikume was enthroned as Emperor Suinin 垂仁 (trad. r. 29 BCE–70 CE). Suinin's record in the chronicles is sparser than his father's, but he still performed some important tasks. One of these was founding the Great Shrine of Ise, which today remains the centre of worship of Amaterasu. Ise is in modern Mie Prefecture, on the Pacific coast south of Nagoya. As the crow flies it is only a few dozen kilometres from Nara, but the rugged Iga Mountains block the way. Even now, any journey to Ise either requires sailing around the Kii Peninsula, or traversing river valleys and

The Inner Shrine of Ise, as seen *c.* 1910–19. The architectural style is believed to reflect ancient Japanese storehouses from the Kofun Period or earlier.

mountain passes to the north. This remote location was selected by Suinin's daughter, Princess Yamatohime 倭姫 ('Princess of Yamato'), when her father asked her to find Amaterasu a home in which the goddess desired to be worshipped. Yamatohime searched for twenty years before settling on the Ise coast. Yamatohime was then appointed the first Saiō, or High Priestess of Ise (often translated as 'Ise Virgin').

The Saiō was an unmarried young woman from the imperial family who traditionally was sent to Ise to be Amaterasu's chief representative. The Saiō would live at Ise until a new one was appointed, usually when there was a change of reign. The transition itself required several detailed ceremonies and purifications, and afterwards, the Saiō was supposed to refrain from impure activities, including sex, for the duration of her term. The institution continued down to the late medieval era before finally lapsing. During the Heian Period, at the height of her role's importance, the Saiō was often portrayed as a romantic figure. Her ritual untouchability made her the subject of tragic romances. Although both the *Kojiki* and the *Nihonshoki* retell Yamatohime's story, evidence from archaeology, as well as a citation in the *Man'yōshū*, date the actual first Ise Priestess much later, to the reign of Emperor Tenmu in the late 7th century CE.[7]

Suinin married a woman named Sahohime 沙穂姫 ('Lady of Fine Plumes'), who was also his niece. Sahohime was very close to her older brother, Sahohiko 沙穂彦. Sahohiko was very upset at his sister marrying their king and demanded that she tell him who she loved more, her brother or her husband. Sahohime was confused, so Sahohiko reminded her that as she aged, Suinin would fall out of love with her, but he, as her brother, never would. Convinced of his sister's loyalty, Sahohiko persuaded her to kill Suinin while he slept. Sahohime waited until the ruler fell asleep across her knees, and then took out her dagger and tried to stab his neck, but found that she could not make herself do it. She tried three times in all, and each time she failed. After the third time, Suinin woke up, and demanded to know what his wife was doing with a dagger. Collapsing in tears, Sahohime told Suinin of the plot against him, and then fled the palace.

Sahohime and Sahohiko sought refuge in their home fief at the northern end of the Nara Basin. Suinin brought an army and besieged them. Sahohime then revealed that she was pregnant with Suinin's son. Suinin held off the siege until Sahohime gave birth. The estranged empress offered to give their son to the emperor. Suinin had men stationed around the gate, with orders to grab her as she passed through it to give up the baby. However, Sahohime, aware of the plot, shaved her head and made a wig from the shaved hair, and then put on clothes rotted by sake. When the men reached out to grab her, everything they touched fell away, and Sahohime was able to wrest free, leaving the baby prince on the ground before fleeing back to her brother. Once again Sahohiko asked his sister whom she loved more, and this time she told him without hesitation in her voice: it was her brother. Suinin then ordered his troops to invade their home and both Sahohiko and Sahohime were killed in the battle.

Suinin's son with Sahohime was named Prince Homutsuwake 誉津別. According to the *Kojiki*, even after he had grown such that his beard 'was eight hand-lengths long', he was unable to speak.[8] One day, Homutsuwake saw a beautiful swan in the sky, and tried to say something. Sujin was amazed and sent a hunter to capture the bird. Eventually the hunter caught it in the land of Koshi (later Echizen, Etchū and Echigo Provinces; modern Fukui, Toyama and Niigata Prefectures). The swan was brought

Depiction of Izumo Shrine that was appended to a request for
permission to repair its premises, dated 1875.

back to the palace and shown to Prince Homutsuwake. The prince once
again struggled to speak but was unable to do so. That night, the disap-
pointed Suinin had a strange dream, in which a voice told him that the
great spirit of Izumo desired a shrine. The emperor woke, and realized
that to fix his son's affliction, he had to build yet another shrine, this one
for Ōkuninushi, who had once ruled in the land of Izumo.

Suinin dispatched Homutsuwake to Izumo, along with several other
princes. The men had several adventures on the journey, but Homutsuwake
still had not regained his ability to speak. Eventually they arrived at Izumo,
where they paid homage to Ōkuninushi and constructed a great shrine,
which became known as Izumo Shrine (in modern Shimane Prefecture).
As they turned to leave, Prince Homutsuwake looked back, and suddenly
exclaimed how beautiful the shrine looked, and asked whether it was truly
in honour of Ōkuninushi. Hearing his voice, the assembled princes and
their men rejoiced. When word reached the emperor, Suinin dispatched
more men to build up the shrine further.

Suinin's reign featured several other notable moments. He first defined the provinces of the empire, naming them and their peoples. Early in his reign, a wrestling tournament – which may or may not have taken place at the foot of the distant Mt Fuji – was the origin of the sport of sumo. Finally, Suinin continued expanding agriculture across southern Honshu. He finally died at 138 years of age and was succeeded by his son Prince Ōtarashihiko-Oshirowake, who was enthroned as Emperor Keikō 景行 (trad. r. 71–130 CE).

Bloody though some of these tales may be, they demonstrate the futility of crossing the court. The emperors were guarded by powerful *kami*, and to rise against them was to risk almost certain defeat. Not even the empress herself (Sahohime) is exempt from this fate. Although neither Emperor Sujin nor Emperor Suinin is believed to have been a real person by modern scholars, both the *Kojiki* and *Nihonshoki* treat their deeds as historical fact. Like most history, this one too has a bias: to show the imperial clan as not only powerful, but inevitable. Yet the importance of the emperors was not only in their divine right to rule. As the stories of the imperial founding of great shrines at Miwa, Izumo and Ise demonstrate, these sovereigns' rule was as much about construction as suppression. This is a pattern that continues into the next ruler, with even more spectacular results.

Violence and Victory: Keikō and Yamato Takeru

Like his father Suinin, Keikō was chosen as emperor over his older brother. Before naming his successor, Suinin asked the two princes what each one wished for the most. The elder brother wished for a bow and arrows, but the younger one (the future Emperor Keikō) wished for the empire itself. Happy with his second son's ambition, Emperor Suinin made him his heir. Keikō made good on his desire, pushing to expand the kingdom like his father and grandfather had done. The *Nihonshoki* records Keikō travelling to southern Honshu and Kyushu, touring his domain and leading armies to put down enemies. Keikō's travel, so far away from his palace, is unusual for an emperor in both the myths and recorded historical practice.

Keikō's reign is most notable, however, for the actions of one of his sons. Prince O'usu 小碓 or 'Little Mortar', later known by the epithet Yamato Takeru 倭猛, 'Brave Man of Yamato', was the younger of two sons by Keikō's first empress. O'usu's older brother was Prince Ō'usu 大碓 or 'Big Mortar'. One day, Keikō noticed that Ō'usu had not appeared at court for some time, so he sent O'usu to check on his older brother. O'usu was renowned for his fierce temper and battle prowess, and when he found Ō'usu ignoring the imperial summons, the younger prince flew into a rage, killed his older brother, and then tore the arms and legs from the corpse before bringing it back to throw before his father's throne.

Keikō was shocked at his son's brutality, and a little afraid as well. However, Prince O'usu only wished to serve his father. In order to allow his son to do so, while keeping him far away from other family members for their safety, Keikō decided to send the prince out to fight enemies of the court. Word had come that in the far south of the realm, at the southern tip of Kyushu, a people called the Kumaso had become strong and proud under a leader named Kumaso Takeru 熊襲猛, the 'Brave Man of the Kumaso'. In the west, in the lands of Izumo (around Izumo Shrine), yet another rebellious leader had arisen: Izumo Takeru 出雲猛, or 'Brave Man of Izumo'. Keikō decided to send Prince O'usu south to defeat Kumaso Takeru, and then west to defeat Izumo Takeru. To mark his son's new status as a general, Keikō bestowed upon him the name Yamato Takeru ('Brave Man of Yamato').

After leaving, Yamato Takeru first journeyed to Ise, and met with his aunt Yamatohime, who was still the High Priestess there. She gave him a set of women's clothing and sent him on his way. He then journeyed to the far south, crossing the Inland Sea to southern Kyushu. Reaching the land of the Kumaso, he dressed himself in the women's clothing gifted him by his aunt; he was of such astounding beauty that he made as gorgeous a woman as he did a man. Kumaso Takeru was instantly infatuated with the new arrival. Not knowing Yamato Takeru's identity, Kumaso Takeru claimed 'her' as his future wife. Yamato Takeru demurely accepted this proposal, but secretly concealed a sword in his bridal clothes. After the bridal feast, when he and Kumaso Takeru were left alone to consummate the marriage, Yamato Takeru threw off his women's clothing, revealing his identity, and killed Kumaso Takeru over the bridal bed. He then sang a poem of victory, by which the Kumaso recognized him and submitted to the authority of the emperor.

After subduing the Kumaso, Yamato Takeru travelled on to Izumo where, to his surprise, Izumo Takeru received him with a warm welcome. Although surprised by Izumo Takeru's hospitality, Yamato Takeru remained focused on his mission, and the following day he secretly replaced Izumo Takeru's sword with a fake blade made of wood before challenging him to a sparring match. Izumo Takeru's fake sword broke, and Yamato Takeru ran him through. Since this is the same trick that Izumo Furune, one of Emperor Sujin's enemies, is said to have used against his own brother two generations earlier, in the same location, the two myths may in fact be echoes of the same story.

Yamato Takeru returned to court, and Emperor Keikō congratulated him on successfully pacifying the west and south. Still scared of his son's

Yamato Takeru (standing), subduing the Emishi of northern Japan.

power, Keikō decided to send him on one last mission. In the far north-east lay the lands of the Emishi, who refused to heed imperial commands. Keikō wished for Yamato Takeru to subdue them as well. Having given the prince his orders, Keikō dismissed him at once. Yamato Takeru, upset at his father's abruptness, once again headed to Ise to seek solace from his aunt. Yamatohime comforted her nephew, and gifted him with a sacred treasure: the sword Kusanagi, the 'Grass-Cutter'. This was the same sword that Susanowo found in the tail of the Yamata-no-Orochi, and which became one of the Three Imperial Regalia (see Chapter 2). In the *Kojiki*'s version of the tale, Yamatohime also gives her nephew a bag containing a flint.

Yamato Takeru's wife, a woman named Oto-Tachibanahime 弟橘姫, asked to accompany him to the land of the Emishi. Here the *Kojiki* interjects a story not found in the *Nihonshoki*. As they travelled north, Yamato Takeru's company arrived in Suruga Province (modern Shizuoka Prefecture) and were welcomed by its governor, who was secretly in league with the Emishi. He sent Yamato Takeru out to a field to go hunting, and then had his men set fire to the field. Realizing his betrayal, Yamato Takeru took out the sword Kusanagi and, with one swipe, cut all the grass in the field, demonstrating the truth of its name. Then he opened the bag his aunt had given him and pulled out the flint. Using the flint, he kindled his own fire in the cut grass, which turned back the larger fire and cleared the way for him to escape.[9]

Both chronicles continue the story with Yamato Takeru's arrival in Sagami Province (modern Kanagawa Prefecture), where his route required

---

Yamato Takeru

- Born as Prince O'usu, 'Little Mortar'; later received the name Yamato Takeru, 'Brave Man of Yamato'.
- Killed his older brother for ignoring imperial summons.
- Sent by his father, Emperor Keikō, on many conquests across the realm to kill and subjugate enemies.
- Both a conquering hero and a violent individual who inflicts suffering.
- Wields the sword Kusanagi, the 'Grass-Cutter,' one of the Three Imperial Regalia.

---

him and his entourage to cross the entrance to what is known today as Tokyo Bay. They hired boats to sail across the bay, but in the middle of their crossing the sky grew dark, and a sudden storm raged over the sea. Yamato Takeru's men were frightened, but Oto-Tachibanahime spoke up suddenly. She claimed that the storm was the doing of Watatsumi, the god of the sea, and that if he could take her instead, he would let Yamato Takeru pass. Yamato Takeru and all his men wept, but they took the brave Oto-Tachibanahime and released her into the ocean. She sank down into the water, and immediately the storm cleared.

Yamato Takeru and his men continued to the north-east, eventually arriving in Kai Province (modern Ibaraki Prefecture). From here they set about subduing the Emishi, slaughtering their chieftains and forcing their villages to submit. Although the task was completed successfully, Yamato Takeru still grieved for his lost wife. Passing by Mt Tsukuba (in modern Tsukuba City, Ibaraki Prefecture), he encountered an old man, also bowed with grief. Together, the two of them composed a famous poem.

Yamato Takeru and his forces turned south-west to head home. In his grief and anger, Yamato Takeru grew reckless, and as they passed Mt Ibuki (on the border of modern Shiga and Gifu Prefectures), he rode up the mountain to go boar hunting. Seeing a great boar, he shot at it, wounding it, but it escaped. Unbeknownst to him, the boar was the *kami* of Mt Ibuki, who was greatly angered at having been shot. As he and his forces continued their journey home, Yamato Takeru suddenly took ill with a strange sickness. He became wan and listless, and over the next few days lost all his strength and health. His men tried to rally him, but every time they fell silent, Yamato Takeru recited a different poem, each sadder than the last. After composing the fourth poem, he shuddered and died. No sooner had his men finished erecting his tomb, than a white bird sprang up out of it and flew southward. According to the *Nihonshoki*, the bird stopped in Yamato, then again in Kawachi before ascending into the sky and vanishing. The men chased after it, noting where it perched. They would later erect shrines at both places it stopped.[10] These are known as Shiratori ('White Bird') Shrines. Hearing of his son's death, Emperor Keikō grieved as well.

The legend of Yamato Takeru is one of the most famous of the Japanese myth cycles. Japanese schoolchildren know it even today, and there have been novels, films, manga and anime that retell the story or incorporate elements from it. The network of Shiratori Shrines still exists, even if it is not exactly popular, and is often associated with prayers for good fortune or good romantic outcomes. Yet for all that the myth of Yamato Takeru is well known, it is not well understood, even by scholars. This is partially due to the tale having many possible meanings, some of which are far less positive towards the early Japanese court than others.

Yamato Takeru is a valiant figure, a loyal son who subjugates enemies of the realm on behalf of his royal father. He fulfils both the image of the conquering hero and Confucian values of filial piety. At the same time, he is violent and unchivalrous, and both his loyalty towards his father and his conquests in Keikō's name result in much death, despair and destruction. Neither chronicle shies away from showing the devastation wrought by Yamato Takeru's conquests, nor the ways in which he uses deceit to achieve them. Yet he also sacrifices everything – his time, his life and even his love – in order to fulfil the emperor's wishes. Perhaps the most important thing about Yamato Takeru is that he is *pure*. He accomplishes the emperor's will with pure devotion, and he defeats the enemies of the realm with pure force. He may not be heroic in the modern sense, but neither is he a villain.

Faith and Conquest: Empress Jingū

Like most of the legendary emperors, Keikō dies at the improbable old age of 143. He is succeeded by a son who rules as Seimu 成務 (trad. r. 131–190 CE). Seimu's annal again only records his palace, tomb, wives and children. He too may be a 'missing emperor', inserted into the historical narrative to push back some of the legendary rulers further into the past. Seimu is succeeded by his nephew, Yamato Takeru's son, who rules under the name Chūai 仲哀 (trad. r. 192–200). Chūai marries a woman named Okinaga-Tarashihime, better known by her later title as Empress Jingū 神宮. Jingū never reigned in her own name (she was not a 'female emperor'); in her case, the title Empress translates the word *kōgō*, literally 'behind the sovereign', the term for the wife with the highest rank in the imperial harem.

Empress Jingū (left) and a retainer.

In the eighteenth year of Chūai's reign, in both the *Kojiki* and the *Nihonshoki*, a pregnant Jingū is overcome with a premonition sent by Watatsumi, the god of the sea. Watatsumi commands Chūai to lead the armies of Japan across the sea to the west and invade Korea. Chūai scoffs at the command, and this angers the god, who declares that the ruler will 'no longer rule over all under heaven'.[11] Chūai is struck dead afterwards, simply falling over his zither (a stringed instrument held in the lap). Jingū takes over as regent, and immediately decides to fulfil the god's command. Although she is already pregnant with Chūai's son, she sets out to lead her armies across the sea and, through force of will, manages to keep her son from being born until the conquest of Korea is achieved.

Jingū's forces initially land in the Kaya region, a confederation of small city-states in what is now South Kyŏngsang Province, South Korea.[12] From there, they proceed to force the subjugation of the kings of both Paekche and Silla, the two southernmost Korean kingdoms. Both chronicles record that after each king surrenders, Jingū accepts their tribute and leaves them in peace as nominal vassals to Japan. One element of tribute is a 'seven-branched sword' presented to Jingū by the king of Paekche. After three years, the empress returns home along with her military forces. During the final crossing she ties rocks to her skirts, keeping the baby inside until she can return to Japanese soil. Once embarking in Kyushu, Jingū immediately gives birth to her son, Prince Homutawake 誉田別. Homutawake will grow up to inherit the throne as Emperor Ōjin 応神 (trad. r. 270–310 CE).

The story of Empress Jingū is possibly the most controversial of the ancient Japanese myths. There is no credible historical or archaeological evidence that any forces from the Japanese islands conquered or in some other way controlled any part of the Korean Peninsula prior to the 16th century. However, there is a lack of detailed sources from Korea prior to the medieval era – the earliest surviving work of history (including mythological history) for this period is the *Samguk sagi* ('Record of the Three Kingdoms', 1145). The Chinese historical sources also contain no records of any Japanese presence on the peninsula, but in general they portray a very different view of Japan, one that does not match up with any of the tales in the ancient Japanese chronicles. In the absence of definitive proof, many Japanese of the early modern and modern eras believed strongly in Jingū as a real and heroic Japanese conqueror. She was therefore used to justify later invasions of Korea and atrocities committed against Koreans.

Jingū's fame in Japan led to her being associated with Watatsumi, and she was enshrined alongside him at Sumiyoshi Shrine, an important Shinto ritual location in modern Osaka. When the Meiji government instituted State Shinto in the 1870s, Jingū, like most legendary imperial figures, was taught as real history. She was also invoked as one of the reasons for the Japanese annexation of Korea in 1910. During the 35 years of often brutal Japanese military occupation prior to the Second World War, Jingū was deployed as a propaganda figure. The totalitarian government portrayed her as a courageous woman whose efforts almost 2,000 years before were now finally paying off in the form of Japanese colonialization. Her legend remains a bitter memory for many Koreans. Attempts to prove or disprove historical context surrounding Jingū remain mired in the history of war and colonization that lies between modern Japan and both Korean nations.

THE SEMI-LEGENDARY EMPERORS

Jingū's son Ōjin is the last of what scholars today call the 'legendary' emperors. Starting with Ōjin's son, the ruler known as Nintoku, we enter the realm of the 'semi-legendary' emperors. This term does not mean that the stories about them are considered reliable history. However, archaeological excavations, as well evidence from the Chinese chronicles, reveal the existence of small kingdoms in the Japanese archipelago in the 4th century CE. In a few cases, there are even traces of names that look suspiciously like those seen in the *Kojiki* and *Nihonshoki*. The first ruler to be considered completely factual is Kinmei 欽明 (509–571, r. 539–571), the 29th ruler in the traditional list of emperors. The thirteen rulers before him, starting with Nintoku, are not considered to be historically accurate, but may be based on real individuals and events. This contrasts with the first fifteen, who are considered completely legendary. This murky situation, where there are legends about figures who may or may not have been real, is what is meant by the term 'semi-legendary'.

Ōjin is the last ruler in the *Kojiki*'s 'Middle Scroll'. The third and final scroll picks up with Nintoku. The *Nihonshoki* is divided into many books, and therefore does not feature so obvious a shift from legendary to semi-legendary emperors. In both chronicles, the descriptions of the rulers become less obviously supernatural starting with Nintoku. Their ages reduce significantly, as do the lengths of their reigns, shrinking to more believable figures. The *kami* still interact with the imperial clan but are increasingly less of an active force. Other clans, and other countries and peoples – such as the Korean kingdoms – also become more prominent players in the narrative.

The Kofun Period (*c.* 200–538) maps onto the same time span associated with these 'semi-legendary' emperors and things we see in the archaeological record from this period do appear in the stories. Tombs and tomb mounds, while always mentioned, become more prominent in the chronicles, along with more detailed descriptions of agriculture and government, which match some of what we can see from the archaeological record as well.

To be clear, mythology is not suddenly being replaced by real history. The transition is subtle and to the people who wrote both the *Kojiki* and the *Nihonshoki* it was probably not a transition at all, since they were compiling the accounts of the legendary and semi-legendary rulers as part of the same official history of the world according to the Nara Period court. But there is certainly more in the tales of the semi-legendary emperors that reflects the realities of 5th- and 6th-century Japan than is the case with any of the previous stories.

The Start of Culture: Ōjin and Nintoku

The reign of Ōjin, the last of the purely legendary emperors, sees the first appearances of continental culture in Japan: writing, art and craftsmanship like that used in China and Korea. Ōjin is less important to the chronicle narratives than are both his mother, Jingū, and his son Nintoku 仁徳, but his reign does have some impressive firsts.

Seemingly ignoring Jingū's prior demand for 'tribute' from the Korean kingdoms of Silla and Paekche, Ōjin receives visitors from the peninsula. One of these visitors is Wani 和邇 (Kr. Wang-in), a man of great learning. Wani brings copies of the Chinese classics, specifically Confucius' *Analects*, and the *Thousand-Character Classic* (Ch. *Qianziwen*, Jp. *Senjimon*). Both of these books were used to teach young children how to read and write Chinese across premodern East Asia. Wani is put to work teaching the crown prince (not the son who would later reign as Nintoku, but his older brother).[13] These immigrants also bring new forms of divination, as well as other technologies known on the continent. Ōjin welcomes them warmly, and they set about teaching these new skills to the court.

The *Thousand-Character Classic* was not actually composed in China until the 5th century CE, so its inclusion in Ōjin's annal is obviously false. Yet the story might still reflect a real cultural memory. Reading, writing and other technologies originally from China arrived in Japan at some time during the Kofun or early Asuka Periods (538–710), brought by immigrants from the continent. By pushing the details of these arrivals back into myth, and connecting them to an early emperor, the creators of the chronicles turned these memories into something more. All the figures who supposedly bring Ōjin these technologies are foreigners, but ones who come to Japan because they want to honour its rulers, not to lord over them as superior. From the perspective of the ancient Chinese, let alone the early Korean kingdoms, the archipelago was a backward place. Yet the chronicles claim even this position as a strength; that the ancient emperors of Japan deserved these gifts from abroad, and that they were brought willingly and given with grace.

Ōjin had eleven wives and many children. His two favourites for the throne were Prince Ōyamamori 大山守, a son of his second wife, and Ōsazaki 大鷦鷯, a son of his highest-ranking wife. Both were strong and true men, devoted to their father. Ōyamamori was older, but Ōsazaki's rank was higher. Ōjin approached both sons and asked them to decide the succession. Rather than squabble over the throne, Ōyamamori withdrew in favour of his half-brother. But then Ōsazaki did the same, claiming that, as the younger brother, it would be unfilial of himself to overlook Ōyamamori's claim. The two went back and forth, each refusing the throne three times. Ōjin was impressed by their respective moral stances. Finally, Ōyamamori passed away, perhaps to settle the question once and for all (the *Kojiki* claims from illness, but the reason is never given in the *Nihonshoki*). Ōsazaki therefore took the throne and reigned as Emperor Nintoku, the first of the thirteen semi-legendary emperors in the chronicles.

Soon upon his accession, Nintoku moved the palace outside of Yamato Province (modern Nara Prefecture) for the first time. The palace had been taken down and moved following each ruler's death to avoid exposing the new sovereign to the ritual pollution caused by the death of the previous one. Nintoku moved his palace to Naniwa, a port in what is now downtown Osaka. He built his palace right above the port and, according to the *Nihonshoki*, had a canal dug to facilitate trade. In the third year of his reign, Nintoku climbed a mountain to look down across the realm. He was shocked to see little smoke, indicating that few hearths were lit, and the poor state of the rooftops and fields. Nintoku immediately declared a five-year amnesty on taxes. In the seventh year of his reign, he once again climbed the mountain and was overjoyed to see columns of hearth-smoke billowing over broad green fields and well-maintained rooftops. His generosity made him beloved across the countryside and is one reason for his two-character Chinese name; 'Nintoku' means 'Just and Virtuous'.

Emperor Nintoku, here dressed in vaguely Heian Period robes, surveying the land.

The most famous story about Nintoku, however, is actually one of adultery. His first wife was a woman named Iwanohime 磐之姫, who came from the powerful Kazuraki Clan. Nintoku courted her and they were very much in love. Then the emperor travelled to the land of Kibi (modern Okayama and Hiroshima Prefectures), where he fell in love with his cousin, Princess Yata 八田. Rumours of their affair reached Iwanohime in Naniwa. Upset, the empress fled into the mountains. While there, she composed four poems of longing, which today are among the most famous in the 8th-century poetry anthology *Man'yōshū*. Her poems are complex, expressing both her longing for the emperor and her refusal to tolerate the situation. Here is one example, the second of the set of four:

> Rather than this –
> This constant yearning of love –
> Better had it been
> To pillow on the mountain crags
> And die, my head among the stones.[14]

Iwanohime's poems are not at all like the other ancient songs preserved in the *Kojiki*, the *Nihonshoki* or the early books of the *Man'yōshū*. Some scholars think that these are actually poems from the 7th or early 8th century that were attributed to Iwanohime in order to connect them to a tragic romance. In the story, they have their desired effect: Nintoku returns to Naniwa, finds that his first wife has left, and chases after her. He eventually promises to change his ways, and Iwanohime returns with him to the palace. Although Princess Yata and three further concubines do end up staying with Nintoku, Iwanohime is the sole empress, and the mother of his eventual heirs.

The legend of Nintoku and Iwanohime puts the composition of poetry at the centre of the narrative. Poetry was considered an essential skill for Japanese aristocrats from the 8th century onwards and is still popular today. Japan has a rich literary tradition, and some of its earliest poetic works feature characters and events from the ancient myths. More importantly, however, poetry was a way for people to communicate emotions. Many of the great romances of Japanese literature involve people sharing poems of seduction, grief, love and longing. From this perspective, Iwanohime's poems offer a mythological example of one way that poetry was 'supposed' to be used.

There are several important monuments from the Kofun Period that are associated with Nintoku, but no verifiable evidence that conclusively connects the ruler – who remains semi-legendary – with these places. They are either historically linked to his reign or hint at the existence of a ruler like him at the proper time. Perhaps the most amazing of these is the Daisenryō Kofun, the largest tomb mound known in Japan. It lies in the modern city of Sakai, in Osaka Prefecture, several kilometres southeast of ancient Naniwa. The location roughly matches that given for Nintoku's tomb mound in the *Kojiki* and *Nihonshoki*, and so scholars in the 19th century claimed that it was in fact the legendary tomb. The truth is that we have no idea who built it, presumably for a powerful local ruler. With a base eight times the size of the Great Pyramid of Giza in Egypt, this immense keyhole-shaped tomb is thought to have taken around 2,000 men more than sixteen years to construct. Due to its official status as a tomb of an ancient emperor, excavations have never been allowed, though as of October of 2020, a proposal for excavations was working its way through the relevant government offices. For the moment, at least, the tomb keeps its mysteries.

From Myth to History

Nintoku and Iwanohime have four sons. The oldest succeeds his father as Emperor Richū 履中 (trad. r. 400–405). Richū is only the second ruler (after the ill-fated Chūai) to have a short reign, and the first whose lifespan is realistic in length. After Nintoku's death, the son of one of his lesser-ranked wives raises a rebellion that results in Naniwa being burned to the ground. Richū flees to Yamato, the ancient heartland of the imperial clan, and as he crosses over Mt Ikoma (on the border of modern Osaka and Nara Prefectures), he sees the palace on fire in the distance. Richū composes a poem of sorrow before continuing onwards:

> Hanifu Slope
> When I stop I take a look
> Shimmering air
> Burning cluster of houses
> Around about my wife's house.[15]

Richū eventually wins the rebellion but dies soon afterwards. Two of his brothers ascend after him, the first example of rulers from the same generation in either chronicle. The first is Hanzei 反正 (trad. r. 406–410), a towering figure at 3 m (9 ft) tall, and with large teeth all the same size, according to the *Kojiki*. Hanzei is enthroned over the claims of Richū's two sons, who quietly disappear from the narrative. However, Hanzei's rule is also brief; five years later he too is dead and a third brother ascends the throne as Ingyō 允恭 (trad. r. 410–453). His reign is once again long, though not unbelievably so. Ingyō is beloved, and his rule is mostly peaceful; when he dies, messengers come from the kingdom of Silla, on the Korean peninsula, offering condolences.

The messy realities of history slowly appear to be overtaking the mythic plots. Indeed, there are few ostensibly supernatural elements in the accounts of the rulers that follow Ingyō. There are another nine rulers before Kinmei, the first considered historically verifiable, but the accounts of these rulers become more human in their details. They build palaces and hold ceremonies to placate the *kami*. They fight off rebellions and construct public works projects. The chronicles proceed gently towards their own present, and slowly cast off their more epic trappings. Some emperors, such as Yūryaku 雄略 (trad. r. 456–479), the 21st ruler, still engage in encounters with the supernatural, in episodes that are usually of a romantic nature or relate to personal duels. Yūryaku is in fact one of the semi-legendary emperors with the strongest claim to having been 'real'. A similar Japanese ruler, from around the same time, is mentioned in Chinese chronicles, and a famous sword found at a tomb in modern Saitama Prefecture, north of Tokyo, features an inscription mentioning an overlord with a very similar name, though the specific details of Yūryaku's reign cannot be verified as the chronicles describe them.

After chronicling Kinmei's 6th-century rule, the *Kojiki* essentially gives up. The text lists only the basic reign information for the next four rulers, ending with Suiko, the first empress regnant (or female emperor). The *Nihonshoki* continues, however, and is the sole surviving text to record the events of the late 6th and 7th centuries. Its final books are of great value to historians, covering the events of the Asuka Period in minute detail. By this point in the narrative, recounting events only a generation or two prior to the lives of its actual compilers, the text seems to be mostly accurate. It is still heavily biased towards the imperial family, but the chronicle now includes evidence that can be corroborated from other sources. As this portion of the *Nihonshoki* is no longer mythological in content, we will stop our journey through the chronicles at this point.

MYTHIC JAPAN IN THE CHINESE CHRONICLES

There is one other important source of 'myths' concerning early Japan: Chinese chronicle sources. Writing was invented in China sometime during the second millennium BCE, and there was already a long history of written texts, including chronicles, by the rise of the Han Dynasty in the late 2nd century BCE. The first mention of Japan comes in the *Sanguo shi* ('Record of the Three Kingdoms') from the 3rd century CE.

The book is a compilation of the histories of the Kingdoms of Wu, Wei and Shu Han, which formed after the Han Dynasty broke up in 220 CE. The annals devoted to the Kingdom of Wei also describe events on the northern steppes, the Korean Peninsula and the Japanese archipelago.

The 'Chronicles of Wei' section of the *Sanguo shi* includes a chapter called the 'Account of the People of Wa' (Ch. *Woren zhuan*). Wa 倭 (pronounced *wo* in modern Mandarin, and represented by a character meaning 'little dwarf people') is the name by which the Japanese archipelago was known to the ancient Chinese. According to the account, Wa is a group of mountainous islands in the eastern sea, populated by a short and savage people. The land was originally divided into over a hundred small countries, but after many years of fighting, one man (unnamed in the chronicle) managed to conquer them all. When he died, Wa descended once again into fighting, until after 70 or 80 more years, the people decided on a female ruler instead. They chose a woman named Himiko 卑弥呼 (also possibly 'Pimiko'; Ch. *Beimihu*), a powerful sorceress, as their ruler. Himiko bewitched the people of Wa with magic, and then occupied herself with her spells, retreating deep inside her palace.

The *Sanguo shi* account explains that Himiko never married, despite being 'mature in years'.[16] She had her younger brother assist her as her public face, while few ever saw her in the flesh. All her other attendants, over a thousand of them, were women. Her brother was the only male in the entire palace. Himiko's brother and his armed guards managed her

---

Himiko and the People of Wa
- Stories of mythic Japan from 3rd-century Chinese chronicle *Sanguo shi*.
- Wa was the name for the Japanese archipelago in ancient China.
- Himiko was a female ruler and sorceress who bewitched the people of Wa into peace after centuries of warfare, then retreated to her palace with 1,000 female attendants. Her younger brother served as her public face.
- No proof of Himiko has ever been found, but aspects of her story match some material culture of the Kofun Period (*c.* 200–538).
- Himiko and her capital Yamatai are well-known in modern popular culture, but were not important stories in earlier periods.

---

capital, a great town surrounded by a wooden stockade. Himiko's land was known as Yamatai. Twice Himiko sent emissaries from Yamatai to the ruler of Wei, who returned with brocades and gold seals.

Few, if any, literate Japanese of the Nara and Heian Periods seemed to care much for the description given in the *Sanguo shi*. It does not have the status as a myth in the same way as the legends of the ancient Japanese chronicles. However, the Chinese descriptions of ancient Japan became more widely known in the early modern and then modern eras. Many Japanese today have heard of Himiko, and many works of popular culture involve her. Nearly every year sees some new book or television documentary discussing whether Yamatai ever existed, and if so, where in Japan it was, and who Himiko might have been. This very different tale raises many questions, such as whether the story of Himiko is any more historically accurate than the myths in the *Kojiki* or the *Nihonshoki*, or whether she is related to any of the legendary emperors or their families. Empress Jingū, the only roughly similar figure in the Japanese chronicles, is portrayed very differently. Jingū may interact with the *kami*, but she is first and foremost a warrior and a leader, not a hidden sorceress. The closest analogue to the portrayal of Himiko in the *Sanguo shi* is Takeru's aunt Yamatohime, the first High Priestess of Ise, who is not a major figure in Japanese lore.

The mysteries of Himiko remain unsolved. What is perhaps most important about her story is how it has grown intertwined with native myths. Himiko is not an ancient mythological figure, but a modern one. Equal parts urban legend, anime superheroine and star of an historical thriller, she exists alongside the legendary emperors and the ancestor *kami* in the imaginations of modern Japanese. In this way, her tale is more than just a historical footnote. As the myths of Japan have evolved with Japanese society over the centuries, Himiko has become more well-known than some of the legendary figures discussed earlier in the chapter. This transition is a pattern that we will see repeated. Japanese mythology is not fixed or frozen, but a growing thing that is still developing, even today. As the next chapter will further show, historical documents, common folklore and even real people can be caught up in the Japanese myths and transformed into a part of them.

4

LIVING *KAMI* AND DIVINE HUMANS

Over the two previous chapters, we have looked at the myths originating in the ancient Japanese chronicles from the 8th century CE. With this chapter, we begin to explore how the Japanese myths evolved over time. There are three important ways in which Japanese mythology developed: through the addition of new features, through the interactions between religious beliefs, and through changes in society and technology. Although the myths we have looked at so far are generally considered 'Shinto' in origin, they already contain references to Buddhist, Confucian, Daoist and other philosophies. In later periods of history, more elements from these other religions, and many of their gods, entered Japanese mythology. Japanese society has advanced and changed over the 1300 years since the ancient chronicles were first written, and continues to do so. As society changes, so too do the ways we tell stories, and what they mean to us. Myths are no exception to these developments.

This chapter will look at some examples of the first way in which Japanese mythology evolved: the addition of new myths and supernatural figures, particularly during the Heian Period (784–1185), also known as the 'classical era' of Japanese history. Perhaps the most striking example of such an addition is when humans are transformed into *kami*. These transformations can be literal, involving a human who ascends to become a god, and is later worshipped. They can be gradual as well, starting with the death of a famous person, after which their spirit is recognized as causing either good events or ill. Over time, the spirit of the deceased begins to be worshipped by ever wider groups of people until it too is considered a powerful deity. This process is as old as the ancient chronicles themselves and was already happening when the Nara Period (710–784) court was creating its official history of the imperial clan, but it did not end this early.

Deification, the act of making a human into a god, is not a simple process. In most cases, it starts with an awareness that a (usually dead) person's spirit still has power. This power can be frightening, such as causing natural disasters, or helpful, such as bringing good fortune to the living. As word spreads about the spirit, people may start to pray to it, petition it or ward against it. Eventually certain aspects of life are more strongly associated with the spirit, depending on who the person was in life, legends surrounding them, or the things their spirit was believed to have done after death. This network of associations and worship becomes the structure for belief in the spirit as the god of a specific place, concept or purpose. The five examples below are some of the most famous Japanese *kami* who were either once human or associated with specific humans. All of them can be linked to historical people who actually existed. Whether the myths about these individuals are true is a different question, and one that we are unable to answer. What we can say, however, is that due to these myths, each of these people was regarded as a *kami* at some point after death. None of them appear among the ancient gods of the 7th-century chronicles, and most of them were not seen as *kami* during their lifetimes. Yet today all of them are well-known *kami* relating to specific aspects of Japanese culture.

PRINCE SHŌTOKU: BUDDHISM'S AVATAR

Prince Shōtoku 聖徳太子 (574–622) is one of the earliest human figures to be deified in Japanese mythology. He lived and died nearly a century before the earliest chronicles were written, and was known for his embrace of Buddhism, then a very new religion in Japan. However, by the mid-8th century, when myths had developed that exaggerated his youth and powers, the prince became seen not only as an early believer in Buddhism, but as its spiritual guardian in Japan. By the Heian Period, Prince Shōtoku was worshipped as the herald of Buddhist learning, and even today he is well known for his magical powers and his religious importance as the first Japanese defender of the Buddhist faith.

The name Shōtoku means 'Holy Virtue'. It was not his original name and, according to the *Nihonshoki*, it was bestowed upon the prince much later in his life.[1] He was born as Prince Umayado 厩戸 (lit. 'Stable Door'), a son of the ruler later known as Emperor Yōmei 用明 (540–587, r. 585–587); the prince was also known as Kamitsumiya 上宮. His father Yōmei was the second of four children of Kinmei (the first historically verifiable ruler; see Chapter 3) to hold the throne. Yōmei succeeded his older brother Bidatsu 敏達 (538–586, r. 572–585), only to die shortly afterwards of an illness. As both brothers had several male children, Prince Umayado was not immediately in the line of succession to the throne.

Umayado was known to be intelligent, but the *Nihonshoki* says little about his childhood. When he was in his teens, the court became embroiled in a feud between the Mononobe 物部, an ancient clan of ritualists who supported worshipping native *kami*, and the Soga 蘇我, an immigrant clan from the continent who were strongly Buddhist. The dispute erupted into a minor military conflict. According to the *Nihonshoki*, Umayado, still a young teenager, questioned whether military might alone could achieve victory for the Soga. On his own, he cut down branches of Chinese sumac (*Rhus chinensis*, Jp. *nurude*), and fashioned

Prince Shōtoku (centre), here portrayed as an adult, with his two young sons.

icons of the Four Heavenly Kings, guardian deities of Buddhism.[2] The prince placed the icons in his hair, and their magic protected the Soga forces, allowing them an easy victory.

The Soga and their promotion of Buddhism would dominate the court from the 580s to the 640s, and Prince Umayado became one of their chief allies. After his father's death, the throne passed to another son of Kinmei, who ruled as Sushun 崇峻 (d. 592, r. 587–592) and died without leaving any heirs. As none of the sons of either Bidatsu or Yōmei were old enough, Bidatsu's widow, who was also his half-sister and therefore of royal lineage herself, assumed the throne as Suiko (554–628, r. 593–628), the first historically verifiable female ruler of Japan. Prince Umayado, now of age, was named Suiko's crown prince. He served his aunt as a regent rather than as simply an heir. The *Nihonshoki* records that the prince issued rulings and judgments and was always exceedingly fair. He gathered together Buddhist monks and nuns and established a network of court-sponsored temples, including two that remain famous today: the Shitennōji in Osaka, and the Hōryūji in Ikaruga, outside of Nara. He also issued a series of seventeen edicts later called a 'Seventeen-Article Constitution'. Although not a constitution in the modern sense of the word, this was the first time that the basic laws of the Japanese court were laid out writing.

Any one of these acts would be enough for the prince to be remembered by history, but given all three, he became known even in his own day as a paragon of religious-minded virtue. This led to him being called Shōtoku, the name by which he is remembered today. The prince died in 622, seven years before his aunt, and never ascended the throne. His children were assassinated in a coup shortly afterwards, and his lineage vanished from Japan. Politically he had very little effect on future developments.

The *Nihonshoki* account is the only detailed record of the prince's life written before he became a religious icon. He died ninety-eight years before the chronicle was compiled, and no contemporary records of his existence have survived. The *Nihonshoki* account contains some elements that are clearly exaggerated. The most notable is the text of the 'Seventeen-Article Constitution' itself, which contains anachronistic terms that would not be used in government until the Nara Period.[3] However, the *Nihonshoki* does not make out the prince to be anything other than a human, albeit an exceptionally talented and devoted one. Yet by the late 8th century, within a generation of the *Nihonshoki*'s completion, Prince Shōtoku began to be honoured as a quasi-divine figure at Buddhist temples. He embodied some of the religion's core values, despite having never been a priest, and because he had never ruled as emperor in his own right, he was not remembered for any mistakes, nor were his descendants still around to tarnish his image. Eventually, he was perceived as one of Buddhism's main proponents in early Japan. By the turn of the 9th century, legends about Shōtoku's brilliance, purity and blessed powers had eclipsed the real history of the historical Umayado.

According to the *Jōgū Shōtoku taishiden hoketsuki*, an 11th-century account of the prince's life, he was blessed even before his birth.[4] By age two he had read the entire Buddhist canon and was able to recite sutras perfectly. His intellect stunned those around him, as did his perfect understanding of Buddhist theology. A figure made of golden light supposedly visited him in his dreams and taught him secrets of magic and doctrine. These visitations encouraged Shōtoku to produce Buddhist monuments on behalf of Japan. His construction of the Shitennōji temple, dedicated to the Four Heavenly Kings, was in gratitude for their magical help during the Soga-Mononobe War. By fulfilling his vow to build a temple on their behalf, the prince obtained even greater merit.

Prince Shōtoku
- Name means 'Holy Virtue'; born as Prince Umayado, a son of Emperor Yōmei (r. 585–587).
- Served as regent to his aunt, who ruled as Empress Regnant Suiko (r. 593–628); he was supposedly the first to codify laws of the Japanese court in writing. Details of his life have been obscured by later myths.
- Became deified within Japanese Buddhism by the 9th century; his cult was at its height in the 12th–14th centuries.
- Said to have read the entire Buddhist canon by age two; often depicted as a baby of two in icons.
- Supernatural visitations encouraged him to build Buddhist monuments, several of which survive today.

The *Jōgū Shōtoku taishiden hoketsuki* was the first of several such texts about the prince that appeared during the Heian Period. Each of these added further to the Shōtoku legend. Among the stories told about the prince include that he foresaw the importance of Buddhism in dreams, and had the ability to discern strangers' true identities. One famous tale goes back as far as the *Nihonshoki* account. Prince Shōtoku was out riding with his attendants when he saw a poor beggar by the side of the road. The attendants all ignored the man, but Shōtoku got off his horse and greeted the beggar as though he was of equal status. He attempted to bring the man with him, but the beggar was nearly dead from starvation and could not move. To the shock of his entourage, the prince took off his own cloak and covered the man's body, telling him to rest well. Upon returning to his home, Shōtoku sent messengers to find the beggar, but they discovered that he had already perished. The prince ordered a tomb mound to be raised and sealed tight around the man's body. Several days later, the prince called his men together again and told them that the beggar had been an immortal sage. He sent a messenger to the tomb, who reported that it had been opened as if from the inside, and now lay empty. Only Prince Shōtoku had the insight to recognize a fellow sage.[5]

The cult of Prince Shōtoku was most prominent in the Heian and Kamakura (1185–1333) Periods. Prayers made to Shōtoku's spirit were believed to save petitioners from illness or calamity. Although he was not the most widely worshipped Buddhist deity, there are a number of famous icons of him.[6] By the eleventh century, it became common to depict the prince as a baby of two years old or younger, with his hair in a pair of pigtailed loops. These statues were not the main objects of veneration at temples, which were

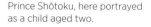

Prince Shōtoku, here portrayed as a child aged two.

99

usually of buddhas or bodhisattvas. Rather, like statues of famous sages and sect founders, depictions of Shōtoku were often placed in alcoves or smaller worship pavilions.

Today Prince Shōtoku is not widely worshipped in Japan, but he is well known as a historical figure. Many elements of his religious cult, such as the details of his mortal life, have now become conflated with stories from texts such as the *Nihonshoki*, or even recent archaeological discoveries about the time in which he lived. A representation of Shōtoku appeared on several banknotes issued during the 20th century. He is also the subject of several popular manga, including the famous *Hi izuru tokoro no tenshi* ('Prince of the Land of the Rising Sun', 1980–1984), which reimagines the prince as a magical but morally ambiguous and sexually deviant figure who manipulates everyone around him to tragic ends.

EN NO GYŌJA: WIZARD OF THE WOODS

The *Shoku nihongi* ('Continued Chronicles of Japan', 797) is an imperial-commissioned sequel to the *Nihonshoki* that covers the years 696–791. In an entry for 699, the *Shoku nihongi* records that a man named En no Ozunu 役小角 (also Otsunu or Otsuno; 634–c. 700 or 707) was sentenced to exile for practising black magic. The record includes a short passage about En no Ozunu. He was known as a master of sorcery and had several disciples. One accused him of using spirits to draw water and cut firewood, and of binding them with spells so they did not disobey.[7] 'Black magic' (an English translation of the term *jujutsu*, literally 'curse technique' – not to be confused with the martial art known in English as jiujitsu) included summoning the dead, as well as natural *kami* or other spirits, and forcing them to labour or murder on behalf of the summoner.

En no Ozunu was exiled to the province of Kii (modern Wakayama Prefecture), a region of steep, forested mountains south of the Nara Basin. The region was sacred to many *kami*, particularly those worshipped at the triple Kumano Shrines. These are three separate shrines, approximately 20 km (13 miles) apart, and considered to be one shrine in three places. The Kumano Shrines are ancient pilgrimage destinations, and the route over the mountains to reach them is likewise an ancient place for mountain ascetics to retreat and train. Known as *yamabushi* ('those who prostrate upon the mountain') or *shugenja* ('those who practise deep training'), these mountain ascetics practise a syncretic mix of Buddhist, Shinto and Daoist beliefs known as Shugendō ('The Way of Deep Training').[8]

Records of the *yamabushi* and their retreats into the Kii mountains go back to the 7th and 8th centuries. However, starting in the 9th century, they begin to claim that their practices derived from a legendary founding figure known as En no Gyōja 役行者, or 'En the Practitioner'. When asked about the identity of this mysterious founder of Shugendō, the *yamabushi* explained that he was none other than En no Ozunu. Earlier legends still depicted him as a morally ambiguous figure, who may have bound one or more mountain gods to his service, and who flew through the sky to China after his exile.[9] However, by the end of the Heian Period he was seen as an unambiguously positive figure. The exiled sorcerer was now revered as the founder of a cult, one that combined aspects of Buddhist hermits, Daoist alchemists and *kami*-worshipping faith healers.

En no Gyōja was believed to have transcended his mortality while living deep in the mountains of Kii. *Yamabushi* and others who practised Shugendō believed that he had become a *kami* with one foot in the world of Buddhist deities and the other in the world of nature spirits.

En no Gyōja opens Mt Fuji with his powers.

Supposedly he often appeared to petitioners as an old man wearing the clothes of a typical mountain ascetic: long robes, a wooden prayer rosary and sometimes a straw hat or raincoat. He also appeared as a young boy of around five years old, usually wearing only smallclothes. In either form, he often rode a large black ox.

En no Gyōja is primarily worshipped as a source of beneficial magic, esoteric knowledge or both. He is not necessarily a mountain *kami*, although he tends to appear in the deep mountains. He is also not a Buddhist deity, but he is tightly linked with esoteric figures from tantric Buddhism, a strain of Buddhism that focuses on the hidden nature of reality by interweaving ideas from multiple sects. The main centre of Shugendō devotion is at Mt Yoshino, at the very southern end of the Nara Basin where the route to the Kumano Shrines begins. The Kinpusenji Temple at Mt Yoshino, which lies high up on the northern slope of the peak, has been the chief temple for Shugendō since the Heian Period. Mt Yoshino was a famous site for astrological rites conducted by the Japanese rulers of the 7th century and was later believed to be an abode of Maitreya (Jp. Miroku), the Future Buddha. Over time, however, En no Gyōja's association with the site led to worship of the mountain *kami* there, himself included.[10]

Faith in En no Gyōja and the myriad other deities of Shugendō (regardless of their religion of origin) gives *yamabushi* great powers. They can bind evil spirits, cure disease, command the forces of nature and, through physical and mental conditioning, maintain great health well into old age. Many of these talents are those for which the original En no Ozunu was supposedly exiled. While *yamabushi* are wild figures, living apart from civilization, they are not evil, and in literature they are often sought out as the last hope of aristocrats suffering from curses or other plights. En no Gyōja likewise appears in later Japanese literature as a mysterious but beneficial figure. Starting in the medieval era, he appears in stories to give cryptic advice or help one of his *yamabushi* save someone; his days as enemy of the early court are long forgotten.

Like Prince Shōtoku, En no Gyōja is not widely worshipped today. Shugendō still maintains practitioners and has experienced new fame with the designation of the ancient Kumano routes as a UNESCO World

Heritage Site. However, actual *yamabushi* remain few and far between in the modern world. Yoshino and the Kumano Shrines are now tourist destinations and the image of the medieval *yamabushi* is a popular one in fiction, manga and anime. Unlike that of of Prince Shōtoku, the history behind En no Gyōja is much less widely recognized in modern Japan. Many people in the present know about him as a deity, but few are aware that he is based on a real person, or even details of why he is worshipped.

PRINCE SAWARA: ARCHITECT OF VENGEANCE

In late 781, Emperor Kanmu 桓武 (736–806, r. 781–806) was enthroned in Nara. The last ruler of the Nara Period, Kanmu would go on to be one of the most famous emperors in Japanese history. Soon after his enthronement, the emperor decided to move the capital away from Nara. Although the exact reasons are unknown, it is thought that one significant factor was Kanmu's desire to get away from the older aristocratic families and the great Buddhist temples, both of which had come to exert strong control over the court. Kanmu chose to make his new capital at a site known as Nagaoka, halfway between the modern cities of Osaka and Kyoto. Nagaoka was along the Yodo river, one of the main trade routes between the Inland Sea and the rest of the Home Provinces. Planning began immediately, and the capital was officially moved in 784, ending the Nara Period.[11]

Emperor Kanmu
(r. 781–806), portrayed
in generic Chinese-style
clothing.

One of the most visible detractors of the plan to move the capital was Kanmu's half-brother Prince Sawara 早良親王 (750?–785), who was a powerful figure at court. Because Sawara was so vocal against the move, it was easy to pin any mishaps on him. In 784, just months before the capital was officially transferred, one of the heads of the committee for its construction was murdered. The *Nihon kōki* ('Later Chronicles of Japan', 840), the official chronicle that follows the *Shoku nihongi* and covers the turn of the 9th century, unfortunately only survives in fragments. However, there is enough evidence remaining in it to reconstruct what happened next more or less accurately.

Prince Sawara does not appear to have been behind the murder, but he was framed for it by Kanmu, who had him executed for treason in early 785. The move to Nagaoka went off as planned. Two years later, the Yodo river flooded during an extremely rainy spring, inundating much of the city; a year later, it happened again, causing even more widespread damage. Today it is understood that the city was located on a natural floodplain, squeezed between the river and a low mountain, but at the time these events were deemed to be the work of angry *kami*. Diviners set to work trying to understand what god might be behind the calamities, and what it wanted. They determined that the *kami* was Prince Sawara's ghost. Unable to rest due to having been framed for murder, the prince was now sabotaging Kanmu's great project – and looked to be winning.

In 788, Kanmu's crown prince, the future Emperor Heizei 平城 (773–824, r. 806–809), fell grievously ill. At this point, Kanmu decided to do whatever it took to appease his half-brother's ghost. This began with a public declaration of Prince Sawara's innocence. A second imperial edict retroactively declared Sawara to have been the crown prince, and post-humously named him Emperor Sudō. Kanmu's edicts basically rewrote history so that Sawara's spirit received the highest honours instead of being remembered as a traitor. These moves appeased the spirit enough that the crown prince recovered, but Nagaoka-kyō remained unlucky, and Kanmu began making plans to move his capital again. In 794, ten years after the ill-fated move, the capital was moved again, to Heiankyō, which would become the modern city of Kyoto.

Prince Sawara represents a cautionary tale: if you frame your relatives for a crime, beware their vengeance from beyond the grave. The early Heian court took this lesson seriously, and it altered the course of Japanese history. However, Prince Sawara was not a unique case. Kanmu had been invested in 'pruning' the imperial clan down to his own descendants, killing a number of distant relations – several of whom came back as angry spirits. Calamities that befell Kanmu and his sons in later decades were likewise blamed on the executions of Kanmu's relatives during the 780s and 790s. After the ninth century, the problem of ghostly vengeance became a mainstay in both fiction and historical records.

Unlike the other examples in this chapter, Prince Sawara has never been worshipped as a god. No modern list of emperors includes him, and he is essentially only an interesting historical footnote today. Yet his legend remains important for two reasons. The first reason is that Sawara's curse was often given as the reason for the founding of Kyoto. The second is his role as one of the earliest and most famous examples of a human becoming an angry *kami* after death. Prince Sawara is referenced in several works of pop culture, including some modern historical fantasy films. Although he does not command the same horror and reverence he did for Heian Period aristocrats, the wronged prince turned vengeful spirit is still able to generate a few screams.

SUGAWARA NO MICHIZANE: HEAVENLY GENIUS

Sugawara no Michizane 菅原道真 (845–903) was born into an illustrious family of scholar-aristocrats. Although not at the top of the aristocracy, the Sugawara clan were well known as studious and capable administrators. Michizane was a genius even by the high standards of the clan. He graduated from the State Academy in 870 with full honours and proved adept at the mid-level bureaucratic jobs that awaited young courtiers.[12] He was also recognized for his literary skills, particularly at writing Classical Chinese poetry (Jp. *kanshi*). Michizane was put in charge of diplomatic relations with Korean and Chinese envoys. Due to his literary skills, he was highly sought after for compositions on behalf of higher-ranking courtiers. His star rose swiftly – and so did the envy of his peers.

Scene from a biography of Sugiwara no Michizane (left), showing the future deity teaching an imperial princess at court.

When Emperor Uda 宇陀 (866–931, r. 887–897) ascended the throne, Michizane wrote several forceful essays backing certain members of the court. These earned him widespread acclaim, and he was given better and better positions. By the 890s, he was in charge of Japan's diplomatic exchanges, and was behind the decision to cut off ties with the faltering Tang Dynasty in China.[13] Michizane's writing in both Chinese and Japanese was popular at the court, and survives in several anthologies, including the *Shinsen man'yōshū* ('Newly Compiled Collection of Myriad Ages', before 913), the *Kokin wakashū* ('Collection of Ancient and Modern Poetry', 920) and the *Shūi wakashū* ('Collection of Gleanings', 1005). Michizane was also known as an outspoken politician who entreated the aristocrats to live more moral, Confucian-style lives.

However, when Uda abdicated in 897, Michizane's star dimmed. Uda's son Emperor Daigo 醍醐 (885–930, r. 897–930) was close to Fujiwara no Tokihira 藤原時平 (871–909), a scion of the powerful Fujiwara clan.

Tokihira framed Michizane for plotting against the new emperor. Although he was not executed, Michizane was demoted in rank and sent into exile. He lived out the remainder of his life in Dazaifu (in modern Fukuoka Prefecture), a settlement in northern Kyushu hundreds of kilometres from the capital.

After Michizane's death, disasters began to befall Daigo's court one by one. First, members of the Fujiwara who had testified to Michizane's crimes died under mysterious circumstances while still in good health. Then Emperor Daigo's sons began to die one after another. A drought descended on the capital in the summer of 930, and just as prayers for rain began, a great storm, more intense than the prayers intended, appeared out of nowhere and the main audience hall of the imperial palace was struck by lightning, burning to ashes.[14] As in the case of Prince Sawara, divinations were performed in order to determine the cause of this string of catastrophes. The culprit was revealed to be Michizane's vengeful ghost, seeking revenge for the politics that cost him his job, his reputation and ultimately his life. Once the spirit behind the disasters was identified, Daigo ordered Michizane's ranks and job titles restored posthumously, and all mention of his exile was stricken from the official record. A special shrine called the Kitano Tenmangū was built to honour him in Kyoto. Once he had been enshrined as a *kami*, Michizane's attacks stopped, and the capital was at peace.

Sugawara no Michizane (Tenjin)

- Born into a family of scholar-aristocrats. Recognized for his literary skill.
- By 890s he was given control of Japanese diplomatic exchanges.
- Severed ties with the Tang Dynasty. Compiled several anthologies of prose and poetry that were popular in Emperor Uda's court.
- Died in exile after being framed for plotting against the new emperor.
- After his death, Emperor Daigo's (Uda's son) court faced many disasters and Michizane's ghost was determined to be the culprit.
- His rank and titles were reinstated posthumously, and a shrine built in his honour. This quelled all further attacks from Michizane's ghost.
- Now worshipped (as 'Tenjin') for job protection and scholarly success.

Over the next 70 years, Sugawara no Michizane's spirit gained worshippers among aristocrats seeking job protection and scholarly aptitude. The Kitano Tenmangū grew into a large shrine, and a second Tenmangū was established at Dazaifu, where Michizane had died in exile. Now known as Tenman Tenjin 天満天神, or 'Heavenly God Who Fills Heaven', Michizane's spirit was formally invested in 973 as the greater *kami* of scholarship and learning. Not only had this bureaucrat surpassed Prince Sawara with the fame of his attacks on the court, but he had also been transformed into an important god in less than a century.

Today the god who was once named Sugawara no Michizane is most often known simply as Tenjin. Tenjin is worshipped across Japan at shrines generally known as Tenmangū ('Heaven-Filling Palace') after the two original ones in Kyoto and Dazaifu. He is a popular god among young people, particularly high school and college students seeking help on exams. Although the story of who Sugawara no Michizane was, and why he became deified as Tenjin, is well known throughout Japan, many people do not actively think of the historical figure and the *kami* as the same being. Tenjin is not often pictured at shrines. When he is depicted, it is often as a man wearing the clothes of a mid-Heian Period courtier. Unlike Western (or even some Chinese) ideas of a sage as a wise old man, Tenjin is more generally associated with youthful brilliance and middle-aged ability rather than the wisdom that comes from long study. Surprisingly, while he is a popular object of worship, Tenjin has little presence in pop culture. Perhaps his worship is too ordinary to be considered an exciting subject for film or manga in contemporary Japan.

MINAMOTO NO YOSHIIE: GOD OF THE BATTLEFIELD

The Heian Period drew to a final close with the rise of the Kamakura Shogunate in 1192, but the seeds of its demise had been planted much earlier. The Fujiwara clan's domination of the inner circles around the emperors was mostly complete by the early 11th century. This in turn led to ever-younger emperors managed by Fujiwara regents, who were the real power behind the throne. Emperors would often retire upon reaching maturity and live their adult lives free of (some of) the fetters of the position. By the turn of the 12th century, this led to the practice of the Insei, or 'retired emperor system', in which a child emperor would be put on the throne and managed by one or more Fujiwara regents (often his maternal relatives); meanwhile, there were one or more living retired emperors, often still fairly young adults. These retired emperors frequently took basic vows as Buddhist lay monks and then pulled their own political strings from within nearby temples.

The Japanese aristocracy had long ago ceased to lead war efforts, which were mostly restricted to the slow conquest of northern Honshu, far from the capital. Over the past 150 years, the former roles of aristocratic warriors had been taken by hereditary professional soldiers based largely in the distant provinces. Two of the most powerful of these warrior clans were the Taira (also known as the Heike) and the Minamoto (also known as the Genji). Both clans, along with other lesser-known ones, were active in the conquest of the north. This protracted effort, begun as early as the late 7th century, took until around 1100 to be completed. Two of its final conflicts were the Zenkunen War (1051–63) and Gosannen War (1086–89). The enemies in these conflicts were the Emishi, the same groups whom Yamato Takeru had to subdue in legends from centuries

The Heiji Disturbance (1150), in which Minamoto no Yoshiie's descendants took part.

The Emishi
- Enemies in the conflicts during the conquests of northern Honshu.
- Term 'Emishi' came to mean anyone from northern Honshu who rejected the authority of the imperial court.
- Most information about them comes from the Japanese imperial court.
- Ethnicities and languages are not known. Many were probably ethnically 'Japanese', however.

---

earlier. By this point, the term 'Emishi' had come to refer to anyone in northern Honshu who did not accept the authority of the imperial court. The actual ethnicities and languages of these populations are unknown, although Japanese from the rest of the archipelago lived among them. As they did not produce many written records of their own, most of what we know of the Emishi, and of the conquest of the north, comes from material produced by or for the Japanese imperial court in Kyoto.

The Minamoto leader in both the Zenkunen and Gosannen Wars was a man named Minamoto no Yoshiie 源義家 (1039–1106). Yoshiie was known as a natural warrior, skilled with both sword and bow and equally at home on horseback or on foot. Leading a relatively small force of highly trained warriors, Yoshiie broke two sieges during the later phase of the Zenkunen War. After cleaning up the final stages of the conflict, Yoshiie travelled to Kyoto to present the court with his spoils, including the heads of powerful Emishi chieftains. Due to Yoshiie's battle prowess, he began to become known as Hachimantarō 八幡太郎 ('Son of Hachiman').[15]

Hachiman 八幡 is the patron god of warriors, and by extension, of war itself. Hachiman does not appear in either the *Kojiki* or the *Nihonshoki*. He is mentioned in records from as early as the Nara Period as a deity who was worshipped in the provinces, primarily by peasants and warriors.[16] As we know very little about what people outside the court believed until the late medieval period, Hachiman could indeed have much deeper native roots. Either way, the warriors under and around Minamoto no Yoshiie in the 11th century believed in this god and attributed their leader's powers to his blessing. Two decades after his spectacular rise, Yoshiie returned to the battlefields of northern Honshu, and commanded

LIVING *KAMI* AND DIVINE HUMANS

imperial forces in crushing the Emishi during the Gosannen War. By the time of his death, Yoshiie's legend had spread far and wide, even among the aristocrats in Kyoto.[17]

In the 1150s the Insei system exploded into violent conflict. Various retired emperors, Fujiwara leaders and even great Buddhist temples brought armed forces into the streets of Kyoto. The Taira and the Minamoto were called into the capital by leaders on opposite sides, and served as the private militaries for the aristocratic families. Eventually the Taira decided to remain, building up their own power base and briefly replacing the Fujiwara in controlling the imperial government. Events came to a second head in 1180, when the Minamoto were called back to depose the upstart Taira. The conflict that followed, known as the Genpei War, saw the destruction of aristocratic power, and laid the groundwork for the military rule that would define the Japanese middle ages.

The Minamoto leader was a brilliant commander named Minamoto no Yoritomo 源頼朝 (1147–1199). Yoritomo was the great-great-grandson of Yoshiie and seemed to have inherited his ancestor's abilities. By the breakout of the Genpei War, Yoritomo was already the veteran of many successful battles against local lords and the remaining Emishi rebels. Yoritomo was known as a brave leader, but he was also a cunning strategist with more than a touch of paranoia. He proved a match for the Taira forces, even though he also ended up turning on several of his own commanders in the process. When the dust settled in 1185, Yoritomo was the last leader of the two great warrior houses left standing. Rather than seize power in Kyoto as the Taira had done, Yoritomo chose to leave for his homeland in the Kantō, the plains around modern Tokyo. He did, however, demand that the emperor name him Shogun in 1190. Two years later, Yoritomo initiated the Kamakura Shogunate, and with it one of Japan's most important historical developments.

Minamoto no Yoritomo claimed his ancestor Yoshiie as a personal and familial patron. However, given his rule over Japan as its first Shogun, Yoritomo's personal worship of his ancestor became mingled with larger issues of faith. The legend of Yoshiie as the son of the god Hachiman led to the view that Yoritomo was similarly protected by the god of war. This in turn led to Hachiman being worshipped on a much larger scale. The figures of both Yoshiie and Yoritomo became merged with the popular idea of Hachiman – as did the figure of the legendary Emperor Ōjin (see Chapter 3). By the mid-13th century, Hachiman was seen as the military protector of Japan, and the guarantor of safety for its people.[18]

Hachiman's association with warriors, and particularly with Minamoto no Yoshiie, also made him into the god of archery. He is usually depicted as an early medieval Japanese warrior, a middle-aged man wearing traditional armour and carrying a sword, a bow and a quiver full of arrows. In some cases, portrayals of Hachiman are explicitly of Minamoto no Yoshiie, or even (more rarely) of Minamoto no Yoritomo. In later centuries all three figures became merged into one syncretic *kami*.

Hachiman is worshipped at Hachimangū Shrines across Japan. The most famous is the Usa Shrine, often called the Usa Hachimangū, in modern Ōita Prefecture on Kyushu. This shrine appears to have been originally dedicated to Emperor Ōjin's spirit. It is mentioned in Nara and Heian Period texts and was patronized by the imperial family.[19] The shrine's association with Hachiman is of uncertain origin and may predate the warrior class's devotion to the

Two portrayals of Minamoto no Yoshiie as the god Hachiman: as a Heian noble (left), and as a medieval mounted warrior (right).

kami. Other important Hachimangū are in the north and east of Honshu, the areas traditionally associated with the medieval warrior clans. These include the great Tsurugaoka Hachimangū in Kamakura (in modern Kanazawa Prefecture), which was one of Minamoto no Yoritomo's own principal shrines.

Today Hachiman is widely worshipped, albeit to a lesser degree than Tenjin or some of the other great *kami*. He had been one of the most important deities during the modern Empire of Japan, between the Meiji Restoration and the end of the Second World War. Named a patron of the imperial family and the Japanese nation-state (both political entities that post-dated his original worship), Hachiman was also the most important *kami* for soldiers in the Imperial Army and Navy. He was invoked during Japan's modern wars up to and including the Second World War and faced equivalent backlash during the American Occupation and in the postwar decades. This modern history makes the worship of Hachiman more emotionally charged than that of other deities, such as Tenjin. This may be one reason why he is no longer as important today. The official pacifism of contemporary Japan may be another.

HUMANS AND GODS; HUMANS AS GODS

The boundary between 'spirit' and 'human' is a porous one. The examples above show how certain people's spirits could be worshipped after death, and in time grow into something larger and more important. But in other cases people's spirits can affect the world while they are still living. The premodern Japanese created a detailed lore concerning the spirits of individuals both living and dead, and the ways in which they interacted with other people. These interactions ranged from very positive to negative and even fatal. Dealing with the spirits of other humans was as fraught with potential danger as dealing with their ordinary living selves.

We know little about early Japanese understanding of local spirits. The 7th-century chronicles are concerned with the origins of the imperial family, the organization of the world, and other big-picture events. The early 9th-century compilations of Buddhist-themed folklore known as the *Nihon ryōiki* ('Record of Strange Tales from Japan', compiled between 787 and 824) is the earliest source that records stories that are not connected to the imperial family. However, the *Nihon ryōiki* is mostly concerned with teaching lessons related to Buddhism through its fables. Other fiction and diaries survive in slightly larger numbers from the late 9th and early 10th centuries. This leaves us a gap between the initial Japanese myths, which date to the early Nara Period (*c.* 700), and records of what nobles believed, which only start appearing in the mid-Heian Period (*c.* 900).

Heian aristocrats were usually literate, but few others in Japan were able to read and write before the 16th century. This means that when we talk about Heian folklore we are still talking only about the stories of the upper classes. There are very few records about what farmers or poor townsfolk believed until much later in Japanese history; their views will be addressed in the next two chapters. Almost all our lore about humans and spirits in Heian and early medieval Japan therefore comes from texts produced by aristocrats, usually living in Kyoto.

Heian aristocrats believed that they shared their world not only with a variety of natural *kami*, but also with the spirits of people. There were two basic types of these spirits: peaceful and aggressive. Peaceful spirits offered little to fear. These were usually the results of karmic bonds between people holding the spirit of a loved one in place after they had died. People who were very much in love, or who shared a similar karmic bond from a previous life, might be held by their attachment to their loved one. This attachment was technically a negative according to Buddhist dogma, as it prevented people from freeing themselves from the cycle of rebirth, but it was far less dangerous than other possible outcomes.

One of the biggest fears of Heian courtiers was aggressive human spirits. Known as *onryō* or *goryō*, these were the spirits of humans who had been betrayed or otherwise bore a grudge against other living beings. *Goryō*, in particular, are the spirits of those unfairly condemned to death – in which case they can also be called *shiryō* ('dead spirits'), like Prince Sawara – or of those who have lost everything due to betrayal but are still alive, in which case they can also be called *ikiryō* ('living spirits'). *Onryō*, while an overlapping term, often refers to spirits who are evil rather than merely angry. *Goryō* and *onryō* are generated either after a violent death, or by violent emotions in someone who is still alive.[20] They appear at night, in abandoned houses, or in otherwise dim and lonely sections of premodern urban environments.

Goryō and *onryō* cause numerous disasters. In cases like those of Prince Sawara or Sugawara no Michizane, these disasters can affect large groups of people. Such calamities might involve floods, fires, storms, earthquakes or illness. In the nightmares of ordinary Heian nobility, these vengeful spirits cause smaller-scale disasters such as collapsing houses, sudden pain or death of individuals, or even the stillbirth of a child. In some cases, a spirit can possess a living person, causing them great agony and/ or death. This phenomenon, known in Japanese as *mononoke* 物の怪, is also another term for the spirits that cause it. *Mononoke* possession can be by either living or dead spirits.

One famous example comes from *Genji monogatari* ('The Tale of Genji', *c.* 1000), one of Japan's most famous premodern works of fiction. It is a long and epic story of an imperial prince turned commoner and his romances with many different women at court. Early in the tale, the main character, Genji 源氏, begins a relationship with an older woman known as Rokujō 六条. Genji eventually stops seeing Rokujō and begins affairs with several other women. During one such tryst, Genji finds himself at an abandoned house with his current paramour, a young woman called Yūgao 夕顔. Yūgao is terrified of the place, but Genji soothes her. Later, he is awakened by a spectral presence. When Genji reaches for Yūgao, he finds her cold and dead; the presence yells at him in a jealous rage and is implied to be Rokujō's living spirit. This is confirmed in a later chapter, when Genji's legal wife, Aoi 葵, also dies under mysterious circumstances.

Goryō and *onryō*

- Aggressive human spirits who have been betrayed or otherwise hold grudges against the living.
- *Goryō*: spirits of those unfairly sentenced to death, or who are still living and have lost everything due to betrayal.
- *Onryō*: more general term for evil spirits
- Cause disasters and illness; can possess the living. The consequences of such attacks can affect many people.

The ghost of Yūgao, pictured against the bottle-gourd flowers that are her namesake, in this chapter cover page of an Edo Period edition of *The Tale of Genji*.

Aoi and Genji have a troubled relationship. They married for political reasons when they were both young. Genji had affairs with other women and Aoi was cold and distant. Things warm up between them, however, when Aoi becomes pregnant with their son. During her pregnancy, Aoi goes to view the Kamo Festival, and her wagon inadvertently blocks Rokujō's wagon. Rokujō, still upset over Genji's having cut off their earlier relationship, is consumed with jealousy at the sight of his wife. When Aoi goes into childbirth soon afterwards, a spirit in the form of a woman shows up to torture her and kills her immediately after the child is born. Genji recognizes this spirit as the same one that killed Yūgao. Rokujō then wakes in her own house with the scents of poppy and smoke on her clothes – the same scents used to ward off evil in Aoi's birthing chamber.

In both cases, Rokujō is still alive when her spirit kills the other two women. Her waking self is unaware of these actions and she is in fact horrified when she learns what she has done to Aoi. However, she is portrayed as being so jealous of Genji's other objects of affection that she cannot help herself. Upon sleeping, Rokujō's anguished spirit leaves her body and becomes a *goryō*, seeking out others whom Genji loves and murdering them in fits of rage. Modern scholars believe that spirit possession, particularly that done by Rokujō, originated as a way to explain sudden deaths that medical knowledge of the time could not. This may be one reason why spirit possession often kills women in childbirth. However, the trope is also known from a variety of other examples, including attacks on men, or by male spirits.

Rokujō is perhaps the most classic example of spirit possession by a living person in Japanese fiction. Her interactions with both Yūgao and Aoi, as well as with Genji, are not only key moments in the narrative of *Genji monogatari* but are also the subject of 15th-century Noh plays and early modern fiction. Other, later stereotypes of jealous female ghosts, those of both living and dead people, are heavily based on the *Genji monogatari* archetype and Rokujō's serial terrors.

Humans are not supernatural beings in the Japanese worldview, but they can become them. Great individuals can become even more legendary after their deaths, until their spirits are worshipped for the miracles that they offer their descendants and worshippers. The wrongfully persecuted can return to wreak spiritual vengeance, driving people to fear and respect them. On a small scale, this results in ghost stories and spirit possessions. On the large scale, we see everything from the adoration of Prince Shōtoku as a deity to the fearful posthumous recognition of Prince Sawara. Respect and understanding of these figures, like the myths themselves, grow and change over time. Sugawara no Michizane went from being a famous person to a fearsome ghost, and finally became a god.

Modern scholars read this process in multiple ways. On one hand, the development of legendary figures who evolve into new objects of worship is not unique to Japan. Catholic saints, Sufi wise men and Hindu gurus (among others) undergo similar transformations into cult figures. On the other hand, the ease with which gods enter or leave the Japanese pantheon makes it a surprisingly fluid one. The ancient chronicles are not the be-all and end-all of Shinto or any other religious mythology. As people's needs change over time, events become legends that then offer hope and power to those who need them. The Japanese myths are very good at incorporating these changes.

Figures like Michizane, and the others presented in this chapter, stand between the worlds of gods and men. There are many like them in Japanese folklore. The founders of great Buddhist sects become revered saints to whom prayers are offered. Real-life analogues of Rokujō become evil spirits that roam the countryside, the stuff of ghost stories and cautionary tales. There are many other types of spirits that live alongside humans, some of which will be dealt with in the following chapter. However, the figures that cross between both worlds form one of the most important elements of Japanese mythology, and of the different forms of faith practised in Japan even today. They are proof of the transformative power of storytelling: legends, when set free, can transform a prince into a saint, and an exiled criminal into a prophet of the wilderness.

5

CANON FOREIGNERS:
THE JAPANESE BUDDHIST PANTHEON

The term 'canon foreigner' describes a phenomenon that occurs in modern films or television series that are based on novels or comics. This term is used for a new character who is introduced as important to the plot, but who did not exist in the original medium.[1] Such a character is 'canon' in that they are officially recognized as a part of the work. They are also 'foreign' in that they were not present in the original version of the story. This concept can also be applied to older works, including mythology. Myths are fluid not only over time, but through space and across national and cultural boundaries. As a people interact with other groups, their native gods, heroes and demons can be transmitted to another culture as characters in stories or be traded like goods. Japan, which embraced Buddhism, Confucianism, Daoism and numerous other traditions from East Asia and beyond, has many examples of such foreign gods. In most cases they have become nativized, with distinctive Japanese names and forms of worship – and in some cases, they even merged with native *kami*.

This chapter explores the most important 'canon foreigners' in Japanese mythology: the Buddhist pantheon. Buddhism has existed in Japan for over 1500 years. During this time, the religion has interacted with other faiths, most importantly the native Shinto. These interactions are not only between people or places. They also take the form of shared or competing philosophies, gods – and mythologies. Buddhist figures, stories and influences have joined with and enriched the native myths of Japan. There are of course foreign deities from other traditions that have also become important to Japanese mythology, but these other *kami* are not part of a single, generally coherent whole in the same way as the Buddhist 'pantheon' (a blanket term for a shifting collection of gods and other supernatural beings) appears. For this reason, they will be addressed separately in Chapter 6.

One quick note on naming: Buddhism comes from India, and was originally recorded in ancient Indian languages, primarily Sanskrit and Pali, but the names used in Japan for Buddhist deities, places and concepts were transmitted via China. They are therefore usually Japanese pronunciations of the Chinese terms, which had themselves been translated or transliterated into Chinese from Indian originals. This chapter will introduce both the Sanskrit (Sk.) and Japanese (Jp.) names for most ideas, as well as the Chinese (Ch.) names where necessary. For basic Buddhist concepts we will use Sanskrit words such as *buddha* or *bodhisattva*, instead of the Japanese *nyorai* or *bosatsu*. However, where the Japanese equivalent is functionally different, or where the Sanskrit name is long and complicated, we will use the Japanese names (as in the cases of the bodhisattva Kannon and the wisdom king Fudō Myōō).

BUDDHISM AND JAPANESE MYTHOLOGY

Buddhism is a widely practised religion with many different sects, multiple mythologies and a history of several thousand years. Here we focus only on the Buddhist deities and mythological figures who have had the greatest impact on Japan. They are not necessarily the most important figures in other Buddhist countries, or in other forms of Buddhism, although many are known outside of Japan.

Japanese Buddhism comprises several different schools, but all are part of the Mahayana or 'Greater Vehicle' tradition. This is one of the three main divisions of Buddhism, along with Theravada ('Way of the Elders') and Vajrayana ('Diamond Vehicle'). Theravada, practised widely in Southeast Asia, focuses on a core set of texts considered to be the oldest, 'original' Buddhist scriptures from ancient India. Vajrayana, practised in Tibet and Mongolia, emphasizes tantric practices. Mahayana, which is practised across East Asia as well as in Vietnam, comprises many schools. All these Mahayana schools believe in 'expedient means' (Sk. *upāya*, Jp. *hōben*), a way to achieve Buddhist salvation in one's own lifetime. Each

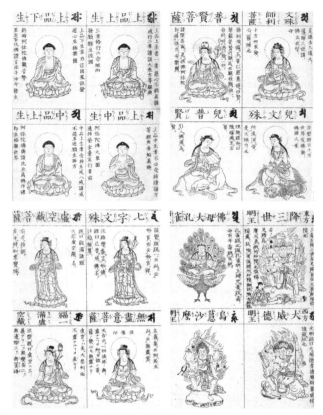

A series of Buddhist figures with names and/or ranks: buddhas (upper left); bodhisattvas (lower left, upper right); devas and wisdom kings (lower right).

school is defined by its focus on one or more specific expedient means: meditation, for example, in the schools of Zen Buddhism.

One other important feature of Mahayana Buddhism is its reliance on divine figures. There are more deities and levels of divinity in Mahayana forms of Buddhism than in either Theravada or Vajrayana schools. Most of these figures fall into four levels. At the top are buddhas (Jp. *nyorai*). Buddhas are mortals who achieved full enlightenment during their lives. They realized the truth of the world and in the process freed themselves from the endless cycle of rebirths. Upon their deaths, buddhas achieve *nirvana* (Jp. *nehan*), a state of positive nonexistence where one simultaneously no longer exists, yet is one with the entire universe. Buddhas are often portrayed as monks, with shaved heads, simple clothing and brilliant and extensive haloes. Most buddhas have specific iconography that allows worshippers to tell which one a given statue or image is supposed to represent.

At the second level are bodhisattvas (Jp. *bosatsu*). These are beings who, like buddhas, began as ordinary mortals, and who turned back at the moment of enlightenment, choosing to forgo the full process in order to have the ability to help other beings. Bodhisattvas are more accessible but somewhat less powerful than buddhas, as they are still enmeshed in the 'worlds of desire' – the universe. Bodhisattvas also exist in Theravada and Vajrayana schools, but are less prominently worshipped in these traditions than they are in forms of Mahayana Buddhism, including those practised in Japan. Bodhisattvas are often portrayed as Indian princes, with flowing hair, gorgeous robes and strands of jewellery. Like buddhas, there are specific items or symbols that allow one to tell which bodhisattva is being portrayed in each statue or image.

Mahayana deities of the third level are known as the wisdom kings (Sk. *vidyārāja*, Jp. *myōō*). These are the only truly violent deities in Buddhism. They are the defenders of the faith, who defeat demons and purge the

---

Four levels of deities in Japanese (Mahayana) Buddhism
- Buddhas: at the top of the hierarchy, they are mortals who achieved enlightenment and are free from the cycle of rebirth. When they die, they achieve nirvana. They are usually portrayed as Buddhist monks.
- Bodhisattvas: mortals who at the moment of enlightenment turned back to the world so they can help others; usually portrayed as Indian princes.
- Wisdom kings: violent defenders of the faith, with terrifying red eyes and weapons; they scare people onto the right path.
- Devas: guardians of Buddhism, often the gods of other religions who have been absorbed into Buddhist cosmology; they are portrayed as men in armour and women in flowing robes. Although they are gods, devas are still stuck in the cycle of rebirth.

---

wicked. They are also those who scare people onto the correct path via fear, rather than persuasion or salvation. Given their nature, wisdom kings are often depicted in East Asia as scary figures with fiery red eyes, skin in primary colours, and brandishing weapons such as swords. They may be surrounded by fire, standing on defeated demons, or otherwise involved in scenes of violence against the enemies of Buddhism. As with portrayals of other Buddhist deities, wisdom kings also have specific iconography that allows one to tell them apart.

The fourth level of Mahayana deities are known as devas (Jp. *tenbu*). *Deva* is the Sanskrit word for 'god' in a general sense, and many devas are Indian deities (some of whom are important in modern Hinduism) who were co-opted by Buddhism. Buddhism considers devas to be immensely powerful figures, but still embedded within the 'worlds of desire', one term for the multiverse. Buddhist devas are not immortal, unlike their equivalents in Hinduism and other Indian religions. Although their lives can stretch for thousands or even billions of years, Buddhist devas each have an origin and eventually a death from which they will be reborn, as will all beings that have not achieved enlightenment. Many devas are guardians of Buddhism, and while they rank below wisdom kings, buddhas or bodhisattvas, they are still important figures of worship. Devas in East Asian Buddhism are often portrayed as figures from ancient China (rather than their original Indian forms), either males in armour or females in flowing robes. Some of the more common figures also have consistent iconography allowing one to tell them apart, but they often come in sets which can be individually identical (or nearly so). There are between one and three yet lower levels of deities between devas and humans, depending on the tradition and sect of Buddhism. These are complex figures who do not often appear in basic explanations of the Japanese (or other) Buddhist pantheon, so we will not address them here.

BUDDHAS: THE ENLIGHTENED ONES

There is more than one buddha. The one to whom most historical text-books refer is known in Mahayana Buddhism as the 'Historical Buddha'. This is Siddhārtha Gautama, whose life provided the model around which

---

Śākyamuni, the Historical Buddha

- Human named Siddhārtha Gautama, who lived *c.* 500 BCE. He later gained the Sanskrit name Śākyamuni, meaning 'Sage of the Śākya Clan', pronounced in Japanese as Shakamuni, sometimes shortened to Shaka.
- The original teacher of Buddhist principles; attained enlightenment.
- Manifested 32 physical attributes that mark a person as a buddha.
- He had many previous lives, each foretelling his future holiness.
- Widely worshipped in Japan as a figure of salvation and enlightenment.

Buddhism coalesced sometime around 500 BCE. The Historical Buddha is considered only one of several figures who attained enlightenment. Depending on the school and tradition within Buddhism, he is variously understood as being the only buddha in our era of history, the only buddha on our plane of existence, or simply the most well-known from either.

The Historical Buddha is also known as Śākyamuni ('Sage of the Śākya Clan') in Sanskrit, transliterated into Japanese (via Chinese) as Shakamuni 釈迦牟尼. In Japan, he is often referred to as Shaka-nyorai 釈迦如来, or just Shaka 釈迦. He is the primary lecturer of most of the principles of Buddhism and many sutras are attributed to him. Many of these sutras are not from the right time period, or even the right country – some are probably Chinese or Central Asian in origin – but they all claim to be Śākyamuni's own words. He is also the main historical example and inspiration for the religion, even in schools that worship other buddhas.

Śākyamuni was born as Siddhārtha Gautama, a prince of the Śākya Clan who ruled a city known as Kapilavastu. The city's location is unknown today but believed to have been in either southern Nepal or near the Nepalese border of northern India. The prince grew up completely isolated from the outside world and had no knowledge of suffering, sickness, old age or death. One day he happened to venture outside the palace walls and became aware of human suffering. In shock, Gautama renounced his royal position and dedicated his life to seeking an answer to suffering. He joined different sects of what we would today call early Hinduism, seeking answers, but found none. One of these sects was a group of priests who practised intense meditation; another, a group of ascetics who starved themselves in the forest. No group gave Gautama any further understanding, but one day he decided to follow a memory of an experience he had as a young child. Meditating under a fig tree, Gautama finally achieved true understanding of suffering and became instantly enlightened.[2]

After his enlightenment, Śākyamuni began to preach Buddhism, quickly gaining a following. He foretold his own death, which came to pass exactly as he had prophesied, further solidifying the movement around his teachings. In the centuries after his passing, as stories of the Historical Buddha spread across Asia, ever more supernatural legends were added to his life. Immediately after his enlightenment, Śākyamuni supposedly manifested the 32 physical attributes said to mark any buddha. These included growing to over 6 ft (2 m) in height, gaining metallic golden skin, a large lump on his head and elongated earlobes, fingers and toes. Most Japanese icons of Shaka preserve these features, using gilt bronze or golden paint for the icon's skin and clothing, and emphasizing the differently shaped elements of the body.

The Historical Buddha supposedly also had a long series of previous lives, each of which predicted his future holiness. The stories about these previous lives are known as *jataka* in Sanskrit (*honshōtan* in Japanese). There are entire books of *jataka* tales; one example is that of the 'Lion Who Showed Compassion for a Monkey's Children and Tore Out His Own Flesh for an Eagle'. The Japanese version recounted here comes from a text known as *Konjaku monogatarishū* ('A Collection of Tales of Times Now Past', *c.* 11th–12th century), although it is based on an earlier Chinese translation from a Sanskrit original.

The Historical Buddha Śākyamuni (Shaka), depicted as a newborn already bearing physical signs of enlightenment. This icon is part of a bowl for cleansing rites.

In the distant past, a lion lived in a cave in the mountains of northern India. Nearby lived a pair of monkeys who had two little babies. The babies had grown too heavy for their mother to take them foraging with her, but she still needed to get food for them. The lion promised to watch them, and this freed both monkeys to go off and look for food. However, an eagle was also watching, and as soon as the monkeys were gone, it swooped down to capture the baby monkeys. The lion started to defend the monkeys, but then the eagle told him that it too had babies, and needed the monkey's babies for food. The lion did not wish either set of parents or babies to go hungry, so he cut out a piece out of his own leg and gave it to the eagle to feed its children. When the mother monkey came back, she found her own children safe, and was overcome with emotion. The lion was a previous life of Śākyamuni, and the monkeys were all the previous lives of several of his disciples (the previous life of the eagle is not stated).[3]

Śākyamuni is still widely worshipped in Japan and is an important figure in most Mahayana Buddhist schools. He does not have any specific domains and is a general figure of salvation and Buddhist enlightenment.

Śākyamuni delivering his famous sermon at Vulture Peak, attended by bodhisattvas, devas and mortal humans.

Parinirvana, or Death of the Buddha: Śākyamuni lies on a bier
surrounded by mourning gods, humans and animals as his mother,
Lady Maya, arrives from the sky to take his soul.

He can be portrayed standing, sitting or lying down, but always takes the
typical form of any buddha icon: a Buddhist monk in simple garb with a
tightly shorn head of dark curls. When standing or sitting, he is usually
on a lotus-blossom pedestal. The lotus, which starts out as a tuber in the
mud at the bottom of a lake and grows up through the water to break
out into the air above, is a metaphor for rebirth and enlightenment in
many Indian religions. The hand gesture that usually marks a statue as
being of Śākyamuni is known as the 'earth-touching gesture', and features
the right hand pointed downwards, palm inside, with the second, third
and fifth fingers outstretched. When the historical buddha is depicted
lying down – rare for Buddhist deities – it is usually a representation of
Śākyamuni's death. These portrayals often show him on his back on a
long bier, surrounded by the weeping figures of gods, men and beasts.[4]

Another important buddha in Japan is Amitābha, the Buddha of Infinite Light, known in Japanese as Amida 阿弥陀. Upon attaining enlightenment, this buddha made a vow to create a paradise in the uttermost west of the multiverse. Through praying to him for salvation, beings can be reborn in this Western Pure Land, following which they automatically achieve enlightenment, attaining *nirvana* on their following death. The Pure Land is a place of living precious metals and growing jewels, bathed in eternal light and free from any sort of sin. It is paradise, but at the same time it is only a stop on the road to enlightenment, as *nirvana*, not rebirth there, is the true goal.[5]

Amitābha is an ancient figure in Buddhism. He and his Pure Land appear in sutras that go back to the last few centuries BCE of India, and he is worshipped in all three broad divisions of Buddhism. China's many centuries at the centre of the Mahayana Buddhist world influenced that tradition's ideas of Amitābha strongly, and his Pure Land is generally portrayed in East Asian art as a Chinese ideal of paradise.[6] In addition to the living metals and brilliant atmosphere, it features Chinese-style palaces, sumptuous food and magical handmaidens who float about playing heavenly music. In Japanese iconography, Amida (Amitābha) is often shown with one of two hand signs: the meditation sign, which features all five fingers of both hands pressed against one another, or the exposition sign, which features both hands outstretched, the left downward and the right upward, with the thumb and forefinger of each making a circle.

Amitābha is usually accompanied by two bodhisattvas, Avalokiteśvara and Mahāsthāmaprāpta. Avalokiteśvara, known in Japanese as Kannon 観音, represents compassion, and is an extremely important

The Buddha of Infinite Light, Amitābha (Amida), seated on a lotus.

deity in Japan who will be discussed at length later in this chapter. Mahāsthāmaprāpta, known as Seishi 勢至 in Japanese, represents wisdom. The triad of wisdom, compassion and salvation (as offered by Amida) is what allows the power of the Western Pure Land to draw in the lost and the desperate. Similar groupings of three figures, usually one buddha and two bodhisattvas, appear throughout Mahayana practice. These groups of three are known as triads, particularly when they form physical sets of three icons. In some cases, the identity of either the buddha or the bodhisattvas is what allows identification of the entire triad.

In China, Korea and Japan, worship of Amida has formed its own schools, known collectively as Pure Land Buddhism. In Japan in particular, these take the form of the Jōdo ('Pure Land') and Jōdo Shinshū ('True Pure Land') schools. Each one rests on the idea that calling Amida's name allows him to hear a petitioner's voice, so that he will usher their soul into the Pure Land for its next rebirth. The expedient means embraced by both schools is repetition of Amida's name, usually in the chant *namu*

The buddha Amitābha (Amida; centre) flanked by the bodhisattvas Avalokiteśvara (Kannon; left), and Mahāsthāmaprāpta (Seishi; right).

amida butsu ('Praise to Amida Buddha!'), although the schools differ in other points of doctrine. Because this type of expedient means is so easy to perform, even for commoners, both Jōdo and Jōdo Shinshū became extremely popular in Japan and remain two of the largest Buddhist sects in the country today.

Bhaiṣajyaguru, the Medicine Buddha, is another important figure in Mahayana Buddhism. He is known in Japan as Yakushi 薬師 or 'Medicine Master', a literal translation of the meaning of his name. Yakushi is known from an ancient sutra (an Indian scriptural or philosophical text) of unknown origins that recounts how he became enlightened upon making twelve vows, all of which involved healing either physical or mental suffering. Due to this emphasis on healing, Yakushi is worshipped as giving physical health in life, rather than facilitating rebirth in paradise like Amida.[7] Yakushi was historically much more important in East Asia than elsewhere in the Buddhist world. He was among the first buddhas worshipped widely in Korea and Japan, perhaps due to the belief that he could cure illness. Some scholars believe that, after Buddhism was brought to a new region but before its doctrine was widely understood, the magical powers of a figure like Yakushi would be the most attractive to new believers.

Yakushi is commonly portrayed sitting down and holding a small container. The container represents a magical jar of lapis lazuli that bears a salve that can cure all the world's ills. Otherwise, Yakushi is depicted very similarly to Shaka (Śākyamuni). The Medicine Buddha is accompanied by two bodhisattvas who represent the sun and moon, known in Japanese as Nikkō 日光 and Gekkō 月光. They are often called the 'nurses' to Yakushi's 'doctor'. Worship of Yakushi was very popular for much of ancient and classical Japanese history but declined during the medieval era. Today he is less widely worshipped than Shaka or Amida.

Vairocana, known in Japanese as either Birushana 毘盧遮那 or as Dainichi Nyorai 大日如来, is yet another important buddha. Birushana is a transliteration of the original Sanskrit name, but Dainichi Nyorai means 'Great Solar Buddha'. This is because Vairocana is a primordial buddha, a figure who was never mortal to begin with. Instead, he is a representation of the light of enlightenment itself as it spreads through the multiverse like rays of light from a sun. According to some doctrines,

Vairocana is the 'true' buddha and all others are merely 'reflections' of enlightenment within different worlds of desire. Vairocana is also said to represent *śūnyatā* (Jp. *kū* 空), or 'emptiness', the true nature of the universe. This is a positive quality. The light that emanates from Vairocana across the universe is in fact the light of emptiness, which reveals the meaninglessness of the 'worlds of desire'.[8]

The most famous statue of Vairocana in Japan is the Great Buddha of the Tōdaiji Temple in Nara. Originally forged in the 740s, it is among the largest Buddhist statues in the world. Vairocana is usually depicted alone or surrounded by many esoteric bodhisattvas. Statues of Vairocana are most often seated on a lotus pedestal. There is a specific gesture associated with Vairocana in which the forefinger of the left hand is clasped by the right hand, whose own forefinger is wrapped around it. This represents the joining of all of existence to itself.

Several other buddhas have been worshipped in Japan, but none as widely so as these four. However, other Buddhist deities of lower levels, such as some bodhisattvas and devas, actually have larger presences in Japanese myth. Buddhas by their very nature no longer exist; they can be called upon for salvation, but they do not interact with the world. Bodhisattvas, wisdom kings and devas, however, all still move within the 'worlds of desire', so they can (and do) act to save people. Although lower in status than buddhas, these deities have more direct effects on their worshippers, and some are widely revered in Japan.

The 'Great Solar Buddha' Vairocana (Dainichi Nyorai or Birushana) making his unique hand sign.

BODHISATTVAS: AGENTS OF SALVATION

Bodhisattvas are figures who, at the moment of enlightenment, turned back towards the worlds of desire just before achieving buddha-hood. As a result, they are not full buddhas, but are the next closest thing, and are able to usher others towards salvation without having left reality entirely. There are bodhisattvas who are worshipped prominently in Japan either alongside buddhas, as part of triads with a buddha and another bodhisattva, or on their own. The most important of all of these in Japanese Buddhist practice is Avalokiteśvara, known in Japanese as Kannon. Kannon is a hybrid, gender-fluid bodhisattva. Avalokiteśvara, also known in Sanskrit as Padmapani, embodies the compassion of all buddhas. This is not the same as earthly compassion or empathy. Instead, 'compassion' here is for the very state of being alive and trapped in the cycle of rebirth. As such, Avalokiteśvara longs to save all living beings from the cycle, and acts in various ways to do so. Although originally male, Avalokiteśvara can be portrayed in Indian art as either male or female. This gender fluidity became more complex when the bodhisattva was brought to China in the 4th or 5th century CE and renamed Guanyin ('Perceiving Cries'), meaning compassion for those in suffering. However, there was already a Daoist goddess known as Guanyin in China at the time. So Avalokiteśvara the (then, usually male) Indian bodhisattva of compassion became mixed with this Chinese female Daoist deity, resulting in the figure of Guanyin as a predominantly female bodhisattva with more active powers than is typical of other bodhisattvas.[9]

Kannon is the Japanese pronunciation of the Chinese Guanyin. As in China, Kannon is most often depicted as female, although she may appear as male, genderless, or any other combination. She also has several different forms, each of which expresses a different way of helping sufferers reach enlightenment. Thousand-Armed Kannon is usually represented with 50 arms, each of which acts 20 times. Each hand bears a different implement – a wheel, a lotus blossom or even more esoteric tools – for saving a specific type of sufferer. Eleven-Headed Kannon has ten smaller heads atop her main head. Each of these heads looks in a different direction, such that no suffering being can escape her sight. Thousand-Armed and Eleven-Headed Kannon are often combined into the same icon.

Thousand-Armed Kannon, Japanese Buddhist deity of compassion, seated on a lotus. Each of the 25 arms represents 40 arms, and bears an implement or symbol of salvation.

Dream-Weaving Kannon has only two or four arms, and usually only a single head. She weaves a net to catch those trapped by delusions such as greed, lust or hunger. There are other, more esoteric versions of Kannon as well. These include the form in which she appears in a triad with the bodhisattva Seishi and the buddha Amida (see page 129).

Kannon is among the most widely worshipped Buddhist figures in Japan. She also often steps in directly to help her worshippers, and there are many tales of Kannon helping individuals in need. Here is one famous tale recorded in the 12th-century collection *Konjaku monogatarishū*. In the province of Bitchū (modern Okayama Prefecture, in central Honshu), there was a man named Kaya no Yoshifuji. He was a merchant who had become rich from trading in metal coins. One day Yoshifuji took a walk and saw a beautiful woman. He asked for her name and when she demurred, he followed her to her home. Although he had lived in his town his whole life, Yoshifuji had never seen the woman's home before; it was a grand mansion on a hill, full of servants. Entranced by the woman's beauty and the house's wealth, Yoshifuji decided to stay with her as her lover.

Yoshifuji's family were worried when he vanished without any explanation. When searches for him proved futile, they built an image of Kannon and prayed to it daily for his well-being. One day, a strange man bearing the staff of a Buddhist lay priest arrived in the town. Without asking for directions, he went straight to the ruins of a house that had been destroyed by fire some years previously. The man aimed his staff at the ruins, and suddenly foxes began to scatter from underneath them, running in terror. After a few minutes, a dirt-covered monkey-like creature came crawling slowly out into the light. It was Yoshifuji! The house he had imagined living in was an illusion conjured by foxes. His family immediately took him home, and the strange man disappeared in the confusion. It was later revealed that the man had been an apparition of Kannon, moved by the family's pleas, who had come to save Yoshifuji from possession and death.[10]

Another widely worshipped bodhisattva who is known to intercede on behalf of ordinary humans is Kṣitigarbha, known in Japanese as Jizō 地蔵. If Kannon vows out of compassion to save all who suffer because of not having reached enlightenment, Jizō vows to instruct all who need help in learning the ways to achieve it. As such, he is commonly depicted as a Buddhist monk on a pilgrimage, bearing a staff with dangling rings and wearing a red travelling habit. His statues often show him with a halo around his shaved head. This halo, along with the red fabric mantles that typically drape his icons, are the main ways to identify Jizō.

The bodhisattva Kṣitigarbha (Jizō), portrayed as a monk holding a sacred jewel.

Avalokiteśvara/Kannon, Bodhisattva of Compassion

- Embodies compassion for all living things, and wants to help them escape the cycle of rebirth.
- Originally a male Indian bodhisattva (Avalokiteśvara), then mixed with Daoist goddess Guanyin in China to produce a gender-fluid, hybrid bodhisattva known in Japan as Kannon.
- Portrayed in art as either male or female, and takes many different forms: Thousand-Armed, Eleven-Headed and Dream-Weaving.

Like Avalokiteśvara (Kannon), Jizō's original Indian figure Kṣitigarbha can be both male and female. In Kṣitigarbha's case, this is due to having had two important past lives. In one, they were a high-caste maiden in ancient India; in the other, a Buddhist monk on the Indian subcontinent. However, when worship of Kṣitigarbha was brought to East Asia, he was primarily envisioned as male, and his association with monks increased.[11]

In Japan, Jizō is seen as a guardian as much as an instructor. He is particularly protective of young children, pregnant women and travellers. Statues of Jizō, singly or in long rows, are placed at crossroads or along thoroughfares, and in some cases strewn across mountainsides, to protect travellers from harm. There are also folktales preserved in *Konjaku monogatarishū* and other Heian and medieval collections that depict Jizō saving children or pregnant women from harm. Starting in the Muromachi Period, Jizō became associated with the River Sanzu 三 途の川, the path taken by dead souls to be judged for their rebirth. When children die, Jizō will find and guard their souls, allowing them either peaceful limbo or a quick rebirth, depending on the tale. Even today people place small piles of stones in cemeteries and at crossroads to symbolize children lost too young, marking sites to pray to Jizō for their salvation.

There is one important bodhisattva who, depending on the form in which he is worshipped, can cross over into buddhahood. This is Maitreya, known in Japanese as Miroku 弥勒, the Buddha of the Future. He is the next buddha to be born into the world, a messiah-like figure; however, since time is an illusion in the wider Buddhist cosmos, Maitreya also exists in the here and now, and can be reached for and prayed to. Before his actual birth into the world to become the next buddha, an event which will happen at some point in the distant future, Maitreya is a bodhisattva. He is often depicted and worshipped in that form. He is also worshipped as the buddha he will become, however, and when depicted in that form he resembles Amida (Amitābha) or Shaka (Śākyamuni). [12]

Maitreya is a pensive bodhisattva, with his mind always on the future he will save. In this form, he is usually depicted with one leg up in the lotus position, and the other dangling, his eyes lost in thought. He has his own Pure Land, the Tuṣita Heaven (Jp. *Tosotsuten* 兜率天), in the extreme north of the multiverse, in which he gathers souls to spur them onwards to enlightenment. Maitreya was the centre of an important cult in the Nara and early Heian Periods, possibly one brought over from the Korean peninsula. Worship of him has reappeared in times of great turmoil, when people long for his future appearance, and there are Maitreya cults from various centuries that have risen and fallen with wars and epidemics. [13] Today he is less widely worshipped than Kannon, Jizō or the buddhas Shaka and Amida, but is still an important figure in Japanese Buddhism.

Maitreya (Miroku), the Future Buddha, here portrayed
as a bodhisattva due to his having not yet been born.

Samantabhadra (Jp. Fugen 普賢) and Manjuśrī (Jp. Monju 文殊) are a pair of bodhisattvas who accompany the historical buddha, Śākyamuni. Fugen represents actions, while Monju represents wisdom. Both are necessary: action without wisdom results in haste and idiocy, whereas wisdom without the will to act is wasted. These two bodhisattvas flank the historical buddha, to represent that he had both qualities, but they also have powers of their own and distinctive appearances. Fugen rides an elephant and imparts the power to achieve lofty goals. Monju rides a blue lion, and sometimes bears both a flaming sword and a lotus blossom in his hands. He brings the wisdom to know truth from falsehood, and cuts through delusions while offering the beauty of enlightenment.

As with buddhas, there are yet more bodhisattvas in the Mahayana Buddhist tradition. However, most of these are esoteric figures, and are not – nor have ever been – as widely worshipped in Japan as any of the five mentioned here. They also rarely appear in Japanese folktales or myths, and do not interact with humans to the extent of Kannon or Jizō.

The bodhisattva Samantabhadra (Fugen, left), riding an elephant, is often paired with the bodhisattva Manjuśrī (Monju, right), who rides a lion.

WISDOM KINGS: FREEDOM THROUGH FEAR

The third tier of Buddhist deities are the wisdom kings, *vidyārāja* in Sanskrit and *myōō* in Japanese. Where buddhas are the distant, enlightened teachers, and bodhisattva are angelic figures who save the needy, the wisdom kings are the angry parents of the Mahayana Buddhist pantheon. These fearsome figures have two roles. The first is to defeat the demons who represent vices such as greed and lust. The second and more important role is to chastise believers into proper behaviour. The wisdom kings bring discipline born of compassion and remind the faithful of the price of straying from the path of righteousness.

Five wisdom kings are grouped together in a set known as the Five Guardians of Buddhism. They are Acāla the Unmovable, known in Japanese as Fudō Myōō 不動明王, and his four subsidiaries: Trailokyavijaya (Jp. Gōzanze Myōō 降三世明王), Kuṇḍali (Jp. Gundari Myōō 軍荼利明王), Yamāntaka (Jp. Daiitoku Myōō 大威徳明王) and Vajrayakṣa (Jp. Kongōyasha Myōō 金剛夜叉明王). Of these five, Fudō Myōō is the most important. He is so virtuous as to be unmoved by anything less than himself, which means that he is unaffected by most of existence and therefore cannot be defeated, avoided or blocked. His role is to crush the demons who try to tempt people, but also to remind those being tempted that there is no easy way out of life's problems. Like a stern parent, Fudō Myōō disciplines the world.[14]

The wisdom king Acāla (Fudō Myō'ō), defends Buddhism from the demons of iniquity with his sword and whip.

All wisdom kings are depicted with scary features, but Fudō Myōō is the most fearsome of them all. His skin is usually blue; his hair is the dark crimson of embers and he is surrounded by wreaths of fire and smoke. He is dressed in a loincloth and may wear skull jewelry. He often carries a sword and a lasso. The sword impales the enemies of Buddhism, while the lasso captures those who try to flee from the paths of righteousness. Fudō Myōō sits on a rock, proof of his immovability. Sometimes he is accompanied by two young acolytes, each of whom is busy decapitating or otherwise crushing a demon.[15] In much of the rest of the Buddhist world, Acāla and his four subsidiary kings are minor (if important) components of the overall pantheon, but in Japan, worship of Fudō Myōō is more significant than that of many other Buddhist deities. Entire temples are dedicated to him and he is also associated with some of the more violent Shinto deities, such as Hachiman.

There are several other wisdom kings who are not associated with the Five Guardians. One is almost as important as Fudō Myōō in Japanese Buddhism: Rāgarāja, known in Japanese as Aizen Myōō 愛染明王, the

The wisdom king Rāgarāja (Aizen Myō'ō) likewise defends Buddhism from evil, here represented by the demon's decapitated head in his hand.

Lust-Tinted Wisdom King. Almost the opposite of Fudō Myōō, Aizen Myōō has crimson skin and dark blue hair, and is wreathed in darkness as often as flame. He is draped in jewelled robes and has six arms, each of which bears a different item used to bring followers to salvation. Where Fudō Myōō represents sternness, Aizen Myōō represents the power of sexual energy honed to a focused point, where it shifts from a distraction into a tool for enlightenment. In Aizen Myōō, sexual lust, bloodlust and ambition are all channelled towards achieving enlightenment, rather than allowed to determine a person's life goals.[16]

DEVAS: GODS OF INDIA, LIVE FROM JAPAN

Buddhism is able to incorporate deities from most other religions, but once incorporated they are no longer considered omnipotent or immortal, because under a Buddhist system even gods must eventually die and re-enter the cycle of rebirth unless they too achieve enlightenment. However, because humans are so much further down in the divine hierarchy, a god can still appear to be omnipotent or immortal by comparison to a human. This understanding allows Buddhism to absorb other religions' gods, or at least to live alongside them in relative harmony.

The gods of ancient India were absorbed very early in Buddhism's history. These are a mix of the Vedic gods of ancient Indian religion and more recent deities who remain important in modern Hinduism. Indian gods were eventually given new identities and tasks in Buddhist belief, and when Buddhism spread to East Asia, it brought the Indian pantheon in its Buddhist form as well. Many of these gods and goddesses were further reinterpreted in China and Korea before being brought to Japan. In some cases, they continued to evolve even after arriving in Japan, or were seen as the same as *kami* who already existed. They form the fourth rank of Mahayana Buddhist deities, known in Japanese as *tenbu*, from Sanskrit *deva*.[17]

Many devas are grouped into sets in Japanese Buddhism. These sets have little to do with relative power. While devas lie below wisdom kings, bodhisattvas and buddhas, all of these various beings are extremely powerful from a human perspective. The most commonly seen set of devas

The Four Heavenly Kings, typically portrayed as ancient Chinese generals. From left to right: Tamonten, Jikokuten, Zōjōten and Kōmokuten.

in Japan are the Four Heavenly Kings 四天王 or Shitennō. These four were originally four deities assigned to guard temple spaces in Indian Buddhism. In China they were made more important, and became the guardians of the four directions, each the equivalent of a king among minor gods. In Japan, they are often depicted as men with brilliantly coloured hair and skin who wear the armour of ancient Chinese generals. They always come as a set and are each associated with specific weapons and one of the four cardinal directions.

To the north is Tamonten 多聞天 (also known as Bishamonten 毘沙門天, from Sanskrit Vaiśravaṇa), He Who Hears All. He is probably derived from Kubera, the ancient Indian god of wealth. Tamonten carries an umbrella or a pagoda as a weapon and is associated with the colours yellow and green. To the south is Zōjōten 増長天, He Who Causes to Grow. Zōjōten's origin is uncertain, but his Sanskrit name, Virūḍhaka, is the term for sprouting grain. His weapons are a sword and a spear, although he usually only bears one or the other, and is often shown trampling a demon. Zōjōten is associated with the colour blue. To the east is Jikokuten 持国天, He Who Upholds the Realm. His origin is likewise uncertain, but as the Sanskrit Dhṛtarāṣṭra he is associated with music in Southeast Asia and Tibet, and may previously have been a god of music. In Japan, Jikokuten is a much fiercer deity who wields a trident and is often portrayed trampling a demon. The last Heavenly King is Kōmokuten 広目天 of the west, He Who Sees All. His Indian original, Virūpākṣa, bears an all-seeing eye, and watches the karma of all sentient beings. In Japan, Kōmokuten holds a brush and scroll, and records the deeds he watches.

The Four Heavenly Kings, like the higher-ranked wisdom kings, can perform violent acts that the bodhisattvas and buddhas cannot. However, unlike wisdom kings, but like the other devas, the Four Heavenly Kings are not close to enlightenment. They are merely much more powerful than humans. They are devoted to Buddhism, and with their powers and armies protect the Buddhist multiverse from all sides. They can be summoned to protect individuals, temples or even entire countries from evil. In the past, they were often invoked to defend against illness, ranging from the individual sickness of an emperor or minister of state to epidemics that ravaged the entire archipelago. According to some legends, Prince Shōtoku's powers were due to the protection of the Four Heavenly Kings. This is supposedly why one of the main temples he built in the early 600s was the Shitennōji, or 'Temple of the Four Heavenly Kings', which stands today in Osaka (although none of its extant buildings are original). Folklore of the Heian Period has the Four Heavenly Kings defending against spirit possession in addition to illness.

In addition to the Four Heavenly Kings, there are larger sets of devas. These include the Twelve Divine Generals 十二神将 (Jūni Shinshō) who protect the Buddha of Healing, and the Twenty-Eight Legions 二十八部衆 (Nijūhachi Bushū) who accompany Thousand-Armed Kannon. Most gods of ancient India are present in these sets, with new Japanese names.

DEVA AND *KAMI* AT THE SAME TIME

Several other devas are individually important in Japan. One of the most worshipped today is Benzaiten 弁財天, often shortened to Benten. Benzaiten originates with the Indian goddess Sarasvatī, who is still an important deity in modern Hinduism. By the time she reached Japan, Benzaiten had become revered as the goddess of eloquence, music, beauty and the arts. Although Indian in origin, and considered a Buddhist deva, Benzaiten does not protect Buddhism specifically.[18] Her worship began to shift away from strict Buddhist associations during the Heian Period, and by the 12th century she was reinterpreted as being another form of a native *kami* – although which *kami* depends on the text making the argument. According to medieval Japanese belief, Benzaiten may be a form of Ugajin 宇賀神, a snake-bodied, human-headed fertility god (who himself may be based on Indian *nāga* snake deities). She may also be a form of Ichikishimahime 市杵島姫, a little-known goddess of islands said to reside in the Inland Sea.[19]

Benzaiten is the patron of the high arts of the Japanese court. These include poetry, music, dance, rhetoric and the visual arts. She is also one of the Seven Gods of Luck 七福神 (Shichifukujin), a grouping of various native and foreign gods that began to be worshipped as a set at some point after the 13th century, to bring luck to their worshippers. Benzaiten's luck-giving powers have in turn been reassigned to her as an individual goddess, and she not only brings artistic inspiration but also wealth from one's endeavours.

Benzaiten is often depicted as a noblewoman wearing medieval Chinese clothing. Her hair is usually up in an elaborate headdress and she wears sumptuous robes, often with multiple shawls, ribbons or skirts. She can also be depicted as a Buddhist nun, with her shorn head covered in a tight hood, and wearing long, simple robes. Sometimes the *kami* Ugajin rests on her head, a tiny coiled snake with a human head (either male or female). Benzaiten has a variable number of arms, although rarely more than six. She may bear a lute, a flute, or the weaponry of Buddhist guardian gods, such as a sword and/or spear.

The deva Benzaiten (left), next to a musician who receives her patronage.

Benzaiten is worshipped at places known as Bentendō, or Benten Halls. These structures may be part of larger shrines or temples but may also be their own sites. Technically a Bentendō is a Shinto shrine, not a Buddhist temple, due to the later association of Benzaiten with specific *kami*. One famous example is the Shinobazu Pond Bentendō in Ueno Park in the heart of Tokyo. This shrine is on an artificial island, surrounded by lotuses, in Shinobazu Lake, an artificial reservoir built over the ruins of the Kan'eiji Temple, which was an important Buddhist site during the Edo Period (1600–1868). Today only its pagoda remains, sitting on a hill overlooking the Bentendō.

Another important deva who is worshipped separately in Japan, as well as being part of a set of guardians, is the goddess Kichijōten 吉祥 天, also pronounced Kisshōten. Like Benzaiten, Kichijōten originates

The deva Kichijōten, here portrayed as a Chinese noblewoman.

144

with an important Indian goddess, in this case Lakṣmī (often romanized as Lakshmi). In modern Hinduism, Lakṣmī is the wife of the god Viṣṇu (Vishnu) and is an extremely important deity. Despite centuries of adaptation in China and then in Japan, Kichijōten still retains some of Lakṣmī's qualities and associations. She is the goddess of happiness, fertility and beauty, and represents women and the feminine in general.[20]

Like Benzaiten, Kichijōten has been subsumed into the Seven Gods of Luck. Due to this association, Kichijōten is also a bringer of good fortune and wealth through beauty. She is usually depicted as a gorgeous woman in Chinese clothing, her hair either up in an elaborate headdress or down and flowing. She sometimes carries a jewel. Her clothing and aura can be inscribed with the *kagome*, a six-pointed star symbol. This is an ancient Shinto symbol that appears in the decor of shrines dating as far back as the 5th century CE. It is possible that it became associated with Kichijōten due to her connections to magical wish-granting jewels, another holdover from her Indian origins. Today the *kagome* symbol and Kichijōten are closely linked: the *kagome* either appears individually on her image, or as part of a lattice constructed of many repeated symbols.

Enma 閻魔, also known as Enma-ō ('King Enma') or Enmaten, is the Japanese equivalent of Yama, the Buddhist celestial judge of the dead. Yama first appears in Indian Buddhist scriptures, but may not be based on an older Indian deity. He exists 'in a mixed state', sometimes with the broad powers of a celestial deva, other times only able to do things related to his duty. Whenever someone still in the cycles of rebirth dies, they are brought before Yama, who assigns them their next rebirth.

Enma
- Japanese equivalent of the Indian Yama, judge of the dead.
- Fearsome and fair, rules at the head of a bureaucracy dedicated to ensuring proper rebirths and punishments. Souls brought before him are judged based on their karmic ties and deeds done in life.
- Depicted as a giant, dressed as a courtier of the Heian Period.
- Appears in modern pop culture, referencing death and ghosts.

When Buddhism was brought to China, Yama quickly merged with a pre-existing Daoist deity known as Taishan Fujun 泰山府君 (Jp. Taizan Fukun), a similar judge figure, who assigned people's fates based on their merits in life. By the time Buddhism came to Japan, it featured Yama not only as a deva who sends people on to their next reincarnation (Yama's original role), but also one who judges their past life (Taishan Fujun's role). [21] In Japan, Enma is a fearsome but fair figure. Depending on the source, he rules over Buddhist hell, or exists in his own domain that links to all worlds. Souls come before him and are judged based on the karma they accrued over the course of their most recent life. His abode is often described as an immense palace hall, full of bureaucratic spirits who work underneath him. Enma himself is typically depicted as a physical giant, towering over the souls he judges. He is usually dressed as a Heian Period courtier, or sometimes an ancient Chinese nobleman wearing Confucian court dress. He bears a stern countenance but is not evil – his job is a necessary one for the universe to function.

Enma is unrelated to any ancient *kami* associated with death, such as Izanami. His afterworld, whether

The deva Enma, portrayed as both a Chinese bureaucrat and the fearsome king of hell, reflecting his dual roles.

146

Buddhist hell or not, is not the same as Yomi, the Shinto land of the dead (see Chapter 2). However, Enma's status as a judge of souls has become separated from his original position as a purely Buddhist figure. Like Benzaiten and Kichijōten, he is often treated more like a native *kami* than a Buddhist deity, and his worship in Japan is very different from that of the Indian Yama. Today he is not often worshipped directly but is a well-known figure in pop culture referencing ghosts, death or the afterlife. He appears prominently in everything from horror stories to fantasy manga and anime: for example, as a supporting character in the popular manga and anime franchise *Yū yū hakusho* (1990–1994).

BUDDHISM AND SHINTO, INTERTWINED

The line between Buddhist and Shinto deities had become very thin by the Japanese middle ages (*c.* 1200–1600). This was not a sudden development; in the earliest surviving records from the Japanese archipelago it is clear that the two religions had already grown intertwined. The Japanese had long been aware of Buddhism's 'foreignness', even as they made it their own. Yet its early importance as a religion in Japanese history meant that Buddhist morals and concepts became dominant ones. In addition, Shinto was not originally conceived as a 'religion' in the same fashion as Buddhism. It was only due to the influence of Buddhism and other continental religions that worship of various *kami* became organized into a system and associated with strict practices and philosophies.

Starting in the 9th century, religious leaders went a step further, and proposed that native *kami* and Buddhist gods were not only similar beings, but the same. This concept was known as *honji suijaku*, or 'original ground and left-behind tracings'. The concept was originally introduced in China during the Tang Dynasty (618–908) as a way to further incorporate Daoist and local folk deities into Buddhism. Rather than simply placing local deities into a position beneath the Buddhist pantheon, the way Indian gods had been, Chinese philosophers thought it would make more sense if these familiar gods were actually 'traces' (Jp. *suijaku*, Ch. *chuiji*) of Buddhist originals (Jp. *honji*, Ch. *bendi*). A Buddhist deity, for example the bodhisattva Avalokiteśvara, might wish to save the people of a given land, such as ancient China. However, without preachers to lead the people to the truth, it was easier for Avalokiteśvara to manifest as a goddess such as Guanyin (Kannon), who could be understood by the locals because she fit into their pre-existing faith. The Chinese goddess would be a 'trace', and the bodhisattva, the 'original'. The two were not separate entities that merged later but had always been the same thing from the start.[22]

Japanese monks who studied in China brought the idea of *honji suijaku* (Ch. *bendi chuiji*) back to Japan. The theory was used to argue for pairing certain buddhas and bodhisattvas with important *kami*. Kannon (Avalokiteśvara) was often paired with Amaterasu during the mid-Heian Period, as both were female deities who represented light and goodness. These pairings are referenced in dreams recorded by courtiers in their diaries, and in actual religious practices that took place at temples. Shinto shrines began to be built inside Buddhist temple complexes, and vice versa. By the early Kamakura Period, *honji suijaku* had become standard theory for several Buddhist schools, even as newer forms of Buddhism, such as Zen, made it less important. Of course, there were always shrine priests and eminent monks or nuns who disagreed with *honji suijaku*, but it remained the most popular explanation for the relationship between the two religions for centuries.[23]

Fourteenth-century developments, such as the rise in popularity of the Pure Land and Jōdo Shinshū schools of Buddhism, led to a shift in how *honji suijaku* was understood. The *kami* had always been the 'traces', the forms that Buddhist deities had to take to appeal to 'Japanese' sensibilities. However, Pure Land doctrine stressed that these traces were far less important than the originals. Now that Japan had Buddhism, and had for so many centuries, were the *kami* even worth worshipping any longer? To counter this argument, a group of priests based at Ise, the great shrine to Amaterasu, began to produce their own narratives. This group, centred on the Watarai family, was among the first to give Shinto an organized doctrine, and argue for it as an equal to Buddhism.[24]

The Watarai began to argue for *honji suijaku* in Shinto terms. For example, they borrowed the doctrine of Vairocana's radiance producing buddhas across the cosmos and applied it to Amaterasu. Since the solar deity was herself the reflection of purity and light, it stood to reason that she could be representative of the purity at the centre of the multiverse, in the same way that various buddhas were supposed to be 'emanations' of Vairocana. Amaterasu was therefore an emanation of Vairocana as well – but one who was uniquely oriented towards Japan and the Japanese. According to this argument, Amaterasu, as well as several other important *kami* – all of whom had ties to the Watarai family and/or Ise Shrine – were the original Japanese manifestations of the same truth as that brought by Buddhism.[25]

Starting with the Watarai philosophies, early medieval proponents of Shinto made the argument that it, and not Buddhism, was the primary source of Japanese values. This was not because Shinto was 'better', but because (according to this new narrative) it was *the same* as Buddhism. It only had a different coat of paint, one that was more 'native'. As the discussion of ancient myths in earlier chapters of this book should prove, however, this was not in fact the case. While no religion is 'better' than any other, the ancient *kami* myths and the imperial mythos are obviously not the same as Buddhism. Yet by the medieval era the two faiths had grown so tightly intertwined that any attempt to elevate one over the other could just as easily be used in the opposite way. *Honji suijaku* theory did not only allow Buddhism and Shinto to become linked but also let them freely and openly borrow from one another.

In the 17th century, the 'nativist' (Jp. *kokugaku*) school of philosophy developed out of an interest in recovering the ancient myths. Scholars of this very influential school were not affiliated with any religion in particular. Instead, they were independent academics from different backgrounds who were very interested in identifying what was 'originally Japanese', and separating it from what was 'originally foreign'. These scholars coined a new term, still used today, for what had happened between Buddhism and Shinto over the previous thousand years: *shinbutsu shūgō*. This means the 'syncretism of Shinto and Buddhism', or, to put it more simply, that the two religions have grown to be part of one another (at least in Japan).

This system of intertwined faiths did not survive fully intact into the modern era. The Meiji Restoration of 1868 triggered Japan's rapid modernization and its opening to the outside world. As part of this process, a new form of Shinto called State Shinto (*kokka shintō*) was developed to emphasize the figure of the emperor and act like a 19th-century European 'national religion'. In order to popularize State Shinto, Buddhism had to be rapidly and radically de-emphasized. In 1872, the Meiji government began the process of *shinbutsu kakuri*, or 'forced separation of Shinto and Buddhism'. Buddhist temples and Shinto shrines that had developed together for over a thousand years were forcibly divided, and often the land was given to the shrine. Temples were closed, moved or even destroyed. Shrines were enlarged, and new ones were built in places that had never before been Shinto religious sites. This process was stopped by the 1920s, and to some extent reversed after the Second World War, but the damage was done. After a millennium and a half as intertwined faiths, Buddhism and Shinto had been severed apart.

6

A WORLD FLUSH WITH SPIRITS

There are more gods in Japan than the *kami* of the ancient myths or the Buddhist pantheon. Some of these are lesser gods of the wilderness outside the towns and cities. Some are other deities of non-native religions. Others are the spirits of everyday life, the gods of the household, or of problems such as illness. The world as understood by the premodern Japanese was one filled with spirits of various types, levels and powers. Even animals or inanimate objects could have – or could be – *kami*. The supernatural world operated around and alongside that of everyday life, and belief in its existence was common sense for much of Japanese history.

This chapter explores these different spirits as part of the Japanese environment (both urban and rural) and moves forward in time through the Muromachi (1333–1600) and Edo (1600–1868) Periods, comprising the end of the Japanese middle ages, as well as the early modern era. The 14th and 15th centuries yielded the first written records of commoner beliefs, rather than those of the aristocracy. Printing started in the late 16th century and exploded during the 17th, leaving an immense body of surviving literature and historical works. These books, which include the first known dictionary of folk monsters and the earliest translations of the ancient chronicles into then-modern Japanese, reveal even more about how Japanese commoners understood their own mythology.

THE FOUR SKY GODS AND THE HEAVENLY MANSIONS

The ancient Chinese believed that heaven mirrored earth. This meant that earth was able to become like heaven, but also that heaven followed a logical order that could be understood on earth. As the night sky offered one view into heaven, it had to be mapped so that a logical order could be found. This mapping eventually led to the system of the four gods, the five regions and the twenty-eight heavenly mansions.

Seen from the Earth, the sun, moon and five planets visible to the naked eye (Mercury, Venus, Mars, Jupiter and Saturn) all move within the same plane. This is known as the ecliptic plane. In Europe, the stars along the ecliptic plane were divided into twelve constellations, which we know today as the zodiac. The moon also moves through the ecliptic plane at a rate of 1/28 of the circuit per day. This adds up to the (roughly) 28-day lunar month. In ancient China, diviners and astrologers also catalogued the stars along the ecliptic, and divided them into 28 'mansions', each of which corresponds to one day of the moon's cycle. These are known today as the lunar mansions or heavenly mansions 宿 (Ch. *su*, Jp. *shuku* or *boshi*). This system was brought from China to Japan around the 6th or 7th century CE and was rapidly adopted by the Japanese.

The 28 mansions were divided into four sets of seven, each set corresponding to one of the four cardinal directions. These four directions surrounded the centre, which was understood as a fifth direction aligned with the pole star, and thus associated with the emperor (both in heaven and on earth; see Chapter 3). Together these made the five regions. Each of the four directional regions as well as the centre was associated with an animal god, as well as with a colour and one of the five elements: earth, fire, water, wood and metal.

The east, associated with the colours blue and green and the element of wood, is the domain of the Azure Dragon Seiryū 青龍, also sometimes read Shōryū (Ch. Qinglong). In ancient East Asia, blue and green were considered to be the same colour, so Seiryū is also sometimes translated as the 'Green Dragon' or even the 'Blue-Green Dragon'. Seiryū represents spring and new life. In depictions, Seiryū is a traditional Asian dragon: long, serpentine and lacking wings. He can be any shade of green or blue but is most often a rich turquoise or aqua colour, occasionally with red and/or black on his mane. The seven mansions (constellations) that make up Seiryū are: the Horn (Su-boshi), the Neck (Ami-boshi), the Root (Tomo-boshi), the Room (Soi-boshi), the Heart (Nakago-boshi), the Tail (Ashitare-boshi) and the Winnowing Basket (Mi-boshi). These mansions lie in the Western constellations Virgo, Leo, Scorpio and Sagittarius.

The north, associated with the colour black and the element of water, is the domain of the Black Warrior Genbu 玄武 (Ch. Xuanwu). Genbu is most commonly depicted as a turtle mating with a snake, the two locked together as one animal. He is also sometimes a turtle alone and has been mistranslated as the Black Turtle of the North. 'Black Warrior' is the most accurate translation. Genbu represents cold, the winter, harshness and power. He may also be portrayed as a Chinese-style warrior in traditional armour, usually decorated with both turtle and snake motifs. The seven mansions that make up Genbu are: the Dipper (Hikitsu-boshi), the Ox (Iname-boshi), the Girl (Uruki-boshi), Emptiness (Tomite-boshi), the Rooftop (Umiyame- or Urumiya-boshi), the Encampment (Hatsui-boshi) and the Wall (Namame-boshi). These mansions lie in the Western constellations Sagittarius, Capricorn, Aquarius and Pegasus.

The west, associated with the colour white and the element of metal, is the domain of the White Tiger Byakko 白虎 (Ch. Baihu). Byakko represents warmth, the autumn, clarity and calm. He is usually depicted as a white tiger, sometimes fringed with gold. In older depictions, he is often serpentine, mimicking Seiryū's form, but has the proportions of a realistic tiger in Edo Period and afterwards. The seven mansions that make up Byakko are: the Legs (Tokaki-boshi), the Bond (Tatara-boshi), the Stomach (Ekie-boshi), the Hairy Head (Subaru-boshi), the Net (Amefuri-boshi), the Turtle Beak (Toroki-boshi) and the Three Stars (Karasuki-boshi). They lie in the Western constellations Andromeda, Aries, Taurus and Orion.

The south, associated with the colour red and the element of fire, is the domain of the Vermillion Bird Suzaku 朱雀 (Ch. Zhuque). Suzaku also represents heat, the summer and passionate emotions such as love. The exact species of the Vermillion Bird is never specified. In premodern depictions, Suzaku is usually a large-winged, long-tailed bird in bright reddish-orange, but in recent times has come to be pictured as a creature resembling a Western phoenix, with which Suzaku is frequently confused. The seven mansions that make up Suzaku are: the Well (Chichiri-boshi), the Ghost (Tamaono- or Tamahome-boshi), the Willow (Nuriko-boshi), the Star (Hotohori-boshi), the Extended Net (Chiriko-boshi), the Wings (Tasuki-boshi) and the Chariot (Mitsukake-boshi). These mansions lie in the Western constellations Gemini, Cancer, Hydrus, Crater and Corvus.

The four sky gods: the Black Warrior of the North (Genbu, bottom); the White Tiger of the West (Byakko, left); the Red Bird of the South (Suzaku, top); and the Blue Dragon of the East (Seiryû, right). Curiously, Genbu and Suzaku are in the opposite positions in this illustration.

The centre, the realm of the Celestial Emperor, is associated with the colour yellow and the element of earth. It is considered a fifth direction but is not divided into sub-regions (although there are of course other constellations in it). It represents peace, rule and totality – the sum of all the pieces that make up the other four regions. At the heart of the centre in East Asian astrology is the northern pole star Polaris, the axis around which the heavens turn.

The four sky gods – Seiryū, Genbu, Byakko and Suzaku – appear early in Japanese history. There are paintings of them on the early 7th-century Kitora and Takamatsuzuka tombs in Asuka (in modern Nara Prefecture). They were portrayed on four of the banners arrayed for the annual New Year's Ceremony throughout the Nara and Heian Periods, along with representations of the sun and moon. The four sky gods were widely used in divination, in both large-scale rituals and personal fortune-telling. However, they have never been worshipped outright. They are astrological signs and representations, but their power does not extend beyond divining the future. Today they are still well known and appear in many different contexts in modern Japanese culture and popular media. One extremely well-known example is the use of the four gods in the manga and anime franchise *Fushigi yūgi* (1994–present), where they form the basis for the geography and magic of a fantasy setting.

ANGELIC BEINGS AND ASTRAL ROMANCES

The ancient chronicles and other proto-Shinto myths are unclear about the nature and location of heaven. Buddhism, Confucianism and Daoism all have much more specific concepts of heaven, but these tended to overlap when brought to Japan. As a result, there are several nonspecific spirits that appear similar to Western angelic beings, but are not the same. Most of these are referred to as *tennin*, or 'heavenly people'. This grouping includes important subsets such as *tennyo* or 'heavenly maidens'. *Tennyo* are beautiful women, sometimes with wings, who descend to the earth. Regardless of whether or not they have wings, they wear feathered robes that allow them to ascend at will. In several different legends, enterprising young men manage to trap a *tennyo* by stealing her cloak when she takes it off to bathe, in similar fashion to Celtic legends about selkies.

Tennin may derive from several different sources. Buddhist heavens often have *apsaras* (Jp. *hiten*), beautiful men and women who float between or on clouds. *Apsaras* usually play musical instruments and wear sumptuous clothes. They are somewhere between angels and celestial entertainers. Daoist folklore in China is likewise full of stories of *xianren* or 'immortals' (Jp. *sennin*). These are people whose mastery of the Way brought them immortality and a host of other magical powers, such as flight and eternal youth. *Xianren* live in gorgeous palaces in distant locales, such as magical hidden valleys far from civilization. Both sources may have generated the Japanese *tennin*.

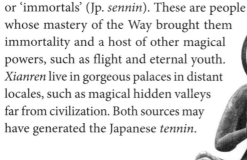

An *apsara*, a heavenly maiden in Buddhist depictions of paradise.

The Cowherd and the Weaver Girl, here dressed as ancient Chinese courtiers.

Two of the most famous legends involving *tennin* are that of the Cowherd and the Weaver Girl, and *The Tale of the Bamboo Cutter*. The story of the Cowherd and the Weaver Girl dates to ancient China and is known from a variety of East Asian countries. The Weaver Girl 織姫 (Jp. Orihime) is the star known in the West as Vega, in the modern constellation Lyra; the Cowherd 彦星 (Jp. Hikoboshi) is the star Altair, in the modern constellation Aquilla. The Weaver Girl and the Cowherd fell in love with one another, apparently violating the rules of heaven, even though both were celestial beings. The pair were banished to opposite sides of the Celestial River (the Milky Way). They can only meet once a year, on the seventh day of the seventh month, when magpies form a bridge across the river. However, if it is cloudy on that day, the magpies cannot fly to heaven, and thus the couple must wait another year to meet.

The original legend is the origin of the holiday still celebrated in Japan as Tanabata. Although it originally referred to the seventh lunar month (roughly modern August), Tanabata is now more commonly celebrated on July 7 as Japan has since adopted the Western calendar. In the 15th century, the legend of the Cowherd and the Weaver Girl was expanded as a fairy tale known as *The Tale of Amewakahiko* (*Amewakahiko sōshi*). The expanded version elaborates on the backgrounds of both characters, as well as introducing a conflict in the form of a giant serpent they have to defeat.[1] This version remained popular into the Edo Period, but is less well known than the original, more vague story today.

The Tale of the Bamboo Cutter (*Taketori monogatari*)is a famous piece of Heian Period (784–1185) literature dating back to the 9th century. By an unknown author, the work appears to be a native Japanese tale. It concerns a bamboo cutter and his wife who long for a child. One day, the bamboo cutter finds a glowing stem of bamboo and cuts it open, revealing a beautiful baby girl, shining like the sun. The couple adopts her and she rapidly grows into a loving, kind, beautiful and intelligent woman

The old bamboo cutter finds the infant Kaguya-hime inside a stalk of bamboo at the start of the *Tale of the Bamboo Cutter*.

Tennin
- 'Heavenly people', spirits that appear similar to Western angels.
- Come from a variety of sources: Buddhist *apsaras* who float in the clouds, Daoist Immortals, and others both native and foreign to Japan.
- Often objects of forbidden love: they are supernaturally kind and beautiful, but marriage between human and *tennin* is not possible.
- Famous *tennin* in legend include Princess Kaguya and the Weaver Girl.

---

whom they call Kaguya-hime かぐや姫 (often translated as 'Princess Kaguya' in English).

Kaguya-hime is pursued by many suitors. She disposes of most of them by sending them on long quests, which they all fail. She then catches the emperor's eye, and against her own desires falls in love with him. Yet their time together is short, as Kaguya-hime reveals that she is a *tennin* from the moon and must return there soon. Her people come to retrieve her, overpowering the emperor and the army with their sheer majesty, and Kaguya-hime leaves her earthly family forever.[2]

As these and other tales about *tennin* make clear, they are objects of forbidden romance. They are beautiful and kind, perfect in ways that normal humans are not. Everyone wants them, both in heaven and on earth. Yet for various reasons, love with a *tennin*, or even between *tennin*, is impossible. They represent the unattainable ideals of paradise, both those of foreign traditions and of Japan itself.

HOUSEHOLD, EPIDEMIC AND DIRECTIONAL DEITIES

It is a sad truth that we know more about the lives of the rich than we do of commoners for much of Japanese history. Literacy expanded slowly before printed texts became widely available in the 17th century. Prior to that, most people who could read and write were wealthy aristocrats and warriors. The majority of them lived in the city of Kyoto, Japan's capital until the Edo Period, so much more is known about urban life in Kyoto than that of the countryside in earlier periods. From these sources it is clear that the urban environment of classical and medieval Kyoto was not solely the domain of humans. Many spirits also lived in the capital and among its citizens.

At the most basic level were the gods of each individual household. These spirits were not specifically named or grouped. They may have included ancestors or deceased family members whose spirits needed to be appeased. In modern Japan, many households have a personal Buddhist altar (*butsudan*) and/or a personal Shinto shrine (*kamidana*). Food and other objects are placed in front of a *butsudan* along with incense, both to share with one's ancestors and to pray for their well-being in future lives. The *kamidana* is less often directly involved in prayer, but is dedicated to the other spirits that may inhabit the home – lesser *kami* of the house and grounds, and the objects in them.[3] Although we cannot confirm the presence of both types of household altars prior to the medieval era, they did exist by the 14th century, and probably much earlier, as aristocrats' diaries and other records from the Heian Period (784–1185) discuss various superstitions related to appeasing local household gods. It makes sense that similar forms of worship to modern household altars were present in homes in late medieval Kyoto, and probably outside it as well.

One group of deities who were widely worshipped by many households in addition to their own ancestors were the Seven Gods of Luck (Shichifukujin 七福神). These are seven distinct gods who started being grouped together as patrons of various professions. Two of them, Benzaiten and Kichijōten (Kisshōten), have already been discussed in the previous chapter. These two are devas, Indian deities who were brought to Japan with Buddhism, and only later grouped with the Seven Gods of Luck. The other five gods were likewise individual deities who became associated with the pursuit of money and success.

The only one of the Seven Gods of Luck with a purely native Japanese origin is Ebisu 恵比寿. Ebisu does not appear in the ancient chronicles but was worshipped as the patron of fishermen starting in the late Heian Period. He rapidly became mixed with two very different gods who do exist in the ancient chronicles: Hiruko 蛭子 and Kotoshironushi 事代主. Hiruko, the Leech Child, is the first offspring of Izanagi and Izanami in both the *Kojiki* and *Nihonshoki* accounts, where he appears only briefly, born without arms or legs and then immediately set adrift in a reed boat

The Seven Gods of Luck, right to left: Kichijōten; Jūrōjin and Ebisu, seated over food; Bishamonten, holding a pagoda; Daikokuten with his mallet; half-naked Budai; and an old man who may be a form of Benzaiten, or a different god substituted for her.

and forgotten (see Chapter 2). Kotoshironushi, on the other hand, has a slightly larger role in the legends about Ninigi's descent, where he advises Ōkuninushi during the negotiations on giving up the earth to the Heavenly Grandson (see Chapter 2).

Hiruko and Kotoshironushi are not related to one another in the ancient chronicles. By the 13th century, however, Ebisu had his own mythical history that incorporated the

A *netsuke*, or decoration for a kimono sash, featuring Ebisu, one of the Seven Gods of Luck, shown as a jolly man in a Heian nobleman's clothing.

legends of both Hiruko and Kotoshironushi, conflated into the same god. As Hiruko, he was born to Izanagi and Izanami in the first days of creation and set adrift. After three years, he grew legs (and presumably the rest of his body) and arrived at the shore near Osaka. He remained somewhat crippled, and was deaf, but neither of these things stopped him from learning the secrets of the shoreline and of the things that wash up on it. As the god of luck and secrets, the former Leech Child then appears as Kotoshironushi to advise Ōkuninushi, before taking his time to wander about Japan, helping the unlucky – particularly fishermen.[4] In the form of Ebisu, these other two very minor deities became newly important for worship. Ebisu is portrayed as a short, fat, jolly man, usually clothed like a Heian nobleman. He often wears a very tall hat, adding further comedy to his capering appearance.

The fourth God of Luck is Daikokuten 大黒天. He too was originally a deva, deriving from the Indian god Śiva (Shiva), today one of the most important in the Hindu pantheon. Śiva is both a creator and a destroyer in different branches of Hinduism and has a wide variety of powers related to both aspects. In Japan, Daikokuten merged with Ōkuninushi, the earth god of the ancient chronicles. He is thus worshipped as the protector of luck and wealth derived from the earth, particularly land ownership.[5] The character 黒 in his name means 'black', and so he has also become associated with positive aspects of darkness. Daikokuten often carries a mallet which brings good fortune and is seated on a pile of rice. Rats sometimes accompany him, signifying ambition and further luck.[6]

The fifth God of Luck is Bishamonten 毘沙門天, who is also one of the Four Heavenly Kings under the name Tamonten. As a god of luck Bishamonten still retains his role as protector of Buddhism as well as of all holy places.[7] The sixth and seventh Gods of Luck, Jūrōjin 寿老人 and Budai 布袋, were supposedly once human. Jūrōjin is the Japanese form of a Daoist sage from ancient China, although his exact identity is unknown. He has a distinctive elongated head, and a long beard and moustache. Jūrōjin rides a white deer, and loves wine and drinking, which are heavily associated with Daoist sages and hermits. Budai is the so-called 'Laughing Buddha', a jolly Buddhist monk with a bulging stomach. He is based on one of several possible progenitors of the Zen 禅 (Ch. Chan) school of

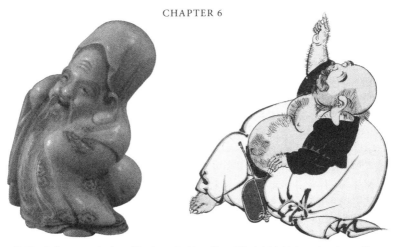

Jūrōjin (left, on a netsuke, with elongated head) and Budai (right, in a drawing, with bulging stomach and sack) are the two Gods of Luck who originated as humans.

Buddhism. Budai carries a bulging sack, representing the luck he brings to his patrons, particularly children.

The Seven Gods of Luck often take the form of trinkets or a series of small statues. They also appear as common subjects of *netsuke*, small decorative objects of ivory or wood that were hung from kimono sashes or sword handles during Japan's Edo Period. *Netsuke* are popular today as collector items, and many famous examples feature one or more of the Seven Gods of Luck. Icons of the Seven are displayed to bring luck to a household or business.

There were also deities who did not help urban citizens, but threatened them. The most obvious of these were the gods of epidemics, such as Gozu Tennō 牛頭天皇, the 'Ox-Headed Emperor'. He is the bringer of calamity, most often in the form of diseases brought by ill winds. As early as the 10th century, portrayals of an ox-headed god bringing wind (representing an epidemic) started to appear at temples in Kyoto. Gozu Tennō remained in the popular imagination for centuries afterwards as a fearsome deity who prowls where he wills. In particular, he brings smallpox and measles, two of the most common scourges of premodern Japan.

Modern scholars believe Gozu Tennō to be a composite deity, like so many others in Japan. He may have started out as a minor Indian god named Gosirsa Devarāja who was worshipped by early Buddhists. In Tibet, this deity became associated with a local god of a mountain that was said to resemble an ox head. Gozu Tennō kept that association through centuries in China, before arriving in Japan, by which point the ox-headed god had incorporated other figures from Daoist and Chinese folk beliefs related to disease. Japanese records from the Kamakura Period (1185–1333) claim that Gozu Tennō was an incarnation of the ancient and powerful *kami* Susanowo, due to both gods' association with violent natural events. Because of this association, Gozu Tennō was worshipped in Kyoto at Yasaka Shrine, which had been originally dedicated to Susanowo.[8] The world-famous Gion Festival, held in the streets around Yasaka Shrine – the neighbourhood of Gion, known in the Edo Period for its *geisha* – may have begun as a ceremony to appease Gozu Tennō in order to protect the capital city from outbreaks of disease.

In addition to Gozu Tennō, there was another type of god who caused trouble for the citizens of premodern Kyoto. These were the gods of the directions, personified by the deity Konjin 金神. Konjin, a mysterious god whose name means only 'Golden Deity', is not the same type of 'directional' god as the four sky gods. Rather, he is a god who moves about the different directions as he pleases. When Konjin or a similar deity – there were many lesser ones known only to diviners – are travelling or residing in a specific direction, that direction becomes taboo or *kataimi* 方忌. No one may travel in the same direction as a current *kataimi*, nor may anyone approach it.

Kataimi was a very strong taboo in Heian society. Heian literature is filled with examples where courtiers were unable to return home because of *kataimi*, and who were forced to stay either at the imperial palace or with friends or family for extended periods of time. Courtiers' diaries also reveal that *kataimi* was seen as a very real danger outside of fiction. Nobles would go to great lengths to set up multiple places to stay around Kyoto in case they could not get to their main home.

The famous work of fiction known as *Genji monogatari* ('The Tale of Genji', *c.* 1000) includes many instances of travel being disrupted by *kataimi*. These travel disruptions often serve as accidental but important moments that drive the plot: for example, when Genji, the protagonist of the book, is forced by *kataimi* to take shelter at the mansion of the Governor of Kii. This change of plans is the trigger for Genji's affair with the Governor's young wife, Utsusemi 空蝉.[9] Several of Genji's other affairs likewise happen when he is forced into close proximity with women of whom he might not otherwise have been aware.

ONMYŌJI: IMPERIAL DIVINERS

Kataimi were determined by divination. In the Heian and Kamakura Periods, and possibly for a good time later (at least among the imperial court), these divinations were performed by *onmyōji*, or 'Yin-Yang Wizards'. *Onmyōji* were officially government workers, assigned to the Bureau of Onmyōdō, or 'Yin-Yang Magic'.[10]

Onmyōdō was a syncretic art that developed in Japan from multiple sources. It included what in China were known as yin-yang theory and five-elemental theory, two ancient practices that perceived all phenomena as comprised of energies in balance. Yin 陰 (Jp. *in* or *on*), the 'female' principle, represents darkness, femininity and passivity. Yang 陽 (Jp. *yō* or *myō*), the 'male' principle, represents light, masculinity and action. In ying-yang theory, these two principles underlie all energies of the world.

Five-elemental theory is similar to yin-yang theory, but instead of two principles, it uses the five East Asian elements: wood, fire, earth, metal and water. These five elements are associated with the five colours (blue/green, red, yellow, white and black, respectively); the five visible planets (Jupiter, Mars, Saturn, Venus and Mercury); and many other natural systems. Bringing them into balance allows one to control and affect phenomena, as a sort of scientific magic. In Japan, yin-yang theory and five-elemental theory were rapidly combined, allowing for yin or yang versions of each element. These systems were associated with other sets of divination tools, such as the twelve-animal Chinese zodiac, to create complex systems of 30–60 phases.[11]

Yin-yang theory, five-elemental theory and the complicated mathematical divinations were then combined with yet other forms of magic. Buddhist rituals for healing and purification, Daoist alchemy, spirit-binding and folk medicine were all brought together to create the set of skills that an *onmyōji* possessed. The government authorized only trained members of the Bureau to use these powers and marked everyone else as 'black magicians'.[12] En no Gyōja, the god of the mountain ascetics, was originally punished for being an unauthorized practitioner (see Chapter 4). Even after the divination of *kataimi* or people's fates was no longer required for the government to function, it was still technically illegal to learn *onmyōdō* without written permission from the Imperial Household Agency until 2006!

Today anyone who applies can study the arts of Yin-Yang Magic. Contemporary Japanese are more interested in *onmyōji* as the Japanese equivalent of wizards from Western fantasy. They feature in several manga, novel series, anime and live-action films and television shows. One of the most well-known figures is Abe no Seimei 安部晴明 (921–1005), the most famous *onmyōji* of the Heian Period, about whom many legends sprang up. He supposedly could travel to hell and back by jumping through a magical well in southern Kyoto. He was able to bind spirits with simple paper charms known as *ofuda* and could summon even greater *kami* to do his bidding. In some tales, he is accompanied by *shikigami*, spirits summoned into paper figures that then take on physical forms as servants or helpers.[13]

The famous *onmyōji* Abe no Seimei (left) casts a divination by torchlight.

Although legends about Seimei have existed since his own lifetime, they became much more widespread in the Edo Period, and remain well known today. His powers have become staples of all *onmyōji* depicted in modern Japanese fiction, and he himself is the main character of many works. One very famous example is the novel series *Onmyōji* 陰陽師 by Yumemakura Baku (b. 1951), which began in 1986 and is still ongoing. The novels feature Seimei as a sort of Heian Period detective, solving mystical crimes with the help of several sidekicks. They remain very popular works, with numerous spinoffs, including manga and a pair of live-action films from 2001 and 2003.

THE HAUNTED COUNTRYSIDE

Premodern Japan was almost entirely rural. Until the 15th century there were few significant towns outside of Kyoto. These included Kamakura, the capital of the first Shogunate, and Dazaifu, the nerve centre of Kyushu. In the 15th century, however, castles began to be constructed in the rural provinces, and by the late 16th and early 17th centuries new towns of significant size and influence had accumulated around them. These castle towns, known as *jōkamachi*, form the cores of many modern Japanese cities.

As castle towns developed, they enabled greater domestic trade and the expansion of literacy, and more records of townsfolk and rural commoners begin to appear as a result. By the mid-16th century, stories and other texts concerning rural Japan were being written and printed. This number only expanded during the Edo Period, as woodblock-printed books became widespread in all areas of the archipelago. These publications are the earliest major sources for what is known about the folklore and mythology of commoners outside the imperial and shogunal courts.

The countryside revealed in these writings is full of spirits. Most of them are Shinto *kami* of some form or another, although they may also build on Buddhist, Daoist and more vaguely 'folk' beliefs. Some of them are spirits of specific landforms; others are more general in their powers, living wherever they will. These spirits are known collectively as *yōkai* 妖怪, *ayakashi* あやかし, *mononoke* 物の怪 or *mamono* 魔物. *Yōkai* is the most common term, and the one most often used today. *Ayakashi* and *mononoke* were both more commonly used in the past; *mononoke* is also the term for possession by another human's spirit.

There are many, many types of *yōkai*. Some were known from across Japan, while others are very specific to the legends of one region or even one village. Starting in the 18th century, scholars began to attempt encyclopaedias of the many spirits of the Japanese countryside, culminating in a series of illustrated *yōkai* compendia by Toriyama Sekien (1712–1788). These books remain the most well-known traditional explanations of the monsters haunting the Japanese countryside. Starting in the late 19th century, modern ethnographers such as Orikuchi Shinobu (1887–1953) made the first systematic investigations of local folklore, which often backed up the tales and creatures portrayed in Toriyama's encyclopaedias. After the Second World War, many of these traditional stories began to be lost due to the increasing focus on urban Japan. Yet the recording of folklore done in both the Edo Period and the first half of the modern era has allowed knowledge of *yōkai* to persist into the present, where these spirits have returned to Japanese popular culture in new forms.

Yōkai are often physical beings with monstrous or bizarre forms. Many modern works translate the term *yōkai* as 'demon', 'devil' or 'monster' in English. This is an easy shorthand for explaining the concept but is also due in part to cultural misunderstanding.

A *mikoshi-nyūdō*, a long-necked *yōkai*, emerges from the forest. This type enjoys scaring humans by peering over folding screens and other tall objects.

Some famous species of *yōkai*

- *Oni*: often translated as 'ogres' in English. Humanoid, with brightly coloured skin and horns. Dress in animal skins or like Buddhist clergy. Haunt mountains and forests, accost travellers and invade villages.
- *Tengu*: often translated as 'goblins' in English. Crow spirits that resemble humans but have long noses or beaks and large black wings. More civilized than *oni*. Skilled swordsmen and harbingers of death in battle.
- *Kappa*: often translated as 'water sprites' in English. Humanoid, with green scaly skin and turtle shells. They try to drown humans and eat their livers, but are otherwise polite, childlike and without malice.
- *Ningyo*: Japanese mermaids, part-human and part-fish. Those who consume their flesh become immortal, but this is usually a curse.
- *Yamanba*: Women living in the mountains, similar to Western witches. Usually crones, but sometimes young and beautiful. They can be good, evil or just uncaring depending on the story.

Yōkai can be terrifying, dangerous or both. However, they are not necessarily evil any more than any wild animal or natural phenomenon. Some prefer to do evil, but that is an individual quality, and not a fixed characteristic of any group or 'species' of *yōkai*. Some are also sources of great good, but once again this is an individual quality. Most *yōkai*, like anything in nature, simply exist, and whether they hurt or help humans is purely incidental.[14] Below are presented some common *yōkai*, as well as historically relevant ones. A complete list of *yōkai* would take many more pages and include many regionally specific examples.

Oni

The single most well-known spirit haunting the wilds of Japan is the *oni* 鬼. *Oni* are often called 'ogres' in English, although this is only the closest possible parallel in Western fairy tales. *Oni* are large humanoid figures, often one and a half to two times the height of a man. They have brutish features and single horns growing out of their heads. *Oni* may have any colour skin, although bright red and bright blue are the most common. Sometimes they have clawed hands and feet, and they may also (or additionally) have extra fingers and toes. *Oni* tend to dress in the skins of wild animals, particularly tigers (which have never existed in Japan, and therefore are rarely depicted accurately). They carry heavy iron clubs known as *kanabō*, which they can use to devastating effect. However, *oni* are also capable of advanced speech and thought.[15]

Oni haunt the mountainsides and forests of Japan. They may accost travellers on deep mountain paths, or invade rural villages to carry people away. One famous *oni* appears in the folktale 'Issun Bōshi'. The version that follows is primarily that told in several late-Muromachi Period (1333–1600) illustrated versions known as *otogi zōshi*. There was a childless couple who desperately wanted a child. They prayed to Watatsumi, the triple god of the sea, at Sumiyoshi (in modern Osaka), and were blessed with a baby boy. However, the boy was born only one *sun* (roughly equivalent to an inch) in height, and he never grew any taller, so they named him Issun Bōshi, or 'One-*Sun* Boy'. When Issun Bōshi was an adult, he set out to find his fortune using a rice bowl for a boat, a chopstick for a paddle, a needle for a sword and a piece of straw as a scabbard.

As he travelled, Issun Bōshi came upon a large and gorgeous house where the governor of a province lived with his beautiful daughter. He asked to meet with the governor, but he was laughed at and dismissed due to his very small height. Sometime later, the governor and his daughter went on a pilgrimage. One night an *oni* came upon their camp and kidnapped the girl. Issun Bōshi chased after the

An *oni* dressed as a Buddhist monk.

oni, feeling no fear, but the *oni* grabbed him and swallowed him up. Issun Bōshi took out his needle sword and stabbed the *oni* again and again from the inside of his stomach. In great pain, the *oni* spat up Issun Bōshi, gave him the governor's daughter, and ran back to the mountains. The governor rejoiced, and Issun Bōshi married his daughter, becoming a noble at the court.[16]

Oni are not worshipped, but they appear in the holiday of Setsubun. Setsubun is observed on the third day of the second month (originally in March, but now 3 February). This ritual involves throwing uncooked soybeans at a person dressed as an *oni*, all while shouting *oni wa soto, fuku wa uchi* ('the *oni* goes outside, good luck comes inside!'). The *oni* must be driven away for the good luck of the new year to enter a house.

Tengu

Tengu 天狗 are often called 'goblins' in English, but this could not be further from their nature and appearance. Although the Chinese characters in their name mean 'heavenly dog', *tengu* are actually crow spirits. In some cases, they are even known as *karasu tengu*, or 'crow *tengu*'. The word *tengu* is a borrowing from an otherwise unrelated monster of Chinese folklore, a magical dog called the Tiangou. The Japanese *tengu* also lives in the forests and mountains, but there the similarities to the Tiangou end. Most often male, *tengu* are humans with exceptionally long noses, or in some cases actual bird beaks, as well as a pair of great black-feathered wings. According to some legends they can switch back and forth between human form and that of a giant crow.[17] In most stories

Masks representing *tengu* feature long, beak-like noses and feathery hair.

they are somewhere in between, sometimes being almost entirely human except for the nose and wings, other times being covered in black feathers or even bearing talons for feet.

Tengu are more civilized than *oni*. They wear clothes, often those of lower-ranking court noblemen, and train in swordsmanship. In fact, *tengu* are said to be the best swordsmen in Japan. They are fierce warriors but also cunning duellists. The earliest references to *tengu* come from 9th-century sources, but they are not pictured in any surviving ones until the 12th century. Although not raging brutes like many *oni*, *tengu* are no less dangerous for their better manners or skilled fighting, and will not hesitate to kidnap or cut down humans. Even when they are behaving, they appear – at least in early medieval lore – as harbingers of death in battle, like the crows they resemble.

The *tengu* are said to be led by a king named Sōjōbō, who lives on Mt Kurama, due north of Kyoto. At its peak is an ancient Buddhist temple, Kuramadera, and the mountain is surrounded by deep forested valleys

Sōjōbō, king of the *tengu*, teaches a young man fighting skills.

with few dwellings, even though it technically lies within the city limits of modern Kyoto. This area has supposedly always been Sōjōbō's domain. According to legends going back to at least the Muromachi Period, the young Minamoto no Yoshitsune 源義経, a brother of the famous Yoritomo and one of the heroes of the Genpei War, came to Mt Kurama as a boy. Sōjōbō took in the young Yoshitsune and trained him in swordsmanship. This is one of the reasons Yoshitsune was supposedly unbeatable in battle.

Today, *tengu* appear in a variety of popular media, retaining their traditional associations with deep forests, crows and swordsmanship. Kuramadera Temple itself has a successful marketing campaign involving *tengu* masks and advertisements for the 'home of Sōjōbō'. *Tengu* have even made it into Western fantasy, as a race in various tabletop role-playing games. Although not as ubiquitous as *oni*, *tengu* remain among the more well-known *yōkai*.

Kappa

Kappa 河童 are *yōkai* who live in or near fresh water. They are often called 'water sprites' in English, but as with *tengu* and 'goblins', this leads to significant misconceptions. *Kappa* are usually humanoid and have scaly green skin and turtle shells. Their faces are also reminiscent of turtles, with short, broad beaks. *Kappa* have a small bowl-like depression on top of their heads which they must keep full of water. Therefore, when one meets a *kappa*, one bows to it. Being naturally polite, the *kappa* will bow back, causing the water to

A *kappa* emerges from a lotus pond.

run out of its head. This may either vanquish the *kappa* or require it not to harm you.[18] This is a good practice, as while *kappa* follow strict rules of etiquette, at the same time they strongly desire to drown humans and then eat their livers out through their anuses. According to some stories, there is a magical jewel, known as a *shirotama*, that exists inside a human's anus, and which *kappa* must remove before they can reach the liver.[19]

Kappa are the size of small children, as reflected in their name, derived from a contraction of *kawa warawa* or 'river child'. When they first appear in medieval records, they are portrayed as more childlike and amoral than strictly malicious. While they do wish to drown and devour people, it is not out of outright malice, hence their exceedingly polite and friendly demeanour, even when facing their prey. In addition to human livers, *kappa* also enjoy fresh produce, in particular cucumbers, and by the Edo Period, they were regarded as ghostly pests on farms as well as mischievous and dangerous water spirits.

Ningyo

Ningyo 人魚 (lit. 'man-fish') are Japan's answer to mermaids. Like their Western counterparts, these creatures are part human and part fish. However, depending on the story, they may be fish with the heads of humans, humans who grew up under the water, or any number of interme- diate forms. *Ningyo* are strictly ocean *yōkai* and do not appear in fresh water. In the most ancient accounts they have monkey-like heads with small

A *ningyo* swims in the ocean; unlike Western mermaids, they are often hideous in appearance.

pointed teeth. By the Muromachi Period, stories about *ningyo* have them appearing more human.

Medieval tales about *ningyo* do not specify whether these creatures are male or female, but they do focus on a different physical quality: the nature of their flesh. Anyone who eats the flesh of a *ningyo* becomes immortal. In most tales, this immortality is a curse. In some cases, lust for a *ningyo*'s flesh drives fishermen or their families and friends to commit depraved acts to obtain it. In other cases, the act of living forever itself becomes a source of pain instead of joy. Because of this, accidentally catching a *ningyo*, or discovering one washed up on shore, was considered a bad omen.

One of the most famous tales about a *ningyo*'s flesh is that of the Yao Bikuni 八百比丘尼, or 'Eight-Hundred [Year] Nun'. In the most common variant of this myth, a *ningyo* was caught off the shore of Wakasa Province (modern Fukui Prefecture). The fisherman who caught it threw a party to celebrate his catch while hiding the nature of the fish, but the party guests found out, and refused to partake. One guest, however, smuggled some of the *ningyo*'s flesh to his daughter, who was very ill. She recovered after eating it and grew up healthy and beautiful. However, once she reached adulthood, the girl stopped ageing. She eventually took Buddhist vows after her husband and children died, and lived for 800 years, wandering Japan as a deathless nun. Eventually she returned to her home village and ended her own life.[20]

Yamanba

Yamanba or *yamauba* 山姥 (lit. 'old lady of the mountains') are akin to the witches of Western fairy tales. These women live deep in the mountains of Japan, where they work magic and interact with the *kami* of the mountains. The stereotypical *yamanba* is an older woman (although not necessarily decrepit with age). She often eats the flesh of both humans and animals and is a fearsome enemy when hunting unfortunate men or women who enter her domain.[21] However, *yamanba* can also give gifts of knowledge or magic to those who help them. They can even possess a house, 'haunting' it in much the way of a household spirit. According to some beliefs in central Honshu and northern Kyushu, a house haunted by a *yamanba* has good fortune. Whether the *yamanba* was originally human or not is another feature that changes with each tale and region. Unlike the witches of Western folklore, *yamanba* are more *yōkai* than human regardless of how they look or act.

Yamanba come in many regional variations as well. Some are aged crones, others beautiful young women, and some are even men. The popularity of these tales during the Edo Period led to a series of famous woodblock prints featuring beautiful young *yamanba*. Such images allowed *yamanba* to escape some of the censorship of bloody folktales by the Shogunate authorities. Regardless of whether they helped or hurt people, these beautiful *yamanba* became popular as erotic figures due to their appearance in these prints, which in turn filtered back into folklore. Several regional *yamanba* myths today still involve beautiful and seductive *yamanba*.[22]

Yamanba are less common than other *yōkai* in modern popular culture, but they do appear. Some of the images of wise old women or witches in contemporary Japanese fantasy owe as much to legends of *yamanba* as they do to Western influences. Several modern Japanese authors have also taken the *yamanba* as a symbol of Japan's traditional bias against older women. The short story 'Yamanba no bishō' ('The Smile of the Mountain Witch', 1976) by Ōba Minako (1930–2007) is a famous example. Set in the modern day, the story equates an

An aged *yamanba* secludes herself in the mountains.

older widow, whose family has withdrawn from her, with the fictional *yamanba*, and questions whether the latter has more freedom due to her status as an inhuman being compared to the life of a woman in modern Japanese society.

Yūrei

In Chapter 4 we addressed the question of human ghosts, as well as the spirits of the living. However, tales from the Muromachi Period and later began to widen the spectrum of what counted as a 'ghost', as well as overlap with *yōkai*. Generally called *yūrei* 幽霊 ('mysterious spirit'), this category includes the previously mentioned *onryō* and *goryō*, vengeful or jealous ghosts who hurt others. *Yūrei* also include certain other spirits who either did not appear in previous folktales or have only now started to be grouped with other 'ghosts'.

Yūrei Okiku, the ghost at the centre of the Edo Period horror tale 'Mansion of Plates'.

Among these other spirits are the *gaki* 餓鬼 or 'hungry ghosts' of Buddhist cosmology. Mahayana Buddhism divides existence into ten 'worlds'. Each 'world' is actually a mode of existence rather than a physical location in the multiverse. From bottom to top, the ten 'worlds' are: hell, hungry ghosts, animals, warring spirits, humans, devas, beings approaching wisdom, beings approaching enlightenment, bodhisattvas and buddhas.[23] *Nirvana* is a state of existence beyond even the tenth 'world'. Hell is at the bottom and is where evil souls are tortured until they can be cleansed and allowed to reincarnate higher up. The next level is that of the *gaki*, and it is almost as horrifying as hell.

Gaki, known in Sanskrit as *preta*, are described as children with immensely distended stomachs and an insatiable hunger. They crawl across their dimension seeking food they can never find. Their existence is less horrible than being in hell, but below everything else, even reincarnation as an animal. However, even in ancient Indian Buddhism, *preta* were able to escape their world and come to ours. They can be nuisances, spirits who crave things that the living have, and in some cases they can become dangerous. By the time the legends of *preta/gaki* came to Japan, they had transformed into more harmful figures. *Gaki* desire to obtain things from humans and will go to great lengths to do so.[24] They may be compared to poltergeists, ghouls or even some notions of Western vampires. They are also considered a type of *yūrei*. Incidentally, the term *gaki* has become the word for 'brat' in modern Japanese, and one can hear it said often in film and television.

Another similar type of *yūrei* is the *zashiki-warashi* 座敷童子 ('storehouse child'). Said to be the ghosts of children who died young, these spirits typically inhabit warehouses and storage spaces. They are mischievous, although not as outright dangerous as *gaki*. *Zashiki-warashi* want to play with humans, and their actions are often driven by a childlike amorality rather than greed or any intent to harm.[25] Many modern Japanese ghost stories draw on traditional stories of these spirits as inspiration, or twist them into more terrifying examples, such as the child spirit in the 2002 horror film *Juon* (Eng. *Ju-On: The Grudge*).

Yūrei are also associated with a different subclass of *yōkai* known as *bakemono* 化け物 or *obake* お化け. The verb *bakeru*, from which both

'Hungry ghosts' (*gaki*) can enter the human world and cause havoc.

names derive, means 'to change'. *Bakemono/obake* are thus beings that undergo a change. In the case of *yūrei*, this can mean the transition into death. Other *bakemono* include some of the animal *yōkai* discussed later in this chapter. The category of *bakemono* is a wide one and includes many types of animal and object spirits that will be addressed below, as well as *yōkai* that are not based on things that exist in the physical world.

Regional *Yōkai*

Many, possibly most *yōkai* in Japan are specific to one region – or, in some cases, to a single town or village. Although some of these regionally specific *yōkai* overlap with the 'species' discussed above, others are unique to their region. The different variations on the *yamanba* mentioned above are one set of examples. Toriyama Sekien's works were among the first to list many of these regional variations on *yōkai*. Some were written about for the first time in his encyclopaedias, and probably came from stories that he gathered from across the archipelago during the mid-18th century. Others were collected in the boom of *yōkai* books that followed Toriyama's publications and lasted into the late Edo Period.

Lafcadio Hearn (1850–1904), one of the first Americans to settle in Japan, made a detailed study of the regional folklore of the Izumo area (modern Shimane Prefecture). Hearn's work, published as the story collection *Kwaidan: Stories and Studies of Strange Things* (1904), was the first English exposure not only to *yōkai* in general, but also to regional *yōkai* of Izumo. Following the Second World War, famed manga author Mizuki Shigeru (1922–2015) made it his life's work to popularize the folklore of that same area through manga. Mizuki's magnum opus, *Gegege no Kitarō* ('Cackling Kitarō', 1960–1969), immortalized the *yōkai* of Shimane for a generation of Japanese children, and the franchise continues to this day (see Chapter 7 for more on Mizuki's works).

Today one can easily buy a dictionary of *yōkai* at Japanese bookstores. These modern books range from pocket guides to heavy tomes, featuring alphabetical entries and detailed anthropological information about the many spirits and lesser *kami* who haunt the countryside. There are also many films focusing on *yōkai*, as well as other popular media, such as anime and manga. Although modern Japan has its own share of urban legends and contemporary variations on *yōkai* – which we will address in the next chapter – the traditional versions are still very popular. The Japanese countryside remains haunted by *yōkai* even now.

ANIMALS, OBJECTS AND THINGS

Astute followers of Japanese traditional culture will have noticed that some key *yōkai* are missing from the discussion above, which focused on *yōkai* with definite supernatural origins. There is, however, another broad class of these creatures: *yōkai* that are based on animals and objects. Such spirits, regardless of their supernatural powers, were thought to be natural developments of ordinary things. Surprisingly, while plants certainly had and have *kami*, there are far fewer legends of plants that are themselves supernatural agents prior to the modern day. Animals and human-made objects, however, are very prone to becoming active spirits themselves.

In many cases, it is age that transforms an ordinary animal or object into a supernatural creature. The most common legend concerning animals is that, should they live for a hundred years or more, they grow extra tails, change colour or otherwise become marked as different. This usually leads to the development of at least human-level intelligence and supernatural abilities. The exact changes depend on the animal and the legend. Objects can also gain sentience as they age. This happens most frequently with swords and mirrors, both of which were already common *shintai* or 'god-bodies' at Shinto shrines. Medieval Japanese legends describe everything from holy jewels to magical living pots achieving spiritual awakening and developing spirits.[26] Those discussed below are only the most common examples.

Foxes

Foxes (Jp. *kitsune*) are among the most famous animal spirits, and possibly the most well-known *yōkai* in Japan today. The red fox (*Vulpes vulpes*) is native to Japan, as it is in much of the northern hemisphere. Foxes are secretive hunters who are rarely seen even when they live nearby, and these traits are played up in folklore. In Japan, foxes are believed to be shapeshifters. They can take many forms other than their real appearance, although most often they transform into beautiful women, elderly men or young children of indeterminate gender. Foxes in human form attempt to swindle or otherwise take advantage of well-meaning humans. This can range from simple schemes, such as pretending to be a poor beggar to steal a human's food or money, to much more complex and dangerous plots. As in the legend of Kaya no Yoshifuji (see Chapter 5), foxes may seduce people and take them to their dens, which appear to be beautiful palaces. While under a fox's spell, the hapless victim is slowly drained of life energy, usually through sex. Without intervention, the victim will eventually die.[27]

Not all foxes are malicious. Inari 稲荷 (also called Inari Ōkami or Ō-inari), a fertility *kami*, is associated with foxes that act as his messengers. Inari's foxes are white with golden eyes. They possess all the powers of traditional foxes, but they use them exclusively to help Inari bring prosperity to farmers and villagers.[28] Worship of Inari derives from a fusion of better-known *kami* from the ancient myths, such as Izanagi and Ninigi. How and when these gods were grouped together as a single protector of agriculture is unknown, but by the 15th century shrines to Inari had appeared across the archipelago. The most famous is the great Fushimi Inari Shrine just outside of Kyoto, which has over 300 bright

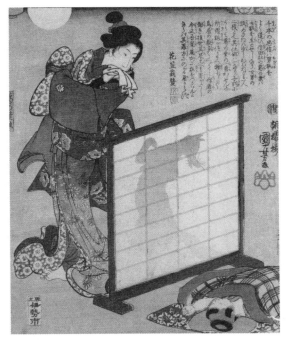

A fox is disguised as a beautiful woman, but her true form
is revealed by her shadow.

red *torii* gates climbing the mountain path to the main shrine. Inari
represents agricultural prosperity, particularly over rice fields and tea
plantations. His association with foxes may derive from their habit of
chasing vermin in fields. He and his foxes remain prominent mythical
figures in Japan today, often with smaller subsidiary shrines at larger
Shinto or even Buddhist sites.

A popular food item sold at sushi restaurants, *inari-zushi* consists
of a tofu-skin coating over vinegar-soaked sushi rice. The edges of the
tofu skin are pointed, and look like fox ears, hence the name. Due to
this connection, tofu skin of similar types is often referred to as *kitsune*
in other contexts. Popular dishes in the Kansai region of Japan (Osaka,
Kyoto, Nara and their environs) include *kitsune udon* and *kitsune soba*,
both noodle dishes featuring tofu skins (not fox meat!).

Tanuki

The *tanuki* 狸 or raccoon dog (*Nyctereutes procyonoides*) is a relative of the dog family native to Japan. These shy nocturnal creatures look similar to the raccoon that is native to North America. However, as members of the dog family they come from a different genetic lineage. Their name is often mistranslated as 'raccoon' in English (the Japanese word for the North American raccoon is actually *araiguma*, 'hand-washing bear'), but they are different animals.

In Japan, *tanuki* have long been considered shapeshifting creatures, similar to foxes. Unlike foxes, however, *tanuki* are generally pleasant or well-meaning. They play pranks on humans but do so in less hurtful ways, rarely anything more than a minor inconvenience to the victim, and in some cases actually improve their lives. *Tanuki*'s magic resides in their testicles, which are often pictured as being very large. How this affects female *tanuki* is not specified in folklore. Real male *tanuki* do have prominent testicles, which may be the origin of the myth, although they are nowhere near as prominent as Edo Period and later art would have one believe.[29]

Shapeshifting *tanuki* appear in records as far back as the *Nihonshoki*. They make occasional but regular appearances in Heian and Kamakura Period literature and are widespread in common folktales as of the late medieval era. They remain popular in the present, and statues of friendly *tanuki* with large testicles can be found outside restaurants and stores in many parts of the country. The 1994 animated film *Pom Poko* by acclaimed director Takahata Isao (1935–2018) is one of several famous modern works that delves

A *tanuki* or raccoon dog, said to be a kinder equivalent of the shapeshifting fox.

into *tanuki* folklore. The film concerns the battle between greedy land developers and a forest of magical *tanuki* who use their magic to try to prevent its destruction.

Dragons and Snakes

Snakes and dragons are separate but sometimes related entities in Japanese myth. Dragon and snake mythologies overlap in much of South and East Asia. Japan absorbed Indian and Chinese snake and dragon lore in addition to its own, and the overlaps are clearly visible in some contexts. Japan has many native snake species, but only a few are venomous, and none are large. There are no native crocodilians in the archipelago, no large lizards and, as far as can be scientifically proven, no dragons. Yet even the early myths found in the *Kojiki* and *Nihonshoki* reference large reptilian creatures. Whether or not these are due to continental influence is unknown.

Both the *Kojiki* and the *Nihonshoki* feature the Yamata-no-Orochi, an eight-headed and eight-tailed reptile with which Susanowo does battle (see Chapter 2). The Orochi is described in detail, yet its actual body shape remains elusive. It has eight heads and eight tails; its body fills eight valleys and covers eight mountains; its back is covered with pine trees; it oozes red fluid from its stomach; and its eyes are brilliant red, like Chinese lanterns. However, legs are never mentioned, only scales. In the *Nihonshoki*, the characters for 'large snake' 大蛇 are used to write the word *orochi*, and so for centuries it has been depicted as a giant multi-headed snake. In fact, the word *orochi* (*worochi* in older Japanese texts) is of unknown origin and meaning. Although the monster has been depicted as a serpent, it could represent many other destructive forces, from a flooding river tainted by runoff from ironworking to a volcanic eruption. Unfortunately, we may never know the 'correct' interpretation, if one ever existed.[30]

The Chinese concept of dragons entered Japan very early. In China, dragons are serpentine creatures with four legs but no wings. They live in water and are attuned to that element. They also fly and are at home in the clouds and sky as well as in lakes, rivers or the sea. Depending on the source, dragons exhale lightning, storms or simply clouds. They are regal creatures, powerful and knowledgable. Dragons can be great allies of humans, but they generally see humans as beneath them, and are just as easily provoked to anger as to helpfulness.

This Chinese description of dragons was brought to Japan at least as early as the 7th century. Dragons in a Chinese style of the Northern and Southern Dynasties (220–589 CE) appear in the architecture at the Hōryūji Temple outside of Nara. These dragons are carved on woodwork dating from around the year 700. Nara Period (710–784) historical texts reference dragons like those seen in Chinese sources. By the early Heian Period, Watatsumi, the three-in-one god of the sea (see Chapter 2), had been fused with the Dragon King of the Sea 竜王 (Jp. Ryūō). The Dragon King, who lives in a palace at the bottom of the sea, is the master of all dragonkind and a powerful god in his own right. After the fusion, Watatsumi gained all these traits, in addition to his earlier status as the protector of sea crossings.

Another famous story involving dragons and the sea, retold often in the Muromachi and Edo Periods, is that of Urashima Tarō 浦島太郎.

A dragon flies through storm clouds. Like most East Asian dragons, it is a creature of water and air, not fire.

Dragons

- Dragons in Japanese myth are minor *kami*, often the gods of seas and rivers, with both Chinese dragon and Indian snake characteristics.
- Chinese dragons have serpentine bodies, four legs and no wings, but can fly. They live in water and in the sky, exhaling storms and lightning. They are wise and powerful, but can be dangerous as well as helpful.
- Indian *nāga* are half-snake, half-human minor deities who live in the Buddhist underworld and are unfailingly moral and compassionate.
- The dragon-like Yamata-no-Orochi described in the ancient Japanese chronicles has eight heads and tails; its body fills eight valleys and its back is covered with pine trees. It may represent destructive floods or volcanoes.

Originally based on a much older tale recounted in works from the Nara and early Heian Periods, this story has been likened to the American 'Rip Van Winkle'. Long ago, a man named Urashima Tarō encountered a group of children on a beach. The children were torturing a small turtle, preventing it from getting back to the ocean. Urashima chased them away and saved the turtle's life. Several days later, Urashima was fishing when a boat magically rose out of the sea and approached him. In it was the small turtle he had saved, who transformed into a beautiful woman. She revealed that she was the daughter of the Dragon King of the Sea, and that the turtle was her less fearsome form (as opposed to either dragon or princess). As repayment for saving her life, she offered Urashima her hand in marriage. He took it, and went with her to the Dragon King's Palace, where they lived as man and wife for a number of days – in some versions, years – in complete happiness.

One day, however, Urashima felt homesick and missed his mother and father, and wished to return to them. His wife let him depart, but gave him a special box, known as a *tamatebako*, and told him only to open it if he could no longer bear living. Urashima returned to the surface but found that his village had changed. No one he knew was still alive, and

The daughter of the Dragon King sees off Urashima Tarō as he
returns home, not knowing how much time has passed.

as he made enquiries, he found out that his parents had died long ago.
How long he had been gone varies with the source, ranging from 80 to
800 years, but he was stuck out of his time regardless. Unable to bear
living when everything he knew and everyone he loved had passed away,
Urashima opened the *tamatebako*, which contained only a white mist.
The mist turned him into an old man, and he died peacefully, able to be
reunited with his family at last.[31]

Dragons have become low-level *kami* in Japan. Many of the gods of
streams or rivers are envisioned as dragons. The sea is likewise their
domain, as are storms. However, dragons have also become associated
with wisdom and Buddhist morality, and linked with snakes, via the
Indian *nāga*. *Nāga* are half-snake, half-human residents of the ancient
Indian underworld. Possessing great wisdom and usually equally great
compassion and goodwill for humans, they are powerful lesser deities.
Nāga still fulfil this role in contemporary Hinduism.

Like so many other facets of ancient Indian belief, the *nāga* were subsumed into Buddhism early in its development. Several ancient *sutras*

discuss the nature of *nāga* and present them as wise and powerful helpers of Buddhism. These ideas were communicated to China, where the image of the *nāga* encountered the pre-existing idea of the dragon. Both creatures were partially snakelike, wise and powerful, and generally aligned with good. Although they remained separate in much of East Asian Buddhist mythology, images of dragons and *nāga* became confused enough that each borrowed aspects of the other. Dragons became representative of the power of Buddhism, whereas *nāga* – and thus snakes – became associated with water.

Snakes thus take on powerful roles in East Asian myth as well. *Nāga* can change into fully human form in Indian myths, and the same appears to happen for snakes in Chinese and Japanese folklore. Unlike the Christian-influenced image of snakes as deceivers popular in the West, snakes in Japan are sources of wisdom. They whisper secrets and can be powerful oracles. However, they are not necessarily good, and when scorned or threatened, can become powerful enemies.

One particularly famous tale is that of 'Lady White Snake', in which a young man falls in love with a woman who is actually a shapeshifted serpent. When the man learns about her true form and is horrified, the woman seeks revenge, transforming into a great white snake bent on killing him. Originally a Chinese folktale from the 4th or 5th century CE, the story of Lady White Snake had arrived in Japan by the mid-Heian Period at the latest. It was the source for a variety of localized folktales, such as the legend of the Dōjōji Temple in the 13th-century *Konjaku monogatarishū*, and the later Noh play *Dōjōji* (*c.* 15th century).

Cats

Stories of pet cats are known from at least as far back as the Heian Period. Cats kept by the emperor appear in several works of Heian literature, such as Sei Shōnagon's (*c.* 966–1017 or 1026) humorous tale collection *Makura no sōshi* ('The Pillow Book', *c.* 1015).[32] By the 14th century, there are tales of magical cats as well. Like foxes, they tend to be individuals who have lived beyond a certain point (usually a century), and often have multiple tails. This may have led to the Japanese practice of bobbing cats' tails, which is still sporadically done, in an attempt to protect humans from their magic. As one native breed of cats, the Japanese bobtail, has a naturally bobbed tail due to a genetic mutation, this superstition may also have been a response to the presence of so many naturally bobtailed cats.

One well-known example of a cat becoming a *yōkai* is the *nekomata* 猫また. These are cats that live for a hundred years or more, upon which they increase in size to that of a wolf and grow a second tail. Once this occurs, *nekomata* run away to the forests, where they seek out humans to hunt and eat. One anecdote, preserved in the 14th-century work *Tsurezuregusa* ('Essays in Idleness'), discusses a man who was attacked by a *nekomata* on his way home at night. He ran screaming through the village, only to find a light source which revealed that what he had believed to be the giant *yōkai* cat was his own dog, trying to welcome him back.[33]

The *bakeneko* 化け猫 or 'shape-shifting cat' is another *yōkai* similar to the *nekomata*. Instead of becoming wolf-sized feral animals, these are long-lived cats whose age and tails give them the power to shapeshift.

A cat that has lived for a hundred years can grow a second tail and become a *nekomata*, able to disguise itself in clothing and wield magical powers.

Magical cats

- Magical cats often have many tails. The Japanese practice of bobbing cats' tails may have developed to protect humans from their magic.
- *Nekomata*: cats that have lived for a hundred years grow another tail and run to the forest, seeking humans to eat.
- *Bakeneko*: shape-shifting cat. Their age and many tails grant them the ability to shape-shift. They are mischievous and do as they will, sometimes hunting or helping humans.
- *Manekineko*: the 'inviting cat' that is often seen in statues welcoming people into stores, restaurants and businesses. It gestures with its paw facing down, inviting good luck in.

As with foxes or *tanuki*, *bakeneko* are mischievous; however, they are more amoral than hurtful foxes or helpful *tanuki*. *Bakeneko* tend to do what they will, whether that is hunting humans or helping them – very like a cat, as cat owners would say.

Starting in the Edo Period, cats also became symbols of luck. This is because a cat's gesture of pawing with a paw face-down is like the Japanese hand signal used to invite people inside a store or home, which led to the idea that cats were inviting good luck. This is the origin of the *manekineko* or 'inviting cat' statue often seen at restaurants and other businesses.

Other Magical Animals

There are many other types of animals who have magical or spiritual powers in Japan. These animals are often counted among *yōkai*. Space constraints prevent addressing most of them in detail, but here are brief descriptions of several that appear frequently in Japanese lore.

Turtles (*kame*) and cranes (*tsuru*) are symbols of longevity. The turtle's association with long life may derive from the Urashima Tarō legend discussed above. There is a common proverb dating back at least into the Edo Period that the turtle 'lives for 100 years, and the crane, for 1,000'. Both animals are often associated with pine trees (*matsu*), another longevity symbol. The word for pine is the same as that for the verb 'to wait', which may be one reason for this association.

Rabbits appear in some ancient myths, particularly takes of the earth god Ōkuninushi, as told in the *Kojiki*. As a young deity, Ōkuninushi rescues a rabbit who lost a race with a crocodile (or perhaps a shark; see Chapter 2) and gives it fluffy white fur to wear as compensation. Rabbits are also lunar symbols, a borrowing from China. In ancient Chinese myth, the dark plains on the moon do not make a shape of a man as in most Western cultures, but a rabbit. This gets conflated with the legend of Chang'e 嫦娥 (Jp. Jōga or Kōga), a Chinese moon goddess. Chang'e

supposedly lives in the moon, where she makes the elixir of immortality by pounding it with a mortar and pestle. The rabbit-shape seen on the moon thus takes over her function, pounding magical food. In Japan, this magical food is imagined as sweet rice paste or *mochi* instead of a liquid elixir.

Centipedes and spiders have negative associations in Japanese myths. Japan is host to a large and colourful species of orb weaver spider known as the Jorō spider (*Trichonephila clavate*). The females, which are the most visible of the sexes, spin huge webs every August. They eat the much smaller males after mating, which may have given rise to the similarly named

Rabbits have been associated with the moon in much of East Asia ever since ancient Chinese myths first linked the two.

jorōgumo 女郎蜘蛛 (lit. 'woman-spider'), a dangerous *yōkai*. These are spiders that transform into beautiful women and lure travellers to their homes, where they have sex with them and then behead them to drink their blood. Centipedes are likewise regarded as dangerous creatures. Although they do not take on human form, they can grow to immense sizes in Japanese folklore. Curiously, centipedes often are the mortal enemies of snakes in late medieval and Edo Period folktales. One example occurs in folklore surrounding the Akagi Shrine in modern Maebashi, Gunma Prefecture. The shrine worships the deity of nearby Mt. Akagi, often pictured as a giant centipede who fought an equally gigantic snake, representing Mt. Futara in modern Tochigi Prefecture, over a lake that lies between their domains. Unfortunately, the centipede lost, and the lake today belongs to the Futara deity and its shrine (Nikkō Futara Shrine, in modern Nikkō, Tochigi Prefecture). Their battle gave its name to Senjōgahara ('Battlefield Plain'), a swampland and current RAMSAR site on the border of the modern prefectures.[34]

The legend that earthquakes were caused by catfish (*namazu*) dates to the late Heian or early Kamakura Period. However, this belief faded from popular folklore until the mid-Edo Period, when a string of natural disasters occurred (including the 1705 eruption of Mt Fuji). Eighteenth- and early 19th-century townsfolk revived the idea that Japan lies atop a giant sleeping catfish whose occasional rolling produces earthquakes and volcanic eruptions. This folk belief even let to a surge in the popularity of protective amulets to help prevent rocking the catfish, or to keep one safe from its earthquakes.

Monkeys, wild boars and various members of the weasel family also take their places in myths. These animals' roles and abilities are usually dependent on specific regional legends. Monkeys frequently appear as human-like characters, or as incarnations of mountain *kami*. Boars are dangerous yet common inhabitants of the forests, and thus can also be invoked as avatars of the equally wild *kami* of mountains and other wild places. Weasels, martins and stoats appear less often in folklore, but are also related to a variety of regional *yōkai*. One example that has become more famous in the modern day is the *kamaitachi* 鎌鼬 ('sickle-weasel'), a scythe- or sickle-bearing weasel who transforms into a whirlwind, and

A *kamaitachi*, a weasel *kami*, creates a whirlwind
with its magical sickle.

can cut people down and kill them before they even know they have
been attacked. *Kamaitachi* legends originate mostly in northern Honshu,
although they can be found around the archipelago.

Tsukumogami and Object Spirits

One final group of spirits in Japanese folklore are those of inanimate
objects. As with animals, objects that survive for a long time can manifest
as *kami* of their own. In general, such object spirits are called *tsukumogami*
付喪神. *Tsukumogami* are most often tools that have been lovingly cared
for and used for more than a century. They can also be weapons, or even
household items such as folding screens or fans. They usually manifest
as human apparitions, whether ghostly or solid. In some cases, this is
driven by sadness that the tool or item is no longer used. In other cases,
a *tsukumogami* forms in order to reward the owner of such an item.

Perhaps the creepiest incarnation of *tsukumogami* are those based on folding screens or paintings, which are said to manifest eyes and heads that watch people like ghostly eavesdroppers.[35]

Forsaken objects can also become *tsukumogami*. Swords left to rust for a century or once-loved tools that were thrown away can, with enough time, become sentient spirits. These are more often dangerous than *tsukumogami* of objects that are still beloved and/or used. Such negative *tsukumogami* may seek revenge against those who discarded them, or otherwise cause problems for people. They are among the *yōkai* that must be sealed away by various magicians such as *onmyōji* or *yamabushi*.

The world of premodern Japan was truly flush with spirits, and this chapter has only scratched the surface of the rich body of Japanese religious and folk beliefs. The skies were host to continental and native gods and *tennin*. The cities were the homes of the gods of luck and industry, as well as those who brought epidemics and calamities. The countryside was haunted by *yōkai* of many types, and even animals and objects were spiritually potent. Stories of this world of spirits spread wider and wider in the modern era. By the Edo Period, the development of woodblock printing and

A *tsukumogami*, an object that has gained sentience as a *kami*, here formed out of various dishware.

Tsukumogami

- Spirits (*kami*) of inanimate objects, usually old ones used for more than a century: weapons, tools, or household items.
- Can manifest as human apparitions, especially when a tool is no longer used, or to reward the owner.
- Unloved and unused objects can manifest more dangerous *tsukumogami*, which often seek revenge.

the spread of education allowed the population of Japan to become much more literate than ever before. The large reading public was hungry for ghost stories, supernatural romances and the great tales of earlier eras. This hunger spread the stories recounted in this chapter far and wide, and encouraged people like Toriyama Sekien to begin collecting those that had never been written down.

Due to this explosion of writing in the Edo Period, as well as a little luck, many of these stories still survive today, and it is thanks to them that we know much about the legends and folklore of Japan. Although not the same as either the ancient Shinto mythology or that of Japanese Buddhism, these legends are important. They reveal the matrix of popular beliefs that surrounded the older myths discussed in previous chapters, at least from the 17th century onwards. They also give context for how premodern Japanese understood the spiritual world, and even how many modern Japanese continue to understand it. As we move on to the most recent developments in Japanese mythology in the next chapter, we need to understand not only the mythic cycles of the main religions, but this wider world of spirits as well.

7

THE NEW MYTHOLOGIES
OF MODERN JAPAN

In 1854, a fleet of American ships led by Commodore Matthew Perry sailed into Edo Bay (modern Tokyo Bay). This was the most egregious Western breach of Japan's isolation in the 225 years since it had been enacted. The Sakoku edicts of 1639 forbade any Westerners to come to Japan other than the Dutch traders at Nagasaki. By breaking them, the Americans guaranteed a dramatic response. However, the Tokugawa Shogunate soon realized that these boats – the so-called *kurofune* or 'Black Ships' – represented technology beyond anything they possessed. To attack them would have been to open Edo itself to invasion, or so the Shogunate feared. Instead, despite centuries of claiming that no foreigner had the standing to meet with the Shogun or his Council of Elders, the Tokugawa government capitulated to American demands for negotiation.

The result, the Treaty of Kanagawa, was signed in 1854. Japan opened five 'treaty ports' to American, British and Russian ships. The rest of the European powers followed suit except for the Dutch, who were left behind as their monopoly fell apart. The arrival of so many Europeans triggered domestic tensions in Japan. People began to feel that the Shogunate was unable to protect them. Several incidents involving foreigners occurred during the late 1850s and early 1860s, and each ended with the Shogunate giving in to foreign demands for compensation. The Shogunate's power-lessness proved to many people across Japan that their fears of Western colonization were well-founded. Reform-minded Japanese eventually gathered around the newly enthroned Emperor Meiji (1852–1912) and demanded a new government. In 1867, the seventeenth Tokugawa Shogun, Tokugawa Yoshinobu 德川慶喜 (1837–1913), abdicated without naming

Emperor Meiji (r. 1868–1912; right), with his son, Prince Yoshihito, and main wife, Empress Shōken (left). The prince's mother, a lower-ranking imperial concubine, was left out of pictures intended to portray a Western-style nuclear imperial family.

an heir, formally ending the Shogunate. Although a brief war followed in 1868, it was mostly a clean-up of Shogunate hardliners. What we know today as the Meiji Restoration had already occurred, and Japan would never be the same.[1]

The decades following the Meiji Restoration saw Japan flooded with new technologies and culture. Much of this was from Europe, which had been unable to trade openly with Japan since the country was closed to foreigners in 1639. The entirety of the later Renaissance, the Enlightenment and much of the European 19th century were thus dumped on Japan all at once. The influx of scientific, artistic, social and philosophical information triggered massive changes, many of which were embraced by the Meiji government. By 1905, when a militarily resurgent Japan defeated Russia in the Russo-Japanese War, the country had been transformed.

The Edo Period had seen an unprecedented number of regional and local legends preserved in printed texts. The great literature of the previous centuries had also become much more widespread. Yet these were all ideas that, to some degree, had already been present in Japan. The Meiji Period (1868–1912), however, saw the introduction of ideas that were very new, and these imported concepts had a strong effect on the country's belief systems. Foreign ideas added to, altered or destroyed many longstanding elements of earlier Japanese culture. Folklore and mythology were no exceptions.

The Meiji government rushed to modernize the country so as to avoid being colonized like so much of the non-Western world had been. This rush led to (among other things) attempts to control and reshape Japan's religions to match those of the European nations. The forced separation of Shinto and Buddhism discussed in Chapter 5 was only one aspect of this process. Scholars trained in Western versions of the scientific method began to study Japanese folklore anew, and in the process added their own interpretations. Finally, the development of modern popular culture led not only to redeployments of older myths, but to new creations as well, such as literary works in the style of Western fairy tales.

This chapter will look at how the mythology of premodern Japan interacted with the sudden influx of 'modern' and 'Western' culture during the late 19th and early 20th centuries, and, later, with the tremendous societal changes that occurred after Japan's loss in the Second World War. Japanese mythology is also still very much alive today. In postwar and contemporary Japan, particularly with the expansion of urbanization and popular cultures, urban legends have grown up in ways that build on and parallel those of the past. Contemporary popular media such as anime and manga also delve deeply into both premodern mythology and the newer developments of modern Japan. Through examining how Japanese mythology survived into the modern era, we can see how and why it remains so vital even now.

STATE SHINTO AND NATIONAL MYTHOLOGY

The major Western powers that Japan encountered during the late 19th century were Britain, Germany, France, Russia and the United States. Several of the European powers had state religions, defined as a religion that is officially supported by the government of a nation and protected and promoted by law. As a source of national pride, focus and identity for citizens, a state religion is a useful way to help bind that country together. The Meiji government thus wanted to have its own national religion to accomplish the same goal of creating a strong, self-identifying citizenry.[2]

There was a problem, however: Japan had no single dominant religion. Buddhism and Shinto provided the two main religious traditions, and Confucianism (especially via Neo-Confucianism) remained strong after the Edo Period. Of these options, Shinto seemed the most obvious choice. It was the only one that was truly native to Japan and that explicitly placed the emperor in a position of authority. Yet Shinto was problematic for other reasons. It lacked a detailed moral and ethical philosophy separate from that brought by Buddhism. It did not have holy texts or a strongly organized moral system. In order to make it into a national religion that resembled the Christian state religions of the European powers, the Meiji government had to either find these elements somewhere else or make them up from scratch. The government chose to do both, issuing a series of decisions that established the doctrine and texts of what became known as State Shinto 国家神道 (*Kokka Shintō*).[3]

The term 'State Shinto' was not actually used until after the Second World War. As far as the Japanese government between 1868 and 1945 was concerned, the practices that we now call State Shinto were just 'Shinto'. Not giving it a different name allowed the government to hide the fact that it was not just reinvigorating an ancient religion but actually making up a new one. The division of Buddhism from Shinto was the first stage of this process (see Chapter 5). The addition of new beliefs, practices and holidays was the second. These additions built up Shinto into a formal religion that was theoretically extensive enough to stand on its own without Buddhism.[4]

The first of these new beliefs, and the most controversial, was the worship of the emperor as a god. The emperor had always been an impor-

---

State Shinto
- State religion introduced by the 19th-century Meiji government.
- The term State Shinto was not used until after the Second World War.
- Government-issued texts and doctrines created a new religion.
- Artificially separated Shinto from Buddhism.
- The emperor was for the first time to be worshipped as a living god.
- Events in ancient chronicles were celebrated by new holidays.
- Reworked folktales such as Momotarō, the 'Peach Boy', were promoted.

The great *torii* gate at the entrance to the main complex of Meiji Shrine.
The simple yet massive architecture is typical of State Shinto shrines
built between 1870 and 1945.

tant figure, even in the ancient myths. He (or she) is descended from the
Sun Goddess Amaterasu and has ritual and political significance because
of his divine heritage. Early emperors were described as *kami*, or interacted
with *kami* as if on the same level to them. However, the emperor himself
had never been a direct object of worship. Even rituals like the great New
Year's Day Ceremony, in which the entire court proclaimed its loyalty to
the emperor at the palace, had previously only been regarded as political pageantry. The closest ancient texts get to outright worshipping the
emperor can be found in funerary poems from the *Man'yōshū* (the earliest
anthology of poetry in Japanese, *c.* 780). Some of these poems refer to
the emperor with specific words that translate into variations on 'godlike
power' or 'manifest deity'. However, this language was not widely used
at any later point until the Meiji Restoration. During his life, Emperor
Meiji was referred to as a living deity using words borrowed from the
Man'yōshū and other early works. After his death, he was enshrined at
a newly built shrine complex in Tokyo, the still-important Meiji Shrine,
where his spirit was worshipped as a guardian of the Japanese people,
and as a source of prosperity.

Emperor Meiji makes a visit to Yasukuni Shrine. Built under State Shinto to enshrine Japan's war dead, today it fuels controversies concerning Japan's colonial past.

The emphasis on the emperor as living god was not the only change in Shinto beliefs. New holidays were created by the Meiji government to honour events in the ancient chronicles. These included the founding of Japan by the legendary Emperor Jinmu, which was now assigned a date: 11 February, 660 BCE. Newly calculated and 'scientifically' explained versions of the ancient myths were taught in schools as official history starting in the 1880s. This not only encouraged a new sense of 'Japanese' pride based on Japan's long and magical national history, but also taught citizens these new interpretations of the myths from an early age.[5]

Japan fought three significant wars during the Meiji Period: the Satsuma Rebellion of 1877, the Sino-Japanese War in 1894–95, and the Russo-Japanese War in 1904–05. The new and modernized Imperial Army was victorious in each engagement, but there were still casualties. These casualties of war were enshrined at another new site in Tokyo, Yasukuni Shrine, which is still important today though also controversial. It enshrines all the war dead from Japan's military conflicts so they can not only be remembered, but actually prayed to as *kami* of war, protection and sacrifice.

The wars of the Meiji Period also resulted in Japan gaining colonies for the first time. The Edo Period had seen the taking of the Ryūkyū Islands (modern Okinawa Prefecture), as well as the entire northern island of

Hokkaido. However, these areas were not colonized in the modern sense of the term until after the Meiji Restoration. Starting in the 1870s, large numbers of Japanese were encouraged to settle in Hokkaido and, to a lesser extent, in the Ryūkyūs. The Sino-Japanese and Russo-Japanese Wars also ended with Japan gaining further territories: Formosa (modern Taiwan) from China, the Kurile Islands and southern Sakhalin from Russia, and eventually the entire Korean Peninsula (formally annexed in 1910). These were all regions populated by non-Japanese who had never been part of a Shinto system. Shinto now needed to expand to accommodate the colonies and their non-Japanese populations. It did so by creating new myths.

Korea was the easiest colonial conquest to justify with new mythology. The chronicles already told the legend of Empress Jingū (recounted in Chapter 3), who supposedly conquered at least the southern half of the peninsula. Jingū's mythical conquests not only justified the annexation of Korea to the Japanese government but also provided a way to include the Koreans in State Shinto. Small numbers of Shinto shrines had been constructed on the Korean peninsula by Japanese traders or exiles since Toyotomi Hideyoshi's invasions in the 1590s, and were now rapidly enlarged under the colonial government. Korean ancestors were enshrined as *kami* (of a sort), like the ancestors of Japanese clans, but of lower status. This allowed Koreans to serve and worship the emperor as

Korea Shrine, a State Shinto construction in occupied Korea, shown here in a surviving photograph from the 1930s.

well, from a lower social level than the Japanese. As the colonial period continued, worship at Shinto shrines became mandatory for most Koreans, as part of a strategic attempt at cultural indoctrination by the Japanese colonial authorities.[6]

Taiwan, Sakhalin and other Japanese territories were the sites of similar new state-sponsored Shinto belief systems. As there was no historical basis for Japanese control over these areas, their native populations were not considered to be long-lost subjects of the Japanese. Instead they were told that they were the lucky ones, protected from being colonized by Europe in order to help the Japanese liberate the rest of Asia. Their own religious beliefs were left alone more than those of Koreans but were still clearly placed below the worship of the Japanese gods, the emperor chief among them. As in Korea, new shrines worshipping local cultural heroes and generalized ideas of 'the state' were founded to promote Shinto, albeit to a lesser extent than elsewhere.[7] State Shinto may not have completely embraced the colonies outside of Korea, but it had no problem subjugating them.

Folktales from later eras were also made into tools of nationalism in the early 20th century. One that became even more famous as a result is the story of Momotarō 桃太郎, the 'Peach Boy'. Originally dating to the 15th or 16th centuries, the legend of Momotarō was a well-known tale by the Edo Period. The tale begins when an old childless couple find a peach floating down a river. They pick up the peach, and it splits open to reveal a baby boy inside. They name him Momotarō after the peach, and he grows up valiant and strong. Once he reaches adulthood, Momotarō decides to set out to Onigashima, the island of *oni*, to defeat the powerful tribe of *oni* bandits who live there. On the way he befriends three different animals: a dog, a pheasant and a monkey. He offers each animal servings of his rations in return for their service and, with their help, defeats the *oni* of Onigashima and returns with their treasure.

The legend of Momotarō remained popular through the Meiji Period, but gained new meaning once Japan had an active colonial empire. In a version first released in school textbooks in the early 1930s, Momotarō was explicitly representative of the Imperial Army. The three animals he befriended each hailed from one of Japan's colonies. In this version, the poor and downtrodden animals begged Momotarō to make them into something greater; by accompanying him, they too had the chance to serve the emperor and achieve glory. The underlying message is clear, even to a contemporary audience: the colonies are lesser beings, but still necessary to ultimate victory so long as they follow and support the homeland. This new version of the Momotarō myth was made into an animated film, one of the first to come out of Japan. Known as *Momotarō's Divine Warriors of the Sea* (1945), it is both a deeply uncomfortable propaganda film and a triumph of early animation.[8]

Many of the greater *kami* were redeployed to serve the nation. As the source of the emperor's power and divinity, Amaterasu was the head of the Japanese pantheon and the most important god to worship. However, she was also female, which created a problem for the prewar government as it was explicitly trying to frame women as a nurturing yet submissive population who existed to support brave and militant Japanese males. Amaterasu herself thus had to be reimagined as a kind yet protective mother figure who invented silk-weaving and other culturally feminine things. In order to promote militarism, other (male) gods also had to be reimagined as important. Hachiman was brought back into the national focus as the patron deity of the military, directly inspiring its success. Susanowo was also celebrated as a source of Japanese martial ferocity, but his lack of subservience to Amaterasu (that is, to the divine ancestor of the imperial line) was a problem, so his role was given less importance than Hachiman's. Worship of Buddhist deities was not outright forbidden but was heavily deemphasized. As foreign gods, they were regarded as responsible for Japan's cultural decline and 'feminization' (as some Meiji scholars notably called it) after the Heian Period.

State Shinto was an excellent propaganda tool prior to the Second World War. It allowed the Japanese state to control the minds and hearts of its citizens while minimizing the chances for religious opposition to political decisions. The increasingly important Japanese military was at one centre of the State Shinto project. The emperor, the source of all peace and prosperity, lay at the other. This system did not survive the war. The American occupation that lasted from 1945 to 1952 made it a priority to demolish State Shinto, viewing it as one of the primary motivations for

Japanese militarism. Textbooks were revised, holidays overhauled, and many other elements – such as the emphasis on military values as a form of worship and the insistence that archaeology and history scholarship should confirm the ancient myths – were simply banned or removed. Yet the legacy of State Shinto remains in Japan.

The major shrines built during the late 19th and early 20th centuries are among the strongest reminders of State Shinto. Yasukuni Shrine remains a source of international controversy today because several war criminals from the Second World War are among the dead enshrined there, and continued visits to the shrine by Japanese politicians appear to mock the suffering experienced by inhabitants of Japan's former colonies. Other State Shinto shrines – such as Meiji Shrine in Tokyo, Heian Shrine in Kyoto and Kashihara Shrine south of Nara – remain important tourist sites. The role of religion generally in Japanese society is problematic today because of State Shinto and its backlash. Ideas of patriotism and militarism, while offensive to some contemporary Japanese for other reasons, are deeply tied to religious ideas put forth prior to 1945. For better or worse, State Shinto and its history is a lens that colours contemporary perceptions of native Japanese mythology and religion.

MYTH AND FANTASY IN POSTWAR JAPAN

Popular culture is often defined as the culture consumed by the majority of people, not just the elite. Recognizable popular culture has existed in Japan since at least the late 17th century. The Edo Period saw woodblock-printed equivalents of popular novels, picture books, pinup posters and even newspapers (in the form of broadsheets). The Meiji Restoration brought new forms of printing and, as the Japanese publishing industry adapted, recognizably modern newspapers and books came into existence. Film technology came to Japan around 1890, and rapidly developed as well. By the 1920s, Japan had popular culture similar to that in the United States or most European countries, with strong publishing and film industries. However, the rise of military rule after 1931 led to a drastic increase in censorship. By the time the Second World War broke out, Japanese popular culture was almost entirely controlled by government censors.[9]

Japan surrendered to the United States on 12 August 1945. Newspapers and magazines began to publish again within days of the surrender. The film industry also rebounded after the war, as directors, staff and actors who had fled the draconian censorship of the wartime government returned to make new films. The American occupation initially censored portrayals of Japanese culture, fearing that it would make people nostalgic for the pre-war system. However, after 1948, as censorship loosened, more films began to take traditional Japanese history and culture as subjects. By 1950, the Japanese film industry was outproducing its pre-war production. Censorship was formally stopped when the American occupation ended in 1952, and the film industry continued to expand dramatically. The 1950s are thus known as the 'Golden Age of Japanese Cinema'.

With the loosening of censorship during the early 1950s, Japanese academics also began to tear into Japanese mythology and folklore. Popular books discussing the 'real' (historical, archaeological, societal) underpinnings of the myths were published. The myths-as-history propaganda system of State Shinto had already been taken apart, but now it was revealed for what it had been. Between the return of traditional folklore to art, and this new academic approach to Japanese mythology, the space grew for fiction based on mythic traditions.[10]

Japanese myths and folklore had been ignored as subjects for cinema immediately after the Second World War, due to their association with militarism and propaganda, but this changed in the late 1950s. One of the most famous works of the postwar era to delve into the Japanese myths was the film epic *The Three Treasures* (Jp. *Nippon tanjō*, 'The Birth of Japan') in 1959. Directed by Inagaki Hiroshi (1905–1980), who had also made several famous samurai films, it featured a star-studded cast including Mifune Toshirō (1920–1997) and Hara Setsuko (1920–2015), two of the most famous actors of the 1950s. The film retold myths from the *Kojiki* and the *Nihonshoki*, including the origins of the archipelago, the conflict between Amaterasu and Susanowo, and the adventures of Yamato Takeru, portraying the events as historical fantasy. Characters wore costumes based on what was known at the time of the Kofun Period (albeit much more glamorous). Special effects brought creatures such as the Yamato-no-Orochi to life and created magical spectacles of the gods' powers. Yet none of this was framed as real or portrayed realistically. Instead, the film adopted the Hollywood style used in big-budget American biblical epics of the 1950s such as *Ben-Hur* and *The Ten Commandments*. *The Three Treasures* was a huge hit in theatres. Although critics today find it unremarkable as an acting showcase, the special effects were groundbreaking for Japan in the 1950s. More importantly, it showed that rather than treating myths like history, they could be woven into a new type of fantasy. This fantasy was based on foreign models but uniquely Japanese in subject matter. Such Japanese-style fantasy would be important in film and other popular media such as manga going forward.

The late 1950s and early 1960s also saw the rise of the manga industry. Comics had come into Japan during the late Meiji Period, paralleling their rise in European magazines. The word *manga* ('idle drawings') originally referred to sketches that helped woodblock artists with their final drawings, but rapidly came to mean this new medium. By the 1920s there were several famous comics running in newspapers and magazines. The modern manga industry did not begin until after the Second World War. New magazines aimed at children began publication in the late 1940s, but comics were only a part of these publications. As manga grew in readership, magazines solely devoted to comics took shape, and by the end of the 1950s, the first modern-style manga magazines appeared. These were telephone-book sized volumes printed on very cheap paper, each containing a single instalment per issue of around twenty different series.[11]

The hit manga *Gegege no Kitarō* ('Cackling Kitarō', also known as 'Kitarō of the Graveyard', 1960–1969), by Mizuki Shigeru (see Chapter 6), was one of the first important series to run in *Weekly Shōnen Magazine*. *Gegege no Kitarō* follows the titular Kitarō, a *yōkai* boy, and his adventures helping other spirits who are now lost in the technologically advanced world of the 1950s. Kitarō and his *yōkai* friends are primarily based on the local folklore of Mizuki's hometown of Matsue, near Izumo in modern Shimane Prefecture. Already famous since ancient times as a location of Susanowo and Ōkuninushi's main shrines, the Izumo region has its own rich set of local legends, *yōkai* and sacred places. Mizuki worked to preserve these elements through his manga. When the work became a huge hit, Mizuki was able to popularize the local mythology of his youth on a national scale. In addition, by showing *yōkai* from the past interacting with the present, *Gegege no Kitarō* set a precedent for using elements of Japan's traditional legends in stories set in other eras, such as Tezuka Osamu's 手塚治虫 masterpiece *Hi no tori* 火の鳥 (*Phoenix*, published intermittently 1954–1988), which moves between the prehistoric past and an imagined future and directly integrates the ancient chronicles with archaeology, similar to the film *The Three Treasures*.

MONSTERS AND METAL MEN

Ancient myths were not the only things reworked into or out of popular culture after the Second World War. Some of the most famous films and manga of the postwar era themselves became additions to Japanese mythology. Although these additions were not seen as 'myths' in a traditional sense, they have since filled similar cultural roles – and have even become reintegrated with older ideas. The two that have received the most attention from fans and scholars alike are *kaijū*, or giant monsters in the vein of Godzilla, and mecha, or giant robots.

Kaijū 怪獣 (lit. 'strange beasts') were originally riffs on American monster films of the 1930s, such as the original *King Kong*. They were strange and mysterious creatures hailing from remote parts of the world – Africa, Southeast Asia or the Pacific Islands. These were places that had been fetishized under colonialism, and were still looked on as backwards in Japan, as in much of the colonizing West at the time. However, the 1954 film *Godzilla* (Jp. *Gojira*) was intended to be more than a horror showcase about exotic monsters. Director Honda Ishirō

Film still from *Godzilla* (1954).

(1911–1993) wanted to make an allegory about the suffering of the Second World War and the dangers of nuclear weapons. The result was a sombre, serious film wherein the monster is a force of nature, unstoppable and indestructible, save through a single scientist's mysterious weapon.[12] In Godzilla and his kin, the Japanese film industry gave birth to a new myth that represents both the fears and hopes of modern society.

The 1950s and early 1960s also gave birth to another modern Japanese myth: that of the giant robot saviour. This paradigm began in the pages of manga aimed at young boys. Its first appearance is often attributed to Tezuka Osamu's 1952–1968 manga *Tetsuwan Atom* ('Atom the Mighty'), published in the United States as *Astro Boy*. This manga, about a robot made in the image of a young boy who saves the world with his techno-logical abilities, was a tremendous hit. An animated television series based on the *Tetsuwan Atom* manga debuted in 1963 and was the first weekly television anime in Japan. Its popularity set up a new phase of Japanese science fiction, wherein robots hold the power to ensure humanity's future.

Tetsuwan Atom was quickly copied by Tezuka's rivals, in both manga and anime. One extremely popular franchise was *Tetsujin 28-gō* ('Iron Giant No. 28', 1956–1966), known in the English-speaking world as *Gigantor*. It features a giant robot controlled via a remote device operated by a young boy on behalf of his late father, the scientist who invented the robot. This set the stage for the boom of so-called 'Super Robots' during the late 1960s and 1970s. Encompassing both manga and television, these series featured young protagonists, usually male, who pilot or control giant mechanical heroes. Series such as *Mazinger Z* (1972–1974), *Getter Robo* (1974–1975) and others made it a winning formula. The human heroes of these works are good-hearted but often powerless without their robots; the robots, while sources of great power, are themselves useless without their human controllers. This new mythology parallels that of the American superhero but is not the same. Through linking ordinary but good-hearted humans with powerful but amoral technology, 'Super Robots' created a belief in the fundamental positivity of human development even in the face of overwhelming odds. These works also envisioned a future in which technology was a powerful force for good. In the decades after the Second World War, this message was not only enjoyed, but needed.[13]

Today, fans and scholars alike call these robots 'mecha' (Jp. *meka*), short for the English 'mechanism' or 'mechanical'. Mecha anime, manga and live-action films have become a genre as wide-ranging and popular as that of *kaijū*. They have also undergone many changes in the subsequent decades. In 1979 the epic animated television series *Kidō senshi Gundam* ('Mobile Suit Gundam') triggered the 'real robot' subgenre. Instead of being technological equivalents of superheroes, the robots (many of which are called 'Gundams') were simply weapons of war such as tanks or jet planes. Their pilots and associated militaries provided the human moral background to the mecha battles. Drawing on the realities of the Cold War, the long-running *Gundam* franchise featured not only individual heroes and villains but entire civilizations with clashing philosophies who waged war using their advanced robots. This new subgenre dominated Japanese science fiction during the 1980s and is still very influential today.

The general societal malaise that followed Japan's economic crash in 1990 also triggered a new subgenre of mecha stories in popular media. This shift began in 1995 with the controversial animated television hit *Neon Genesis Evangelion* (*Shinseiki Evangelion*), which featured levels of gore, psychological torture and philosophical depth beyond that of most prior mainstream anime successes. Combining Jungian philosophy, Christian religious imagery and a focus on the psychology of teens forced into warfare, the series portrayed a world of technology gone amok amid human greed and failures to communicate. The robots – biological monstrosities that were as much metaphors as actual devices – only highlighted the society's problems, rather than bringing about solutions. Reflecting the uncertainties of Japan's new status, and that of the post-Cold War world more broadly, *Neon Genesis Evangelion* set the tone for other works about 'psychological robots' that followed. Just as *kaijū* reflected the anxieties of confronting forces of nature beyond human control, 'psychological robot' mecha fiction is about the breakdown of the dream of a better future through technology first realized in 'super robots'.

Describing both *kaijū* and mecha fiction as myths is not an exaggeration. Godzilla, *Tetsuwan Atom* and their descendants maintain a huge impact on Japanese culture and society. Several generations have grown up surrounded by stories of giant monsters and robots battling for the future of humankind. While these new mythological figures are not worshipped, they do focus the hopes, fears and dreams of people both inside and outside of Japan. These stories also reflect how Japanese society has adapted to the rapid changes of the modern world. They offer a new folklore for contemporary Japan that is obviously fictional and yet emotionally resonant.

URBAN LEGENDS AND DIGITAL MONSTERS

The 'Economic Miracle' is the term used for Japan's rapid reconstruction out of the ashes of the Second World War. Starting around 1965, the Japanese economy began to boom, and by 1980 Japan had regained its place among the wealthiest and most advanced nations in the world, despite having been completely ruined only thirty years before. As Tokyo and the other major cities rebuilt, they were completely transformed. Skyscrapers and modern apartment blocks created the steel and concrete cityscapes of modern Japan.[14] These new urban environments generated their own folklore. In some cases, the urban legends are based on pre-existing folklore, but in other cases they are entirely original.

Ghosts and hauntings are among the most common themes in these new urban legends, which are often retold person to person rather than being transmitted entirely by popular media. The Edo Period fostered a lively tradition of telling ghost stories, and this has remained strong even today. One popular traditional practice is the *hyakumonogatari kaidankai*, or 'hundred ghost stories meeting', when a group of people get together to pass the night telling ghost stories to one another. Traditionally a hundred stories are told, and a candle is snuffed out each time someone finishes. The goal is for listeners to make it to the final candle without feeling so scared that they must leave. The practice originated in the mid-Edo Period as a test of courage for young townspeople. Today it is more often a fun event, mostly done by high school or college students looking for good scares.

Modern urban Japan is just as full of spirits and horrors as was premodern Kyoto (see Chapter 6). Its new *yūrei* and *yōkai* fit alongside equivalent figures from older legends who also still fill the streets. This mix of old and new urban hauntings has deeply influenced modern and contemporary Japanese fiction, including literature, film, live-action television, anime and manga. Japanese horror film, which rose to worldwide fame as a genre during the 1990s, draws heavily from this melding of ancient and modern urban legends. Influential films such as *Ringu* (*The Ring*, 1999) and its sequels were influenced by *onryō* tradition going back to the Heian Period. The success of the so-called 'J-horror' movement may be due to its compelling mix of ancient fear and modern settings.

REMAKING MYTHS FOR THE PRESENT DAY

Ancient mythology is frequently reimagined in popular culture. Myths are larger than life, which makes for good storytelling, particularly for fantasy, science fiction or historical fiction. The mythology of the ancient Japanese chronicles, as well later folktales, have been explicitly retold in manga form on several occasions, particularly through educational manga that repackage the texts with simple visuals and modern dialogue. These retellings are primarily for children who cannot read modern translations, let alone the original texts of the ancient chronicles. In line with postwar developments, they use as much real history as can be safely fit in alongside the myths. Stories about Amaterasu and Susanowo, for example, may feature people wearing Yayoi Period clothing and living in what archaeologists believe Yayoi settlements to have looked like. These retellings are different than popular reworkings of the myths into other genres, such as science fiction or fantasy.

The *Kojiki*'s myths, in particular, have become an important source for both modern reworkings and straight retellings. The *Kojiki* is favoured over the *Nihonshoki* for popular retellings because it not only has a more straightforward narrative but also comes across as bloodier and more visceral to many readers. When stripped of their more questionable details, figures like Yamato Takeru become valiant heroes for young Japanese to look up to – and thus merge very well with heroes of the mecha genre.

The 1990s saw a surge in Japanese myth-based anime and manga series that mingled figures from the ancient chronicles with mecha tropes. The anime television series *Yamato Takeru* ヤマトタケル (1994) is a straightforward retelling of the Yamato Takeru legend, except that it is set in a futuristic outer space. Yamato Takeru is a boy, not an often-enraged man, and controls a powerful robot to defeat enemies (who include Kumaso Takeru and Izumo Takeru). Another television anime, *Blue Seed* ブルー・シード (1995) is both a retelling of and a sequel to the myths concerning Amaterasu and Susanowo's conflict. A newly reawakened Susanowo sends plant-monsters known as *aragami* (lit. 'raging *kami*') to attack Tokyo. A team of military agents and magic-bearing Shinto priestesses must gather to take out Susanowo's forces on behalf of Amaterasu.

The myths of the *Kojiki* and the *Nihonshoki* are reused in other ways, beyond simple retellings. The names of the greater *kami* are often given to weapons or superpowers in modern fictional works. Anyone who knows the basics about Amaterasu, for instance, will have an easier time accepting her name for powers related to fire or light, and the same goes for other well-known gods. In the popular manga and anime franchise *Naruto* ナルト (1999–2017), which concerns the adventures of teenage ninjas in an alternate world, several main characters use a series of techniques named after Amaterasu, Tsukuyomi and Susanowo (among other Shinto deities). The technique 'Amaterasu' enables the user to emit black fire that burns anything, even normal fire. The technique 'Tsukuyomi' traps the target in an illusion. The technique 'Susanowo' creates a skeletal being that acts as a giant suit of armour, almost like a magical mecha. Although these powers are not directly those of any of the *kami* who are their namesakes, they still make sense to anyone with even basic knowledge of the ancient myths.

Video games engage with the *Kojiki* and *Nihonshoki* myth cycles as well. The most obvious example is the *Ōkami* 大神 ('Great God') franchise, which began with a game for the PlayStation 2 in 2006 and continues to the present. The *Ōkami* games see Amaterasu trapped in the form of a wolf. The player must help Amaterasu re scue the other *kami* from villains ranging from the Yamata-no-Orochi to 'Yami', an invented god of darkness. The gameplay uses a 'celestial brush', with which techniques drawn from ink painting produce tangible effects such as creating fire or water, further tying the game to other traditional Japanese cultural elements.

THE PAST, PRESENT AND FUTURE OF JAPANESE MYTHOLOGY

Japanese mythology is not a straightforward system. It combines several different religions, some of which come from far afield. The Japanese myths have also grown and changed over time and continue to do so. They contain layers going back over 1,500 years – not only stories and beliefs sanctioned by different governments, but also the folklore and legends of people in many parts of society.

As this book has attempted to show, these layers can be taken apart and examined. We can read the ancient chronicles for the origins of native myths. We can understand the influx of Buddhist, Confucian, Daoist and other continental faiths, and how each contributed to Japan. We can follow the growth of folklore from when it was first written down into the present. We can even see how the events of Japan's history have shaped its myths and continue to do so today. No matter which way we try to look at the different pieces individually, however, Japanese mythology also remains a single, messy whole that is more than the sum of its parts. And this continuous, organic interweaving of so many different elements remains the most important lesson we can take away from studying Japanese mythology.

It is easy to forget that ancient societies were just as alive as our own. Classical Greece and Rome were many different cultures at many different times. Norse peoples did not have a static belief system, and neither did the ancient Egyptians. Things are always added; meanings continue to change; faiths grow. The mythology of any society is a tangle that may make sense in some ways and be completely impenetrable in others. Yet without studying a living example we can only see the clean lines of a fossil. Japanese mythology gives us that living example.

Modern Japanese popular culture contains many references to older ideas. The myths and legends of Japan from different periods are reworked in modern anime, manga, film, literature and video games. Yet even these works are not the end of Japanese mythology. Instead, they are just another stage, another layer being added on top of older ones. By interacting with these modern works, we bring our own ideas to them – and then we too, whoever we may be, become part of mythology.

NOTES

Chapter 1

1 Piggott, 81.
2 Ibid., 143–44.
3 LeFebvre, 190–91.
4 Breen and Teeuwen, 2.
5 Ibid., 2–4.
6 Cali and Dougill, 20.
7 Gardner, 6–7.
8 Adler, 5.
9 Gardner, 14–15.
10 Wong, 3–5.
11 Laozi, 5–6.

Chapter 2

1 Heldt, *Kojiki*, pp. xvi–xviii.
2 Duthie, *Imperial Imagination*, pp. 111–12.
3 Heldt, *Kojiki*, 7. For the *Nihonshoki* equivalent, see: Aston, *Nihongi*, 2.
4 Heldt, *Kojiki*, 7. All names of deities in the *Kojiki* will use Heldt's translations of their names.
5 Aston, *Nihongi*, 3. All names found in the *Nihonshoki* only will use Aston's translations of their names.
6 Heldt, *Kojiki*, 16.
7 Examples include the animated television series *Blue Seed* (1995–96) and *Kannazuki no miko* ('Priestesses of the Godless Month', 2006).
8 Heldt, *Kojiki*, p. 23.
9 Heldt, *Kojiki*, p. 27.
10 Matsumae, 'The Origin and Growth of the Worship of Amaterasu', p. 5.
11 Gadeleva, 'Susanoo', pp.167–68.
12 'Unearthed Pillar', *Japan Times*, 29 April 2000.
13 Torrence, 'Infrastructure of the Gods', p. 13.
14 Heldt, *Kojiki*, p. 67.

Chapter 3

1 'Constitution of Japan', Office of the Prime Minister of Japan and His Cabinet, http://japan.kantei.go.jp/ constitution_and_government_of_ japan/constitution_e.html, accessed 20 July 2020.
2 Piggott, 91–92.
3 *Nihonshoki 4*, 313.
4 Thakur, 263.
5 *Nihonshoki 1*, 270–71.
6 *Kojiki*, 84–85.
7 Duthie, 319–20.
8 *Kojiki*, 92.
9 *Kojiki*, 102.
10 *Nihonshoki 1*, 386–87.
11 *Kojiki*, 112.
12 *Nihonshoki 1*, 427.
13 *Nihonshoki 1*, 484.
14 Cranston, 162.
15 Cranston, 46.
16 Tsunoda, 13.

Chapter 4

1 Como, 4.
2 Como, 19.
3 Como, 86.
4 Como, 166.
5 Como, 102.
6 Como, 134–35.
7 Keenan, 343–44.
8 Keenan, 348.
9 Keenan, 347.
10 Keenan, 346.
11 Van Goethem, 108–10.
12 Borgen, 89–91.
13 Borgen, 240–43.
14 Borgen, 308.
15 Oyler, 48–50.
16 Scheid, 33–34.
17 Oyler, 51.
18 Oyler, 53.
19 Scheid, 34.
20 Faure 2016a, 140.

Chapter 5

1 'Canon Foreigner', *TV Tropes*.
2 Carrithers, 2–3.
3 *Traditional Japanese Literature*, 535–37.
4 *Japanese Architecture and Art Net Users System*, 'Shaka'.

5   Atone and Hayashi, 9.
6   Inagaki, xiii–xiv.
7   Thành and Leigh, xii.
8   Hodge, 39.
9   Yu, 'Introduction'.
10   *Traditional Japanese Literature*, 545–47.
11   Glassman, 6–8.
12   Kitagawa, 108–110.
13   Lee, 349–350.
14   Faure 2016a, 116–117.
15   Faure 2016a, 125.
16   Faure 2016a, 169.
17   Faure 2016b, 7–9.
18   Faure 2016b, 163.
19   Faure 2016b, 192–195.
20   Faure 2016b, 40.
21   Faure 2016b, 56–57.
22   Faure 2016b, 4–5.
23   Faure 2016b, 6.
24   Teeuwen, 231–233.
25   Rambelli 2008, 254–255.

Chapter 6

1   Reider 2015a, 266–67.
2   *Traditional Japanese Literature*, 169–70.
3   Roemer, 34–35.
4   Rambelli 2018, chapter 5.
5   Faure 2016b, 51.
6   Faure 2016b, 53–54.
7   Faure 2016b, 23–26.
8   Saitō and Premoselli, 279.
9   Tyler, 36.
10   Yamashita and Elacqua, 83.
11   Shigeta and Thompson, 68.
12   Yamashita and Elacqua, 82–83.
13   Miller, 32–33.
14   Foster 2015, chapter 1, section 2b 'Researching *Yōkai*'.
15   Reider 2015b, 7.
16   Reider 2015b, 26.
17   Foster 2008, 89.
18   Foster 1998, 4.
19   Foster 1998, 6–7.
20   Frasier, 181–182.
21   Reider 2015b, 63.

22   Reider 2015b, 85, 88–89.
23   Bowring, 123. Warring spirits, or *asuras*, are immortals who wage eternal war against one another. Beings approaching wisdom or *śrāvakas* and beings approaching enlightenment or *pratyekabuddhas* are stages towards *bodhisattva*-hood that are difficult to define outside of specifics of Mahayana doctrines.
24   Teiser, 126–27.
25   Yoshimura, 149.
26   Foster 2008, 5–7.
27   Foster 2008, 42–43.
28   Smyers, 103.
29   Foster 2008, 36.
30   Weiss, 5, 11.
31   Holmes, 1.
32   *Traditional Japanese Literature*, 250–53.
33   *Traditional Japanese Literature*, 836.
34   Kuribara, 'Hitobito wo tanoshimaseru Akagiyama', 145–47.
35   Foster 2008, 7–8.

Chapter 7

1   Jansen, chapter 10, section 1d 'The Tokugawa Fall'.
2   Hardacre, 30.
3   Hardacre, 52–53.
4   Jansen, chapter 14, section 5 'The State and Culture'.
5   Jansen, chapter 12, section 5 'Mori Arinori and Meiji Education'.
6   Nakajima, 32–33.
7   Nakajima, 38–39.
8   Reider 2015, 108–10.
9   Jansen, chapter 16, section 7 'Urban Culture'.
10   Jansen, chapter 19, section 7 'Postwar Culture'.
11   Power, 10–11.
12   Anderson, 25.
13   Lunning and Freeman, 277.
14   Jansen, chapter 20, section 2 'The Rise to Economic Superpower'.

BIBLIOGRAPHY

Adler, Joseph. 'Confucianism as a Religious Tradition: Linguistic and Methodological Problems'. Gambier, Ohio, USA: Kenyon College (2014). Presentation.

Anderson, Mark. 'Mobilizing *Gojira*: Mourning Modernity as Monstrosity'. *In Godzilla's Footsteps: Japanese Pop Culture Icons on the Global Stage.* Ed. by Tsutsui, William M., and Ito, Michiko. New York: Palgrave Macmillan, 2006.

Atone, Joji and Hayashi, Yoko. *The Promise of Amida Buddha: Hōnen's Path to Bliss.* Boston: Wisdom Publications, 2011.

Borgen, Robert. *Sugawara no Michizane and the Early Heian Court.* Honolulu: University of Hawai'i Press, 1994.

Bowring, Richard. *The Religious Traditions of Japan 500–1600.* Cambridge: Cambridge University Press, 2008.

Breen, John, and Teeuwen, Mark. *A New History of Shinto.* Hoboken, New Jersey, USA: Wiley-Blackwell, 2011.

Cali, Joseph, and Dougill, John. *Shinto Shrines: A Guide to the Sacred Sites of Japan's Ancient Religion.* London: Latitude, 2012.

'Canon Foreigner'. *TV Tropes – the All-Devouring Pop Culture Wiki.* TV Tropes. Web: 10 November 2020. https://tvtropes.org/pmwiki/pmwiki.php/Main/CanonForeigner

Carrithers, Michael. *Buddha: A Very Short Introduction.* Oxford: Oxford University Press, 2007.

Como, Michael I. *Shōtoku: Ethnicity, Ritual and Violence in the Japanese Buddhist Tradition.* Oxford: Oxford University Press, 2008.

'Constitution of Japan'. Office of the Prime Minister of Japan and His Cabinet. http://japan.kantei.go.jp/constitution_and_government_of_japan/constitution_e.html

Cranston, Edwin A. *A Waka Anthology, Volume One: The Gem-Glistening Cup.* Stanford, California, USA: Stanford University Press, 1993.

Duthie, Torquil. Man'yōshū *and the Imperial Imagination in Early Japan.* Leiden: Brill, 2014.

Farris, William Wayne. *Japan to 1600: A Social and Economic History.* Honolulu: University of Hawai'i Press, 2009.

Faure, Bernard. *Gods of Medieval Japan, Volume 1: The Fluid Pantheon.* Honolulu: University of Hawai'i Press, 2016.

— *Gods of Medieval Japan, Volume 2: Protectors and Predators.* Honolulu: University of Hawai'i Press, 2016.

Foster, Michael Dylan. 'The Metamorphosis of the Kappa: Transformation from Folklore to Folklorism in Japan'. *Asian Folklore Studies,* vol. 57 no. 1 (1998).

— *Pandemonium and Parade: Japanese Monsters and the Culture of Yokai.* Berkeley: University of California Press, 2008.

— *The Book of Yokai: Mysterious Creatures of Japanese Folklore.* Berkeley: University of California Press, 2015. Amazon Kindle Edition.

Frasier, Lucy. 'Lost Property Fairy Tales: Ogawa Yōko and Higami Kumiko's Transformations of "The Little Mermaid."' *Marvels and Tales,* vol. 27 no. 2 (2013). 181–93.

Gardner, Daniel K. *Confucianism: A Very Short Introduction.* Oxford: Oxford University Press, 2014.

Glassman, Hank. *The Face of Jizō: Image and Cult in Medieval Japanese Buddhism.* Honolulu: University of Hawai'i Press, 2012.

Hardacre, Helen. 'Creating State Shinto: The Great Promulgation Campaign and the New Religions'. *Journal of Japanese Studies*, vol. 12 no. 1 (1986). 29–63.

Hodge, Stephen. *The Mahā-Vairocana-Abhisambodhi Tantra: With Buddhaguhya's Commentary*. London: Routledge, 2003.

Holmes, Yoshihiko. 'A Chronological Evolution of the Urashima Tarō Story and its Interpretations'. Victoria University of Wellington, 2014. M.A. Thesis.

Hudson, Mark. *Ruins of Identity: Ethnogenesis in the Japanese Islands*. Honolulu: University of Hawai'i Press, 1999.

Inagaki, Hisao. *Three Pure Land Sutras*. Berkeley, California, USA: Numata Center for Buddhist Translation and Research, 2003.

Janssen, Marius B. *The Making of Modern Japan*. Cambridge, Massachusetts, USA: Harvard University Press, 2000. Amazon Kindle Edition.

Japanese Architecture and Art Net User System. Ed. by Parent, Mary Neighbor. http://www.aisf.or.jp/~jaanus/

Keenan, Linda Klepinger. 'En the Ascetic'. *Religions of Japan in Practice*. Ed. by Lopez, David S. Princeton, New Jersey, USA: Princeton University Press, 1999.

Keown, Damien. *Buddhism: A Very Short Introduction*. Oxford: Oxford University Press, 2013.

Kitagawa, Joseph M. 'The Career of Maitreya, with Special Reference to Japan'. *History of Religions*, vol. 21 no. 2 (1981). 107–25.

Kuribara, Hisashi. 'Hitobito wo tanoshimaseru Akagiyama no miryoku 2: Akagiyama wo meguru densetsu to sono rūtsu no kōsatsu'. *Tōkyō fukushi daigaku daigakuin kiyō*, vol. 4 no. 2 (March 2014).

Laozi. *Dao De Jing: The Book of the Way*. Trans. by Moss Roberts.

Berkeley, California, USA: University of California Press, 2001.

Lee, Junghee. 'The Origins and Development of the Pensive Bodhisattva Images of Asia'. *Artibus Asiae*, vol. 53 no. 3/4 (1993). 311–57.

Le Febvre, Jesse R. 'Christian Wedding Ceremonies: 'Nonreligiousness' in Contemporary Japan'. *Japanese Journal of Religious Studies*, vol. 42 no. 2 (2015). 185–203.

Lunning, Frenchy and Freeman, Crispin. 'Giant Robots and Superheroes: Manifestations of Divine Power, East and West'. *Mechademia*, vol. 3 (2008). 274–82.

Miller, Laura. 'Extreme Makeover for a Heian Era Wizard'. *Mechademia*, vol. 3 (2008).

Ministry of Land, Infrastructure, Transport and Tourism. 'Land and Climate of Japan'. https://www.mlit.go.jp/river/basic_info/english/land.html Accessed June 04, 2020.

Nakajima, Michio. 'Shinto Deities that Crossed the Sea: Japan's 'Overseas Shrines' 1868–1945, *Japanese Journal of Religious Studies*, vol. 37 no. 1 (2010). 21–46.

Nihonshoki 1–3. Ed. by Kojima, Noriyuki, et. al. *Shinpen Nihon koten bungaku zenshū*, vols. 2–4 (1994).

Ō no Yasumaro. *The Kojiki: an Account of Ancient Matters*. Trans. by Gustav Heldt. New York: Columbia University Press, 2014.

O'Dwyer, Shaun. 'The Yasukuni Shrine and the Competing Patriotic Pasts of East Asia'. *History and Memory*, vol. 22 no. 2 (2010). 147–77.

Oxford English Dictionary Online, Oxford University Press, June 2020, www.oed.com

Oyler, Elizabeth. *Swords, Oaths and Prophetic Visions: Authoring Warrior Rule in Medieval Japan*. Honolulu: University of Hawai'i Press, 2015.

Piggott, Joan R. *The Emergence of Japanese Kingship*. Stanford, California, USA: Stanford University Press, 1997.

Power, Natsu Onoda. *God of Comics: Osamu Tezuka and the Creation of Post-World War II Manga*. Jackson, Mississippi, USA: University Press of Mississippi, 2009.

Rambelli, Fabio. 'Before the First Buddha: Medieval Japanese Cosmogony and the Quest for the Primeval Kami'. *Monumenta Nipponica*, vol. 64 no. 2 (2009). *The Sea and the Sacred in Japan*. London: Bloomsbury Academic, 2018. Amazon Kindle Edition.

Reider, Noriko T. 'A Demon in the Sky: The Tale of Amewakahiko, a Japanese Medieval Story'. *Marvels and Tales*, vol. 29 no. 2 (2015). 265–82. *Japanese Demon Lore: Oni from Ancient Times to the Present*. Logan, Utah, USA: Utah State University Press, 2015.

Roemer, Michael K. 'Thinking of Ancestors (and Others) at Japanese Household Altars'. *Journal of Ritual Studies*, vol. 26 no. 1 (2012). 33–45.

Saitō, Hideki, and Premoselli, Giorgio. 'The Worship of Gozu Tennō and the Ritual World of the Izanagi-ryū'. *Cahiers d'Extrême-Asie*, vol. 21 (2012). 277–301.

Scheid, Bernhard. 'Shōmu Tennō and the Deity from Kyushu: Hachiman's Initial Rise to Prominence'. *Japan Review*, no. 27 (2014). 31–51.

Shigeta, Shin'ichi, and Thompson, Luke. 'Onmyōdō and the Aristocratic Culture of Everyday Life in Heian Japan'. *Cahiers d'Extrême-Asie*, vol. 21 (2012). 65–77.

Smyers, Karen. A. ''My Own Inari:' Personalization of the Deity in Inari Worship'. *Japanese Journal of Religious Studies*, vol. 23 no. 1/2 (1996). 85–116.

Sundberg, Steve. 'Shirokiya Department Store, *c*. 1910–1940'. *Old Tokyo*. http://www.oldtokyo.com/shirokiya-department-store/ Accessed September 30, 2020.

Teeuwen, Mark. 'Attaining Union with the Gods: The Secret Books of Watarai Shinto'. *Monumenta Nipponica*, vol. 48 no. 2 (1993). 225–45.

Teiser, Stephen F. *The Ghost Festival in Medieval China*. Princeton, New Jersey, USA: Princeton University Press, 1988.

Thakur, Yoko H. 'History Textbook Reform in Allied Occupation Japan, 1945–52'. *History of Education Quarterly*, v. 35, no. 3 (1995). 261–78.

Thành, Minh and Leigh, P. D. *Sutra of the Medicine Buddha, Translated & Annotated under the Guidance of Dharma Master Hsuan Jung*. Taipei: Buddha Dharma Education Association Inc., 2001.

The Aoi Festival in Kyoto. Kyoto Prefectural Government. https://p.kyoto-np.jp/kp/koto/aoi/index.html Accessed 20 July 2020.

Traditional Japanese Literature: an Anthology, Beginnings to 1600. Ed. by Shirane, Haruo. New York: Columbia University Press, 2007.

Tsunoda, Ryūsaku, and Goodrich, L. Carrington. *Japan in the Chinese Dynastic Histories: Later Han Through Ming Dynasties*. South Pasadena, California, USA: P. D. and I. Perkins, 1961.

Van Goethem, Ellen. *Nagaoka: Japan's Forgotten Capital*. Leiden: Brill, 2008.

Weiss, David. 'Slaying the Serpent: Comparative Mythological Perspectives on Susanoo's Dragon Fight'. *Journal of Asian Humanities at Kyushu University*, vol. 3 (2018). 1–20.

Wong, Eva. *Taoism: An Essential Guide*. Boulder, Colorado, USA: Shambhala, 2011.

Yamashita, Katsuaki, and Elacqua, Joseph P. 'The Characteristics of Onmyōdō and Related Texts'. *Cahiers d'Extrême-Asie*, vol. 21 (2012). 79–105.

Yoshimura, Ayako. 'To Believe *and* Not to Believe: a Native Ethnography of Kanashibari in Japan'. *The Journal of American Folklore*, vol. 128 no. 508 (2015). 146–78.

Yu, Chün-fang. *Kuan-yin: The Chinese Transformation of Avalokitesvara*. New York: Columbia University Press, 2001. Amazon Kindle Edition.

ACKNOWLEDGMENTS

This book has been a joy to write, and a light in some dark times. Even so, I could not have accomplished it without the help and support of numerous people. Edward Kamens brought this opportunity to my attention and supported my efforts, as he has throughout my career. My colleagues Robert Lemon, Elyssa Faison, Dylan Herrick and Shizuka Tatsuzawa each supported the initial research and planning behind this book in their own ways, and I remain grateful to all of them.

Tateno Kazumi, of the Osaka Prefectural Chikatsu Asuka Museum, and Sakaehara Towao, of the Osaka City Council on Cultural Properties, provided invaluable insights into ways in which Japanese scholars understand their own ancient myths, and the potential pitfalls in explaining them to foreign readers. Department Chair Nian Liu as well as the staff of the Department of Modern Languages, Literatures and Linguistics at the University of Oklahoma were instrumental in providing me further support to finish this monograph.

Ben Hayes, Isabella Luta, Flora Spiegel, Rowena Alsey, Celia Falconer and everyone else at Thames & Hudson helped me to shepherd this project from initial suggestions through to finished work. They provided the freedom to present Japanese mythology in a novel way, and the resources to finish it at breathtaking speed without sacrificing clarity or detail.

And finally, I need to thank my family – Elyse and Alan; Jaime, Julian and Esme; Jared and Stephanie; Mary, who read over every line of this book to catch my errors; and, of course, my husband Nathan – who have stood by me throughout this project, as they have for every other.

SOURCES OF ILLUSTRATIONS

INDEX